Transformative Advances in Educational Methods

How Cutting-Edge Techniques, Practical Strategies, and Revolutionary Ideas Shape Modern Learning and Teaching

Megan Dennis

ISBN: 978-1-77961-878-8
Imprint: Telephasic Workshop
Copyright © 2024 Megan Dennis.
All Rights Reserved.

Contents

Introduction   1
Overview of the Book   1
Importance of Educational Methods   1
Evolution of Educational Methods   1
Structure of the Book   1

Chapter 1: Understanding Student-Centered Learning   3
Definition and Principles of Student-Centered Learning   3
Advantages and Challenges of Student-Centered Learning   47
Technology and Student-Centered Learning   74

Chapter 2: Inquiry-Based Learning   103
Principles and Process of Inquiry-Based Learning   103
Inquiry-Based Learning Models   122
Technology and Inquiry-Based Learning   162

Chapter 3: Integrating Technology in the Classroom   183
Benefits and Challenges of Technology Integration   183
Blended Learning and Flipped Classroom Models   201
Emerging Technologies in Education   235

Index   255

Introduction

Overview of the Book

Importance of Educational Methods

Evolution of Educational Methods

Structure of the Book

Chapter 1: Understanding Student-Centered Learning

Definition and Principles of Student-Centered Learning

Learner Autonomy

Learner autonomy refers to the ability of students to take charge of their own learning and make informed decisions about their educational journey. It is based on the belief that students should be active participants in the learning process, rather than passive recipients of information. Learner autonomy empowers students to set their own learning goals, select appropriate strategies, and monitor their progress towards achieving those goals. This approach nurtures students' critical thinking, problem-solving, and decision-making skills, preparing them for lifelong learning.

Principles of Learner Autonomy

Learner autonomy is grounded in several key principles that shape its implementation:

1. **Self-regulated learning:** Learners are encouraged to develop self-regulation skills, such as setting goals, planning their learning, monitoring their progress, and reflecting on their achievements. This process helps students become independent and proactive learners.

2. **Choice and reflection:** Learners are given opportunities to make choices regarding what, how, and when they learn. This promotes a sense of ownership and motivation, as students can tailor their learning experiences to suit their interests, needs, and learning styles. Additionally, learners are encouraged to reflect

on their learning experiences, identifying strengths, weaknesses, and areas for improvement.

3. **Collaborative learning:** While learner autonomy emphasizes individual responsibility, it also recognizes the value of collaborative learning. Students benefit from engaging in discussions, sharing ideas, and collaborating with their peers. Collaboration fosters deeper understanding, creativity, and problem-solving skills.

4. **Teacher as facilitator:** In learner autonomy, the role of the teacher shifts from being a knowledge provider to that of a facilitator or guide. Teachers create a supportive environment, foster students' autonomy, and provide guidance, resources, and feedback.

Promoting Learner Autonomy

Promoting learner autonomy requires a holistic approach that addresses various aspects of the learning environment. Here are some strategies:

1. **Gradual release of responsibility:** Teachers gradually transfer responsibility for learning from themselves to the students, providing support and scaffolding as needed. This gradual release allows students to develop independent learning skills at a pace that suits their individual needs.

2. **Goal-setting:** Encourage students to set realistic and meaningful goals that align with their interests and aspirations. These can be short-term or long-term goals and can focus on both academic and personal development.

3. **Choice and flexibility:** Provide students with choices in their learning activities, assignments, or projects. This can be done through menu-based assignments, project-based learning, or personalized learning plans. The flexibility allows students to explore topics that interest them and take ownership of their learning.

4. **Metacognition development:** Teach students metacognitive strategies, such as planning, monitoring, and evaluating their own learning. This helps them become aware of their thinking processes and develop strategies for effective learning.

5. **Reflection and self-assessment:** Encourage students to reflect on their learning experiences, identify their strengths and weaknesses, and set goals for improvement. Self-assessment tools, such as rubrics or checklists, can help students evaluate their progress.

6. **Promote collaboration:** Provide opportunities for students to collaborate with their peers, engage in group projects, and participate in discussions. Collaboration enhances students' social and communication skills while fostering a sense of community in the classroom.

Challenges in Promoting Learner Autonomy

Despite its numerous benefits, promoting learner autonomy can present challenges. Some common challenges include:

1. **Resistance to change:** Students may be accustomed to traditional teacher-centered approaches, leading to initial resistance towards learner autonomy. It may take time for students to adapt to the new learning paradigm and take ownership of their learning.

2. **Time constraints:** Teachers face time constraints in developing and implementing learner autonomy strategies. It requires careful planning, preparation of resources, and ongoing monitoring and feedback.

3. **Unequal access to resources:** Learner autonomy can be hindered by unequal access to resources, such as technology or learning materials. Teachers must ensure equitable access and provide alternative options for students with limited resources.

Case Study: Implementing Learner Autonomy in a Language Classroom

Let's consider a case study where a teacher is implementing learner autonomy principles in a language classroom. The teacher believes that enabling students to take ownership of their language learning will result in enhanced motivation and proficiency.

1. **Goal-setting:** At the beginning of the semester, the teacher encourages each student to set personalized goals for their language learning. These goals are specific, measurable, attainable, relevant, and time-bound (SMART goals). For example, a student might set a goal of improving their speaking skills by participating in classroom discussions.

2. **Choice-based assignments:** The teacher provides a range of assignment options related to the language skills being taught. Students choose assignments that align with their interests and learning preferences. For example, students can choose to write a research paper, create an audio podcast, or design a visual presentation to demonstrate their understanding of a specific topic.

3. **Collaborative projects:** The teacher assigns collaborative projects that require students to work in pairs or small groups. These projects involve tasks such as creating a dialogue, preparing a skit, or conducting an interview in the target language. Collaborative projects promote communication, negotiation, and sharing of ideas among students.

4. **Self-assessment:** Students are encouraged to assess their own language skills periodically. The teacher provides self-assessment tools, such as rubrics or checklists,

to guide students in evaluating their progress. Students reflect on their strengths and areas for improvement, setting goals for further development.

5. **Reflection journals:** Students maintain reflection journals where they write about their language learning experiences, challenges faced, and strategies employed to overcome those challenges. The teacher provides feedback on these journals, guiding students' reflection and providing suggestions for improvement.

This case study demonstrates how learner autonomy principles can be implemented in a language classroom. By promoting goal-setting, choice, collaboration, self-assessment, and reflection, students become active participants in their language learning process, leading to increased motivation and proficiency.

In conclusion, learner autonomy is a powerful approach that empowers students to take ownership of their learning and become independent, lifelong learners. By promoting self-regulation, choice, collaboration, and reflection, learner autonomy prepares students for success in the rapidly evolving educational landscape. Teachers play a crucial role in fostering learner autonomy by providing guidance, resources, and a supportive learning environment. By embracing learner autonomy, educators can transform the learning experience and empower students to reach their full potential.

Individualized Instruction

In the realm of education, a one-size-fits-all approach does not always lead to optimal learning outcomes. Each student has unique strengths, weaknesses, learning styles, and interests. Individualized instruction aims to tailor the educational experience to meet the specific needs of each student, acknowledging their individuality and promoting personalized learning opportunities.

Definition and Principles of Individualized Instruction

Individualized instruction, also known as personalized learning, is an educational approach that recognizes and addresses the diverse learning needs of students. It is grounded in the belief that learners thrive when they are actively engaged in the learning process and have opportunities to explore topics that genuinely interest them.

The principles of individualized instruction include:

1. **Assessment of Prior Knowledge:** Before designing individualized instruction, educators need to understand each student's current knowledge and skills. Pre-assessments help to identify areas of strength and areas that require further support or intervention.

2. **Flexible Pace and Pathways:** Individualized instruction allows students to progress at their own pace, ensuring that they have sufficient time to master each concept. It also provides multiple pathways for students to achieve learning objectives, taking into account their preferred learning styles and interests.

3. **Differentiated Content:** Individualized instruction provides content that is appropriate to students' current level of understanding and skills. It offers a range of materials, resources, and activities to cater to diverse learning needs and preferences.

4. **Varied Learning Approaches:** Individualized instruction recognizes that different students learn in different ways. It incorporates a variety of instructional methods, such as visual, auditory, kinesthetic, and tactile approaches, to ensure that all students can access and engage with the content.

5. **Continuous Monitoring and Feedback:** Individualized instruction involves ongoing assessment and feedback. Teachers monitor each student's progress, provide timely feedback, and make adjustments to the instruction based on individual needs. This iterative process supports continuous improvement and promotes student success.

Advantages of Individualized Instruction

Meeting Diverse Needs: Individualized instruction addresses the unique learning needs of each student, allowing them to progress at their own pace and focus on areas where they need additional support. This approach helps to prevent students from falling behind and ensures that they are appropriately challenged.

Enhancing Motivation and Engagement: When students have a say in what and how they learn, they feel a greater sense of control and ownership over their education. This autonomy boosts motivation and engagement, leading to deeper learning experiences.

Promoting Self-Directed Learning: Individualized instruction fosters learner autonomy and self-directed learning skills. Students develop the ability to set goals, plan their learning, and reflect on their progress. These skills are invaluable not only in academics but also in their future careers and personal lives.

Catering to Different Learning Styles: Each student has a preferred learning style, whether they learn best through visual, auditory, kinesthetic, or other means. Individualized instruction provides opportunities for students to engage with the content in ways that align with their learning preferences, maximizing their learning potential.

Challenges and Strategies for Implementing Individualized Instruction

Implementing individualized instruction presents challenges for educators. It requires careful planning, use of resources, and continuous monitoring of student progress. Some challenges include:

Time Constraints: The personalized nature of individualized instruction demands more time and effort from educators. Providing customized materials, assessing student progress, and providing timely feedback can be time-consuming. To address this challenge, teachers can leverage technology tools, collaborate with colleagues, and streamline administrative tasks.

Classroom Management: Managing individualized instruction within a classroom setting can be challenging. Students may require varying levels of support and guidance, and teachers need to find a balance between providing individual attention and maintaining a classroom community. Strategies such as small group instruction, peer tutoring, and collaborative learning activities can help address this challenge.

Resource Availability: Implementing individualized instruction requires access to a variety of resources, including digital tools, materials at different reading levels, and multimedia resources. Schools and educators can seek partnerships, apply for grants, or tap into open educational resources to expand the range of resources available.

Engaging Parents and the Community: For individualized instruction to be successful, collaboration between educators, parents, and the community is crucial. Engaging parents in the learning process and seeking their input can provide valuable insights into students' individual needs. Regular communication, parent-teacher conferences, and events that showcase student work can help foster a strong school-home partnership.

Assessing Student Learning in Individualized Environments

Assessing student learning in individualized instruction requires a multifaceted approach that aligns with the principles of personalized learning. Some assessment strategies include:

Formative Assessments: Ongoing formative assessments provide valuable insights into students' understanding and progress. These assessments can take the form of quizzes, discussions, projects, or one-on-one conferences. Formative assessment data guides instructional decisions and helps educators tailor instruction to individual needs.

Authentic Assessments: Authentic assessments reflect real-world tasks and challenges, allowing students to apply their learning in meaningful ways. Examples include project-based assessments, portfolios, presentations, and performances. Authentic assessments provide a holistic view of student capabilities and promote the transfer of knowledge and skills.

Self-Assessment and Reflection: Encouraging students to self-assess their progress and reflect on their learning promotes metacognitive skills. Journals, learning logs, and self-assessment rubrics can support students' ability to analyze their strengths and areas for growth, setting goals for future learning.

Evaluating the Impact of Individualized Instruction

Measuring the impact of individualized instruction requires a comprehensive evaluation plan that considers various aspects of student learning and engagement. Some evaluation methods include:

Quantitative Measures: Analyzing student performance data, such as standardized test scores or grades, can provide insights into the overall impact of individualized instruction. It is essential to compare data from previous years or other classes to assess growth and progress accurately.

Qualitative Measures: Qualitative data can offer a more in-depth understanding of students' experiences in individualized instruction. Interviews, surveys, focus groups, and observations can capture students' attitudes, engagement levels, and perceived benefits.

Teacher Reflection: Teachers' reflection on their instructional practices is a valuable source of information. Regular reflection sessions, journaling, and peer collaboration can help teachers identify what works well and areas for improvement.

Technology and Individualized Instruction

Technology tools can enhance individualized instruction by providing personalized learning experiences at scale. Some technologies that can support individualized instruction include:

Adaptive Learning Platforms: Adaptive learning platforms utilize artificial intelligence algorithms to adjust the learning content and activities based on students' responses. These platforms deliver personalized instruction and provide immediate feedback, allowing students to work at their own pace and receive targeted support.

Online Learning Resources: Online platforms offer a wealth of resources that can be tailored to individual student needs. Interactive simulations, educational games, videos, and digital textbooks provide engaging and flexible learning opportunities.

Learning Management Systems (LMS): LMS platforms streamline administrative tasks and provide a centralized hub for teachers to deliver individualized instruction. They allow teachers to monitor student progress, provide feedback, and facilitate communication and collaboration among students.

Data Analytics Tools: Data analytics tools help educators track and analyze student performance, identify areas of concern, and make data-informed decisions. These tools provide insights into student learning patterns, enabling teachers to customize instruction to meet individual needs.

While technology can greatly enhance individualized instruction, it is essential to ensure equitable access to technology resources and address privacy and security concerns.

Conclusion

Individualized instruction empowers students to take ownership of their learning and provides a pathway for personalized growth and success. By recognizing and addressing students' diverse needs, educators can create a learning environment that celebrates individuality, fosters engagement, and promotes deep learning. With the support of technology tools and thoughtful implementation strategies, individualized instruction holds the potential to transform education and prepare students for the challenges and opportunities of the future.

Active Engagement

Active engagement is a crucial aspect of student-centered learning. It involves creating a dynamic and interactive learning environment that promotes student involvement, participation, and collaboration. In this section, we will explore the principles, strategies, and benefits of active engagement in the classroom.

Principles of Active Engagement

Active engagement is based on the belief that students construct knowledge by actively participating in the learning process. It emphasizes the following principles:

DEFINITION AND PRINCIPLES OF STUDENT-CENTERED LEARNING

- **Hands-On Learning:** Active engagement encourages students to physically interact with learning materials, such as conducting experiments, manipulating objects, or engaging in practical tasks. This hands-on approach enhances understanding and retention of concepts.
- **Critical Thinking:** Active engagement promotes critical thinking skills by challenging students to analyze information, evaluate evidence, and form independent judgments. It requires students to go beyond rote memorization and encourages them to apply higher-order thinking skills to solve problems.
- **Collaborative Learning:** Active engagement encourages collaboration among students. Through group discussions, peer teaching, and cooperative projects, students learn from each other, develop communication skills, and gain diverse perspectives.
- **Authentic Context:** Active engagement connects learning to real-life situations and contexts. It helps students see the relevance and applicability of what they are learning, increasing their motivation and interest in the subject matter.

Strategies for Active Engagement

Promoting active engagement requires a variety of instructional strategies. Here are some effective strategies that can be implemented in the classroom:

1. **Think-Pair-Share:** In this strategy, students are given a question or problem to think about individually. Then, they pair up with a partner to discuss their ideas. Finally, pairs share their thoughts with the whole class. This strategy encourages active participation, reflection, and collaboration.
2. **Socratic Method:** The Socratic Method involves using a series of questions to stimulate critical thinking and promote deeper understanding. The teacher asks thought-provoking questions that challenge students to analyze, evaluate, and articulate their ideas. This strategy fosters active participation and enhances higher-order thinking skills.
3. **Debates and Discussions:** Organizing debates or class discussions on controversial topics encourages active engagement. Students research and prepare arguments, listen to different perspectives, and defend their positions. This strategy promotes critical thinking, communication skills, and tolerance for diverse viewpoints.

Benefits of Active Engagement

Active engagement offers numerous benefits for both students and teachers. Here are some key advantages:

- **Increased Motivation:** Active engagement makes learning more enjoyable and meaningful for students. It taps into their natural curiosity, encourages ownership of learning, and boosts motivation and enthusiasm.

- **Enhanced Understanding:** By actively participating in the learning process, students deepen their understanding and retention of concepts. Active engagement allows students to connect new information with prior knowledge and apply it to real-world situations, improving comprehension and problem-solving skills.

- **Improved Social Skills:** Collaborative learning environments foster teamwork, communication, and interpersonal skills. Students learn to work effectively in groups, respect diverse opinions, and develop empathy and cooperation.

- **Higher-Level Thinking Skills:** Active engagement promotes critical thinking, creativity, and problem-solving skills. It challenges students to analyze, evaluate, and synthesize information, cultivating higher-order thinking skills necessary for success in the 21st century.

Overall, active engagement is a powerful approach that empowers students to become active participants in their own learning. By integrating various strategies and principles, teachers can create an engaging and enriching learning environment that promotes deep understanding, critical thinking, and collaboration.

Example: Active Engagement in Science Education

To illustrate the concept of active engagement, let's consider an example in science education.

In a biology class, the teacher wants to teach the concept of photosynthesis and its importance in plant growth. Instead of relying on a traditional lecture, the teacher designs an active engagement activity.

First, the students are divided into small groups and given plant specimens, magnifying glasses, and microscopes. They are instructed to examine different parts of the plant and identify chloroplasts. This hands-on exploration allows students to observe plant structures and reinforce their understanding of the topic.

Next, each group is assigned a specific question related to photosynthesis, such as "How does the intensity of light affect the rate of photosynthesis?" Students are asked to design a simple experiment to investigate their assigned question. They formulate hypotheses, plan their experiment, collect data, and analyze the results.

After conducting the experiments, each group presents their findings to the class. The whole class engages in a discussion, comparing and contrasting the results, and drawing conclusions. The teacher facilitates the discussion, asking probing questions to stimulate critical thinking and deeper understanding.

This active engagement activity immerses students in the process of scientific inquiry, fostering critical thinking, collaboration, and hands-on learning. By actively participating in the learning process, students develop a deeper understanding of the concept of photosynthesis and its relevance to plant growth.

Resources

Here are some additional resources on active engagement in the classroom:

- National Education Association (NEA) - Active Learning: https://www.nea.org/professional-excellence/student-engagement/tools-tips/active-learning

- Edutopia - Active Learning: https://www.edutopia.org/article/what-active-learning

- TeachThought - 10 Strategies for Engaging Students in the Classroom: https://www.teachthought.com/pedagogy/10-strategies-start-engaging-students-day/

Conclusion

Active engagement plays a vital role in student-centered learning. By implementing strategies that encourage hands-on learning, critical thinking, collaborative activities, and authentic contexts, teachers can create a dynamic learning environment that promotes active participation, deeper understanding, and higher-level thinking skills. Embracing active engagement in the classroom empowers students to become active learners, preparing them for success in an ever-evolving world.

Collaborative Learning

Collaborative learning is an educational approach that emphasizes group work and cooperation among students. It is based on the belief that students learn best when they actively engage with their peers, share their ideas, and work together to solve problems. In collaborative learning, the classroom becomes a community of learners where students can benefit from each other's strengths and perspectives.

Benefits of Collaborative Learning

Collaborative learning offers numerous benefits for students, both academically and socially. Here are some key advantages:

1. **Enhanced Learning Outcomes** When students work together in groups, they can exchange ideas, clarify concepts, and deepen their understanding of the subject matter. Collaborative learning provides opportunities for peer teaching and learning, which can reinforce learning and promote higher levels of thinking.

2. **Development of Social Skills** In collaborative learning environments, students develop crucial social skills such as communication, teamwork, and conflict resolution. They learn to express their ideas, listen actively to others, and work towards common goals. These skills are essential for success in the 21st-century workforce, where collaboration is becoming increasingly important.

3. **Increased Motivation** Working in groups can increase students' motivation and engagement with the learning process. Collaborative learning allows students to take ownership of their learning and fosters a sense of responsibility towards their peers. When students feel valued and supported by their peers, they are more likely to actively participate and stay involved in the learning activities.

4. **Development of Higher-Order Thinking Skills** Collaborative learning promotes critical thinking and problem-solving skills. When students work together, they can analyze complex problems, generate creative solutions, and evaluate different perspectives. They learn to think critically, ask meaningful questions, and justify their reasoning, leading to deeper learning outcomes.

5. **Preparation for Real-World Situations** Collaborative learning prepares students for the realities of the real world, where collaboration and teamwork are essential. In today's interconnected society, professionals often work in teams to accomplish complex tasks. By engaging in collaborative learning experiences, students develop the skills necessary for effective collaboration in various professional settings.

Strategies for Implementing Collaborative Learning

To effectively implement collaborative learning in the classroom, educators can utilize the following strategies:

1. **Clear Learning Goals** Clearly communicate the learning objectives to students before engaging in collaborative activities. Ensure that students understand the purpose of working together and how it relates to their overall learning goals.

2. **Structured Group Activities** Provide structured and well-defined group activities that require active participation from all group members. Carefully design tasks that encourage students to interact, share ideas, and work collaboratively towards a common goal.

3. **roles and group dynamics** Assign specific roles to each group member to ensure equal participation and accountability. Encourage students to rotate roles in subsequent activities to promote shared responsibility and a sense of fairness. Additionally, promote positive group dynamics by fostering a supportive and inclusive learning environment.

4. **ongoing monitoring and feedback** Monitor group interactions and provide feedback to individual students and groups. Offer guidance and support when needed, and encourage students to reflect on their group processes and dynamics.

Challenges of Collaborative Learning

While collaborative learning offers numerous benefits, it also presents challenges that educators need to address:

1. **Uneven Contribution** In some group settings, there may be differences in knowledge, skills, and motivation among students. This can result in an uneven distribution of workload and contributions. Teachers must implement strategies to ensure that all students actively participate and contribute to the group's success.

2. **Conflict Resolution** Collaborative learning can sometimes lead to conflicts or disagreements among group members. Teachers should provide guidance on effective communication and conflict resolution strategies to help students navigate these challenges.

3. **Time Management** Collaborative learning activities may require more time than traditional individual tasks. Teachers need to plan lessons carefully to ensure that sufficient time is allocated for group work while balancing the completion of curriculum requirements.

4. **Assessment of Individual Learning** Assessing individual learning within a collaborative learning context can be challenging. Teachers should consider a

combination of individual and group assessments to evaluate students' understanding and skill development.

Real-World Example: Designing a Sustainable City

To illustrate the concept of collaborative learning, let's consider a real-world example: designing a sustainable city. In this project, students work in groups to create a plan for a city that promotes environmental sustainability and addresses societal needs.

Each group member takes on a specific role, such as an architect, urban planner, or environmental engineer. They collaborate to design the city layout, incorporating green spaces, renewable energy sources, and efficient transportation systems. They conduct research, analyze data, and make informed decisions regarding the city's infrastructure and resource management.

Throughout the project, students engage in discussions, share their expertise, and make joint decisions. They learn to consider multiple perspectives, negotiate conflicting ideas, and reach consensus. The project culminates in a presentation where each group showcases their sustainable city design and explains their decision-making process.

This collaborative learning experience not only enhances students' knowledge of sustainability but also develops their critical thinking, problem-solving, and teamwork skills. It encourages them to take responsibility for their learning and fosters a sense of collective achievement.

Resources for Collaborative Learning

Here are some resources that educators can use to support collaborative learning in the classroom:

1. **Online Collaboration Tools** Platforms like Google Docs, Padlet, and Trello enable students to collaborate and share ideas in real-time. These tools facilitate online discussions, document sharing, and project management.

2. **Cooperative Learning Structures** Cooperative learning structures, such as Think-Pair-Share, Jigsaw, and Roundtable, provide a framework for structured group work. These structures promote active engagement and equal participation among students.

3. **Collaborative Projects** Collaborative projects, both online and offline, provide opportunities for students to work together on meaningful tasks. Project-based learning platforms like Edmodo and Seesaw offer project management tools and facilitate peer collaboration.

4. **Professional Development Opportunities** Teachers can enhance their understanding of collaborative learning by participating in professional development workshops, webinars, or online courses. These resources provide educators with strategies and tools to implement collaborative learning effectively.

Wrap-Up

Collaborative learning is a powerful educational approach that fosters student engagement, critical thinking, and social skills. By working together in groups, students can develop a deeper understanding of the subject matter and prepare themselves for real-world collaboration. Implementing collaborative learning requires thoughtful planning, clear learning goals, and strategies to address challenges. With the right support and resources, educators can create dynamic and inclusive learning environments that promote collaboration and empower students to become active learners.

In the next chapter, we will explore another transformative educational method: inquiry-based learning. We will examine the principles, benefits, and strategies for implementing inquiry-based learning in the classroom. Stay tuned for an exciting journey into the world of inquiry-based education!

Assessment for Learning

Assessment for learning is an integral component of student-centered learning. It refers to the ongoing process of gathering evidence about students' knowledge, skills, and understanding in order to provide feedback and guide instruction. Unlike traditional assessments that focus solely on measuring students' performance at a specific point in time, assessment for learning aims to enhance learning by helping students understand their areas of strength and areas for improvement. It also enables teachers to adjust their instruction to meet the specific needs of individual students and the class as a whole.

Principles of Assessment for Learning

The principles of assessment for learning are rooted in the principles of student-centered learning. Here are some key principles to consider:

1. **Clear Learning Targets:** Assessment for learning begins with clearly articulated learning targets or objectives. These targets provide students with a clear understanding of what they are expected to learn and enable teachers to assess whether students have achieved these targets.

2. **Formative Nature:** Assessment for learning is formative in nature, meaning it takes place during the learning process. It provides ongoing feedback to students about their progress, identifies areas of strength and weakness, and guides instruction based on individual learning needs.

3. **Active Student Involvement:** Assessment for learning promotes active student involvement by encouraging self-assessment and reflection. Students are encouraged to monitor their own learning, set goals, and take ownership of their progress.

4. **Varied Assessment Methods:** Assessment for learning utilizes a variety of assessment methods to gather evidence of student learning. These methods include observations, interviews, discussions, portfolios, quizzes, tests, and projects. By using multiple sources of evidence, teachers can gain a comprehensive understanding of students' learning.

5. **Timely and Effective Feedback:** Feedback is a crucial component of assessment for learning. It should be timely, specific, and focused on providing guidance for improvement. Effective feedback highlights areas of strength, identifies areas for improvement, and suggests strategies for further development.

6. **Peer and Self-Assessment:** Peer and self-assessment are important aspects of assessment for learning. By involving students in the assessment process, they develop a deeper understanding of the criteria for success and enhance their metacognitive skills.

7. **Use of Technology:** Technology can play a significant role in assessment for learning. Online platforms, educational apps, and digital tools allow for immediate feedback, interactive assessments, and the collection of data for analysis.

Assessment Strategies for Learning

There are various assessment strategies that can be employed to promote learning. Here are a few examples:

1. **Rubrics:** Rubrics are scoring guides that outline criteria for success and provide a clear description of performance expectations. They help students understand what is expected of them and enable teachers to provide constructive feedback.

2. **Checklists:** Checklists are useful tools for tracking student progress and providing feedback. They allow both teachers and students to monitor the completion of specific tasks or skills.

3. **Peer Feedback:** Peer feedback involves students providing feedback to their classmates. This strategy promotes active engagement and helps students develop critical thinking and communication skills.

4. **Self-Assessment:** Self-assessment encourages students to reflect on their own learning and assess their progress. It helps students develop metacognitive skills and take ownership of their learning.

5. **Group Projects:** Group projects provide opportunities for collaborative learning and assessment. By working together, students learn from and with each other, while also being assessed on their individual contributions to the project.

Challenges and Considerations

Although assessment for learning offers many benefits, there are also challenges and considerations to keep in mind:

1. **Time Constraints:** Implementing assessment for learning requires time for planning, feedback, and reflection. Teachers need to carefully manage their time to ensure effective implementation.

2. **Standardization:** Balancing the need for standardized assessments with the principles of assessment for learning can be challenging. Educators must find ways to meet curriculum requirements while still providing individualized and meaningful feedback.

3. **Assessment Bias:** It is important to ensure that assessments are fair and free from bias. Educators need to be mindful of potential biases that may arise when interpreting and evaluating student work.

4. **Support and Training:** Teachers may require support and training to effectively implement assessment for learning strategies. Professional development opportunities can help educators develop the necessary skills and knowledge.

Case Study: Implementing Assessment for Learning

Consider a high school math class where the teacher wants to implement assessment for learning strategies to promote student engagement and learning. The teacher decides to use a combination of rubrics, peer feedback, and self-assessment.

The teacher starts by creating a rubric that clearly outlines the criteria for success in math problem-solving. This rubric is shared with students at the beginning of the unit, allowing them to understand the expectations and learning targets.

Throughout the unit, students work on math problems individually and in small groups. As they work, they refer to the rubric to self-assess and monitor their progress. They also provide feedback to their peers, discussing strengths and areas for improvement.

At the end of the unit, the teacher collects students' self-assessments, peer feedback, and completed math problems. Using the rubric as a guide, the teacher provides timely and specific feedback to each student, highlighting areas of growth and suggesting strategies for improvement.

The teacher also meets with each student individually to discuss their progress and set goals for future learning. This individualized feedback supports student growth and helps them take ownership of their learning.

By implementing assessment for learning strategies, the teacher creates a supportive and engaging learning environment. Students develop a deeper understanding of math concepts, receive timely feedback, and actively participate in their own learning.

Conclusion

Assessment for learning is a powerful tool for promoting student-centered learning. By providing timely feedback, involving students in the assessment process, and using multiple assessment methods, educators can effectively support student growth and achievement. Through the implementation of assessment for learning strategies, educators can create a culture of continuous improvement and help students become lifelong learners.

Personalized Learning

Personalized learning is an innovative approach to education that tailors instruction and learning experiences to the unique needs and interests of individual students. In a personalized learning environment, students have the opportunity to learn at their own pace, explore topics that are relevant to them, and receive targeted support and feedback. This section will explore the principles of personalized learning, its

DEFINITION AND PRINCIPLES OF STUDENT-CENTERED LEARNING

benefits and challenges, as well as strategies for implementing personalized learning in the classroom.

Principles of Personalized Learning

Personalized learning is based on several key principles that aim to meet the diverse needs of every student. These principles include:

1. **Individualized Instruction:** Personalized learning recognizes that each student has different learning needs and preferences. It emphasizes differentiated instruction, allowing students to learn in ways that are most effective for them.

2. **Student Agency:** Personalized learning promotes learner autonomy, giving students more control over their learning. It encourages students to set goals, make decisions, and take ownership of their learning journey.

3. **Flexibility:** Personalized learning provides flexible pathways and resources to accommodate students' diverse learning styles and interests. It allows students to choose from a variety of learning activities and materials that align with their individual needs and goals.

4. **Data-Informed Instruction:** Personalized learning uses data to inform instructional decisions and provide targeted support. Through ongoing assessment and data analysis, teachers can identify students' strengths and areas for growth and adjust their instruction accordingly.

5. **Collaboration:** Personalized learning recognizes the importance of collaborative learning experiences. It encourages students to work with their peers, engage in group projects, and learn from one another through peer feedback and discussion.

6. **Real-World Relevance:** Personalized learning connects classroom learning to real-world contexts, making learning meaningful and applicable. It provides opportunities for students to apply their knowledge and skills to authentic problems and projects.

Benefits of Personalized Learning

Personalized learning offers a range of benefits for students, teachers, and the educational system as a whole.

For students, personalized learning:

- Increases student engagement and motivation by allowing them to pursue their interests and passions.
- Fosters a deeper understanding of concepts and skills as students can learn at their own pace and in ways that resonate with them.
- Enhances critical thinking and problem-solving skills by encouraging students to take ownership of their learning and make decisions.
- Promotes self-directed learning and independent thinking, preparing students for lifelong learning.
- Supports the development of 21st-century skills, such as collaboration, communication, and creativity, through personalized learning experiences.

For teachers, personalized learning:

- Allows for more targeted instruction and individualized support, enabling teachers to meet the diverse needs of all students.
- Provides valuable insights into student progress and understanding through ongoing assessment and data analysis.
- Fosters stronger relationships and connections with students as teachers work closely with each student to personalize their learning experience.
- Frees up time for teachers to focus on higher-order instructional tasks, such as facilitating discussions and providing timely feedback.
- Promotes professional growth and innovation as teachers explore new instructional strategies and technologies to personalize learning.

For the educational system, personalized learning:

- Increases student achievement and graduation rates by tailoring instruction to individual student needs.
- Reduces achievement gaps by addressing students' unique learning challenges and ensuring equitable educational opportunities for all.
- Encourages innovation and experimentation in teaching and learning practices, leading to a more dynamic and responsive education system.
- Prepares students for the demands of the future workforce, where personalized learning will play a crucial role in lifelong learning and career development.

Challenges in Implementing Personalized Learning

While personalized learning holds great promise, it also presents challenges that educators need to address in order to successfully implement personalized learning in the classroom. Some of these challenges include:

1. **Infrastructure and Resources:** Implementing personalized learning requires adequate technological infrastructure and resources, such as devices, software, and reliable internet access. Lack of these resources can hinder the effective implementation of personalized learning.

2. **Teacher Professional Development:** Personalized learning necessitates a shift in instructional practices and pedagogical approaches. Providing teachers with comprehensive and ongoing professional development is essential to equip them with the knowledge and skills to effectively implement personalized learning strategies.

3. **Assessment and Evaluation:** Assessing and evaluating student learning in a personalized learning environment can be challenging. Traditional assessment methods may not accurately capture the full range of students' knowledge and skills. Educators need to explore alternative assessment strategies that align with personalized learning principles.

4. **Privacy and Data Security:** Personalized learning relies on the collection and analysis of student data. Ensuring the privacy and security of student data is of utmost importance. Educators must establish robust data protection policies and practices to safeguard student information.

5. **Parent and Community Engagement:** Building a culture of personalized learning requires collaboration and engagement from parents, families, and the wider community. Educators need to communicate the benefits of personalized learning to parents and involve them in the educational process.

Strategies for Implementing Personalized Learning

Implementing personalized learning requires careful planning and strategic implementation. Here are some strategies that can help educators effectively integrate personalized learning in their classrooms:

1. **Know Your Students:** Get to know your students' strengths, interests, and learning preferences. Use formative assessments and student surveys to gather information about their prior knowledge and learning goals.

2. **Differentiate Instruction:** Tailor instruction to meet the diverse needs of students. Provide multiple pathways for learning, offer choice in assignments and assessments, and adapt teaching strategies to address individual learning styles.

3. **Use Technology Purposefully:** Leverage technology to enhance personalized learning experiences. Utilize adaptive learning platforms, online resources, and educational apps to provide tailored instruction and immediate feedback.

4. **Create Collaborative Learning Opportunities:** Foster collaboration among students by incorporating group work, peer feedback, and cooperative projects. Encourage students to learn from each other and collaborate on problem-solving activities.

5. **Encourage Self-Reflection:** Promote self-reflection and metacognitive skills by having students set goals, monitor their progress, and reflect on their learning. Provide opportunities for students to assess their own work and identify areas for improvement.

6. **Provide Timely Feedback:** Offer timely and meaningful feedback to students to guide their learning. Use a variety of feedback methods, such as written comments, verbal discussions, and rubrics, to support students' growth and progress.

7. **Build a Learning Community:** Establish a positive and inclusive classroom environment where all students feel valued and supported. Encourage collaboration, respect, and empathy among students to foster a sense of belonging and engagement.

8. **Collaborate with Colleagues:** Work with colleagues to share best practices, resources, and ideas for personalized learning. Collaborative planning and professional learning communities can help educators learn from one another and refine their personalized learning practices.

9. **Involve Parents and the Community:** Engage parents and the community in the personalized learning process. Communicate the goals and benefits of personalized learning, involve parents in decision-making, and provide opportunities for them to support their child's learning at home.

10. **Continuously Reflect and Improve:** Regularly reflect on the effectiveness of your personalized learning practices. Seek feedback from students, colleagues, and parents, and make adjustments based on evidence and student needs.

Examples of Personalized Learning in Action

To better understand how personalized learning can be implemented in the classroom, here are a few examples:

- **Student Choice Boards:** Provide students with a choice board that includes a variety of learning activities related to a particular topic. Students can choose the activities that align with their interests and learning styles, allowing for personalized learning experiences.

- **Individual Learning Plans:** Develop individual learning plans for each student, based on their unique strengths, goals, and areas for improvement. These plans outline the specific learning objectives, strategies, and resources that will support each student's personalized learning journey.

- **Flexible Grouping:** Use flexible grouping strategies to accommodate different learning needs and abilities. Provide opportunities for students to work in small groups or independently, allowing for personalized instruction and peer collaboration.

- **Student-Led Projects:** Assign open-ended projects where students have the freedom to explore a topic of interest. This allows students to take ownership of their learning, conduct research, and present their findings in creative ways.

- **Adaptive Learning Software:** Incorporate adaptive learning software that adjusts to students' individual needs and progress. These digital tools provide personalized instruction, practice, and feedback based on students' responses, adapting the learning experience in real-time.

Resources for Personalized Learning

Here are some recommended resources for further exploration of personalized learning:

- **Books:**

- "Personalized Learning: A Guide for Engaging Students with Technology" by Peggy Grant and Dale Basye
  - "Pathways to Personalization: A Framework for School Change" by Shawn Covel and Brian Stack
  - "Personalized Learning: A Practical Guide for Teachers in School" by Vali Lalioti

- Websites:
  - Personalized Learning https://www.personalizedlearning.org
  - Edutopia: Personalized Learning https://www.edutopia.org/topic/personalized-learning
  - Getting Smart: Personalized Learning https://www.gettingsmart.com/topics/personalized-learning/

- Online Courses:
  - Coursera: "Personalized and Student-Centered Learning" https://www.coursera.org/learn/personalized-and-student-centered-learning
  - edX: "Designing and Implementing Personalized Learning" https://www.edx.org/professional-certificate/michiganx-designing-implementing-personalized-learning

In conclusion, personalized learning is an effective approach to education that puts students at the center of the learning process. By tailoring instruction to meet their diverse needs, personalized learning empowers students to take ownership of their learning, fosters deep understanding and critical thinking skills, and prepares them for future success. While implementing personalized learning comes with challenges, with careful planning, supportive resources, and ongoing professional development, educators can create engaging and impactful personalized learning experiences for their students.

Differentiated Instruction

Differentiated Instruction is a teaching approach that recognizes and supports the diverse learning needs, interests, and abilities of students. It emphasizes tailoring instruction and assessment to accommodate the unique strengths and challenges of each learner. In this section, we will explore the principles, strategies, and benefits of differentiated instruction, and discuss how it can be effectively implemented in the classroom.

Principles of Differentiated Instruction

Differentiated instruction is grounded in several key principles, which guide the design and implementation of instructional activities. These principles include:

1. **Acknowledging learner variability**: Differentiated instruction recognizes that students have different learning styles, preferences, and readiness levels. It embraces the idea that a one-size-fits-all approach to teaching may not be effective for all students.

2. **Building on prior knowledge**: Differentiated instruction acknowledges that students come to the classroom with varying levels of knowledge and experiences. It promotes the use of pre-assessments to identify students' prior knowledge and skills, and uses this information to tailor instruction accordingly.

3. **Flexible grouping**: Differentiated instruction encourages flexible grouping strategies, such as small groups, individualized instruction, and peer tutoring, to meet the diverse needs of students. Grouping can be based on readiness, interests, or learning preferences.

4. **Varied instructional strategies**: Differentiated instruction utilizes a variety of instructional strategies to engage students and address their different learning needs. These strategies may include hands-on activities, visual aids, technology integration, and real-world connections.

5. **Multiple assessments**: Differentiated instruction is accompanied by a variety of assessments that allow students to demonstrate their understanding and progress. These assessments should align with the instructional goals and accommodate different learning styles and abilities.

Strategies for Differentiated Instruction

Differentiated instruction employs various strategies to cater to the diverse needs of students. Here are some effective strategies:

1. **Learning stations or centers**: Setting up learning stations or centers in the classroom can provide students with different activities to choose from based on their learning needs and interests. Each station can target specific skills or concepts.

2. **Tiered assignments**: Tiered assignments provide different levels of complexity or depth, allowing students to choose tasks that challenge them appropriately. This approach ensures that all students are engaged and appropriately challenged.

3. **Flexible pacing**: Allowing students to work at their own pace is an essential aspect of differentiated instruction. Some students may need more time to grasp a concept, while others may need to move ahead. Providing opportunities for self-paced learning supports individual progress.

4. **Learning contracts**: Learning contracts are individualized agreements between teachers and students that outline specific goals and activities for each student. Students have a degree of choice in how they demonstrate their learning, which promotes engagement and ownership.

5. **Varied materials and resources**: Providing a range of materials, such as textbooks, online resources, manipulatives, and multimedia, ensures that students can access information in ways that align with their learning preferences and needs.

6. **Scaffolding and support**: Differentiated instruction requires teachers to provide appropriate support and scaffolding for learners. This can be done through modeling, guided practice, providing examples, or utilizing graphic organizers.

Benefits of Differentiated Instruction

Differentiated instruction offers several benefits for both teachers and students. These include:

1. **Improved student engagement**: Differentiated instruction increases student engagement by providing learning experiences that are relevant and meaningful to individual students. When students feel that their unique needs and interests are acknowledged, they become more motivated and invested in their learning.

DEFINITION AND PRINCIPLES OF STUDENT-CENTERED LEARNING

2. **Enhanced learning outcomes:** With differentiated instruction, students receive targeted instruction and support that aligns with their individual needs. This leads to improved learning outcomes as students are more likely to grasp and retain concepts.

3. **Increased student ownership:** Differentiated instruction empowers students to take ownership of their learning. By providing choices and opportunities for self-directed learning, students develop important skills such as self-regulation, decision-making, and goal-setting.

4. **Promotion of positive classroom environment:** Differentiated instruction promotes a positive classroom environment where diversity is celebrated and respected. Students feel valued and supported, which leads to a sense of belonging and a collaborative learning culture.

5. **Meeting individual learning needs:** By differentiating instruction, teachers can effectively address the diverse learning needs of students, including those with learning difficulties or exceptional abilities. This ensures that all students can access and achieve success in their learning.

Implementing Differentiated Instruction

Implementing differentiated instruction in the classroom requires careful planning and intentional design. Here are some strategies and considerations for effective implementation:

1. **Know your students:** Take the time to get to know your students individually, including their learning styles, interests, and strengths. This will help you tailor your instruction to meet their unique needs.

2. **Pre-assessment:** Use pre-assessments to gauge students' prior knowledge and skills. This will help you determine appropriate starting points, identify gaps in understanding, and plan differentiated activities.

3. **Provide clear learning goals:** Clearly communicate learning goals and expectations to students. Ensure that they understand the purpose of the differentiated activities and how they align with the overall curriculum.

4. **Offer choices:** Provide students with choices whenever possible. This could include choosing from different learning activities, resources, or assessment options. Offering choices promotes autonomy and engagement.

5. **Ongoing assessment and feedback:** Continuously monitor students' progress and provide timely feedback. Adjust your instruction and support based on formative assessment data to ensure that students are making progress towards their learning goals.

Conclusion

Differentiated instruction is a powerful approach that allows teachers to target the diverse needs of students while promoting engagement, ownership, and academic growth. By recognizing and accommodating learners' variability, educators can create inclusive classrooms that foster a love for learning and support all students in reaching their full potential. Implementing differentiated instruction requires careful planning, ongoing assessment, and a commitment to individualized learning experiences. As educators, it is our responsibility to embrace this approach and create meaningful learning opportunities for every student.

Project-Based Learning

Project-Based Learning (PBL) is an educational approach that emphasizes the active and collaborative learning of students through real-world projects. It allows students to apply their knowledge and skills to solve authentic problems, integrating different subject areas and fostering critical thinking, creativity, and collaboration. PBL provides a more student-centered and inquiry-based learning experience.

Principles of Project-Based Learning

Project-Based Learning is guided by several key principles:

1. **Authenticity:** Projects should be relevant to real-world problems or scenarios to engage students and make learning meaningful. Authenticity can be achieved by connecting projects to the students' lives, professional contexts, or global issues. For example, students may design and build a sustainable architecture model for a local community.

2. **Inquiry and Investigation:** PBL encourages students to ask critical questions, conduct research, gather data, and seek answers or solutions independently. This process develops their investigative and problem-solving skills while fostering a sense of curiosity and ownership of learning. For instance, students may investigate the impact of pollution on local wildlife and propose solutions to minimize its effects.

3. **Collaboration:** PBL promotes collaborative learning, allowing students to work together in teams to brainstorm ideas, share knowledge, distribute tasks, and communicate effectively. Collaborating on projects helps students develop social and interpersonal skills, such as teamwork, leadership, and conflict resolution. An example could be students working together to create a website promoting environmental awareness in their community.

4. **Reflection and Revision:** PBL encourages students to reflect on their learning process, evaluate the outcomes, and revise their work based on feedback. Reflection helps students develop a deeper understanding of the subject matter, identify strengths and weaknesses, and refine their approaches. Students may reflect on their experience in creating a marketing campaign for a local business and revise it based on their analysis.

5. **Presentation and Communication:** PBL requires students to present their project outcomes or findings to an authentic audience. This audience can include fellow students, teachers, experts in the field, or the community. Through presentations, students develop communication skills, confidence, and the ability to articulate their ideas effectively. For example, students may present their research findings on climate change to a panel of experts in a public seminar.

Benefits of Project-Based Learning

Project-Based Learning offers numerous benefits to students, educators, and the educational system as a whole. Some of these benefits include:

- **Enhanced Engagement and Motivation:** PBL makes learning more engaging and meaningful for students, as they have a sense of purpose and ownership over their projects. It increases their motivation to learn, leading to improved academic outcomes.

- **Higher-order Thinking Skills:** PBL promotes critical thinking, problem-solving, and decision-making skills. By working on complex and open-ended projects, students develop their ability to analyze information, think creatively, and make reasoned judgments.

- **Integration of Knowledge:** PBL allows students to connect knowledge across different subject areas. It breaks down the traditional silos of education and fosters interdisciplinary thinking, helping students understand how concepts and skills are applicable in various contexts.

- **Collaboration Skills:** PBL provides opportunities for students to work collaboratively, promoting teamwork, communication, and interpersonal skills. These skills are essential for success in the workplace and in society.

- **Real-world Application:** PBL bridges the gap between theory and practice by allowing students to apply their knowledge and skills to real-world problems. This prepares them for future careers and cultivates their sense of social responsibility.

- **Intrinsic Learning:** PBL encourages intrinsic motivation, as students are motivated by the joy of learning and the desire to solve meaningful problems. This type of motivation leads to deeper and more long-lasting learning.

Challenges in Implementing Project-Based Learning

While Project-Based Learning offers significant benefits, implementing it effectively can pose some challenges. It is essential for educators to be aware of these challenges and be prepared to address them. Some common challenges include:

- **Time Management:** PBL requires careful planning and time management, as projects may extend over an extended period. Educators need to allocate enough time for project planning, team collaboration, research, and project completion within the given curriculum constraints.

- **Assessment:** Assessing student learning in PBL can be challenging, as it involves multiple dimensions such as content knowledge, critical thinking, problem-solving, collaboration, and presentation skills. Educators need to design authentic assessment methods that align with the objectives of the projects.

- **Teacher Training and Support:** Implementing PBL effectively requires training and support for teachers. Educators need to understand the principles and strategies of PBL, learn how to integrate it into the curriculum, and develop the necessary skills to facilitate student-centered learning.

- **Resource Constraints:** PBL often requires additional resources such as materials, technology, and community partnerships. Limited resources can pose challenges in implementing and sustaining PBL initiatives. Educators need to find creative solutions and leverage available resources effectively.

Strategies for Successful Project-Based Learning

To overcome the challenges and implement Project-Based Learning successfully, educators can consider the following strategies:

1. **Well-Defined Learning Goals:** Clearly define the learning goals and outcomes of the project. Ensure that they align with the curriculum standards and provide opportunities for students to develop essential skills and knowledge.

2. **Scaffolded Support:** Provide scaffolds and support as students engage in the project. Gradually release responsibility to students, promoting their independence and self-directed learning. Scaffolded support can include guiding questions, templates, graphic organizers, and peer collaboration.

3. **Effective Collaboration:** Help students develop effective collaboration skills by setting clear expectations, establishing group norms, and fostering a positive and inclusive learning environment. Encourage regular communication, reflection, and peer feedback among team members.

4. **Integration of Technology:** Integrate appropriate technology tools and resources to enhance project-based learning. For example, students can use online platforms for research, collaboration, and project management. Technology can also facilitate the presentation and dissemination of project outcomes.

5. **Authentic Assessment:** Design assessment methods that align with the project goals and objectives. Use a variety of assessment strategies, such as rubrics, portfolios, presentations, and reflections, to holistically evaluate student learning and growth.

6. **Reflection and Revision:** Incorporate reflection and revision activities throughout the project. Encourage students to reflect on their learning experiences, identify strengths and areas for improvement, and revise their work based on feedback and self-assessment.

Example: Design Thinking Project

To illustrate the concept of Project-Based Learning, let's consider an example of a design thinking project. In this project, students will work together to solve a real-world problem using design thinking principles.

Objective: Design an innovative product that addresses an environmental issue in the local community and promotes sustainability.

Steps of the Project:

1. **Understanding the Problem:** Students start by researching and understanding a specific environmental issue in their local community, such as plastic pollution in rivers.

2. **Ideation and Brainstorming:** Students engage in brainstorming sessions to generate ideas for a product that can help address the identified problem. Ideas may include a floating trash collection device or a biodegradable alternative to single-use plastics.

3. **Prototyping:** Students create initial prototypes of their product ideas using design tools and materials. They test and refine their prototypes based on feedback and evaluation.

4. **User Testing and Feedback:** Students conduct user testing sessions to gather feedback on their prototypes. They analyze the feedback and make iterations to improve their designs.

5. **Presentation and Showcase:** Students prepare a compelling presentation to showcase their final product designs. They present their ideas, prototypes, and the rationale behind their designs to an authentic audience, such as community members, industry professionals, or environmental organizations.

6. **Reflection and Evaluation:** After the presentation, students reflect on their learning experiences, evaluate their growth, and identify the challenges and successes encountered throughout the project.

Additional Resources

To further explore Project-Based Learning and its implementation, educators and students can refer to the following resources:

- **Books:**
    - "Project-Based Learning Design and Coaching Guide" by Suzie Boss and John Larmer.
    - "The PBL Playbook: A Guide to ACTion Learning in the Classroom" by Jenny Pieratt.

- "Project Based Learning Made Simple: 100 Classroom-Ready Activities that Inspire Curiosity, Problem Solving and Self-Guided Discovery for Grades 3-12" by PBLWorks.

- Websites:

  - PBLWorks (https://www.pblworks.org) provides a wide range of resources, including project ideas, professional development opportunities, and research articles on project-based learning.
  - Edutopia - Project-Based Learning (https://www.edutopia.org/topic/project-based-learning) offers a collection of articles, videos, and guides dedicated to project-based learning.
  - Buck Institute for Education (https://www.bie.org) provides a wealth of project-based learning resources, including project planning templates and rubrics.

Conclusion

Project-Based Learning is a powerful educational approach that engages students in meaningful, authentic, and collaborative learning experiences. By working on real-world projects, students develop critical thinking, problem-solving, collaboration, and communication skills. While implementing PBL may have challenges, careful planning, support, and effective strategies can lead to successful integration. Project-Based Learning prepares students for the complexities of the modern world, fostering a love for learning and empowering them to become active contributors to society. So, embrace PBL and transform your classroom into a hub of creativity, innovation, and active learning!

Problem-Based Learning

Problem-Based Learning (PBL) is an innovative and student-centered teaching approach that focuses on active engagement and critical thinking. It is an inquiry-based method in which students learn through solving real-world problems or addressing complex issues. PBL encourages self-directed learning and promotes higher-order thinking skills by presenting students with authentic and relevant challenges.

Principles of PBL

PBL is based on several key principles that guide its implementation:

- **Real-world problems:** PBL involves the use of authentic problems that reflect real-life situations or challenges, making the learning experience more meaningful and relevant. These problems are open-ended and often require interdisciplinary knowledge to solve.

- **Student autonomy:** PBL places a strong emphasis on student autonomy and self-directed learning. Students take ownership of their learning by actively exploring and investigating the problem, researching and synthesizing information, and formulating their own solutions.

- **Active learning and collaboration:** PBL encourages active learning through collaborative group work. Students work together in teams to analyze the problem, share perspectives, and collectively develop solutions. This fosters effective communication, teamwork, and interpersonal skills.

- **Problem-solving skills:** PBL aims to develop students' problem-solving skills. By engaging in the process of identifying problems, formulating hypotheses, conducting research, and evaluating solutions, students build critical thinking, analytical reasoning, and decision-making abilities.

- **Reflection and metacognition:** PBL encourages students to reflect on their learning process, metacognition, and personal growth. Students are prompted to assess their own progress, identify strengths and weaknesses, and adjust their strategies accordingly. This promotes self-awareness, self-regulation, and continuous improvement.

Steps in the PBL Process

PBL follows a structured process that guides students through the problem-solving journey. The steps involved in PBL can be summarized as follows:

1. **Problem identification:** The teacher presents a real-world problem or scenario to the students, which serves as the driving force for learning. The problem should be challenging, open-ended, and relevant to the curriculum and students' lives.

2. **Defining the problem:** Students work collaboratively to analyze and define the problem, clarifying key terms, identifying underlying issues, and brainstorming potential solutions. This step helps students develop a deep understanding of the problem's context and scope.

3. **Research and investigation:** Students engage in independent and group research to gather information and resources related to the problem. They may utilize various sources such as books, articles, websites, interviews, or experiments to deepen their knowledge and generate potential solutions.

4. **Solution development:** Based on their research, students design and develop potential solutions to the problem. This stage involves creativity, critical thinking, and interdisciplinary approaches. Students evaluate and refine their solutions, considering different perspectives and limitations.

5. **Implementation and evaluation:** Students select the most promising solution and implement it. They assess the effectiveness of their solution through experimentation or other forms of evaluation. This step allows students to reflect on their learning, analyze the outcomes, and make adjustments if needed.

6. **Reflection and presentation:** Students reflect on their learning experience and outcomes, and present their findings to their peers and/or the wider community. This step solidifies the learning process and provides an opportunity for students to share their insights, reasoning, and solutions.

Advantages of PBL

PBL offers several advantages over traditional instructional methods. Some of the key benefits include:

- **Real-world relevance:** PBL makes learning more meaningful and applicable to real-life scenarios. By working on authentic problems, students can directly observe the practical value and relevance of their learning, enhancing their motivation and engagement.

- **Critical thinking and problem-solving skills:** PBL fosters the development of critical thinking, problem-solving, and analytical skills. Students are actively involved in research, analysis, and decision-making, promoting higher-order thinking abilities.

- **Collaboration and communication skills:** PBL encourages collaboration and teamwork. By working in groups, students develop effective communication, cooperation, and interpersonal skills, which are applicable in various personal and professional settings.

- **Autonomy and self-directed learning:** PBL empowers students to take ownership of their learning. They become independent learners, responsible for managing their time, setting goals, and evaluating their progress. This cultivates self-directed learning skills that are essential for lifelong learning.

- **Engagement and intrinsic motivation:** PBL offers an engaging and motivating learning environment. The authentic problems and active involvement foster intrinsic motivation, curiosity, and a sense of accomplishment, leading to deeper learning and retention.

- **Application across disciplines:** PBL can be applied across various subjects and disciplines, promoting interdisciplinary connections and holistic understanding. It encourages students to draw upon knowledge from multiple areas to solve complex problems, reflecting the integration of knowledge in the real world.

Challenges and Strategies in PBL Implementation

While PBL offers numerous benefits, implementing it effectively can pose challenges. Some common challenges include:

- **Time management:** PBL is a time-consuming approach that requires careful planning and coordination. Teachers need to allocate sufficient time for problem-solving, research, and project work while ensuring coverage of curriculum standards.

- **Assessing individual contributions:** Assessing individual contributions in group settings can be challenging. It is important to design assessment methods that evaluate both collaborative skills and individual learning outcomes.

- **Student resistance:** Some students may initially find the shift to PBL unsettling, as they may be unfamiliar with this approach or prefer a more traditional classroom setting. It is crucial to provide proper orientation, guidance, and support to address students' concerns and build their confidence in PBL.

To overcome these challenges, teachers can employ various strategies:

- **Proper planning and scaffolding**: Teachers should carefully plan the PBL process, breaking it down into manageable steps. Scaffolding techniques, such as providing guiding questions or resources, can support students' understanding and progress.

- **Reflection and formative feedback**: Regular reflection and formative feedback sessions help students monitor their progress, identify areas of improvement, and provide opportunities for teacher guidance and intervention. This enables continuous learning and growth.

- **Teacher facilitation and support**: The role of the teacher in a PBL classroom shifts from being the sole source of knowledge to a facilitator and coach. Teachers provide guidance, resources, and support to students, ensuring that the learning process remains on track.

- **Collaboration and peer learning**: Encouraging collaboration and peer learning allows students to support each other, share ideas, and learn from different perspectives. Peer feedback and assessment can deepen students' understanding and foster a positive learning environment.

- **Authentic assessment methods**: Designing authentic assessment methods, such as portfolios, presentations, or exhibitions, ensures that students' knowledge, skills, and creativity are adequately evaluated. Assessments aligned with real-world contexts provide a comprehensive view of student achievement.

Example of PBL in Practice

Let's consider an example of PBL in a high school biology class. The students are asked to investigate the causes and effects of a local environmental issue, such as water pollution in a nearby river. The PBL process could unfold as follows:

1. The problem is presented: Students are introduced to the problem of water pollution and its impact on the local ecosystem. They discuss the significance of the problem and its relevance to their lives and the community.

2. Problem definition: Students work in groups to define the problem more specifically, identifying the sources and consequences of water pollution. They explore related scientific concepts, such as the water cycle, pollution indicators, and the ecological impact on aquatic life.

3. Research and investigation: Students conduct research to gather information on the causes and effects of water pollution. They might collect water samples, perform experiments, analyze data, interview experts, or explore case studies. They synthesize the information and identify potential solutions.

4. Solution development: Students propose potential solutions to address water pollution. They consider different strategies, such as promoting public awareness, implementing pollution control measures, or advocating for policy changes. They evaluate the feasibility, effectiveness, and potential challenges of each solution.

5. Implementation and evaluation: Students implement their chosen solution, such as organizing a community cleanup event or creating educational campaigns. They assess the impact of their solution by monitoring changes in water quality, conducting surveys, or documenting community engagement.

6. Reflection and presentation: Students reflect on their learning process, analyzing the strengths and weaknesses of their solutions and identifying areas for improvement. They prepare presentations to share their findings, recommendations, and personal reflections with their peers, teachers, and community stakeholders.

This example illustrates how PBL allows students to apply their knowledge and skills to a real-world problem, fostering deeper understanding, engagement, and ownership of their learning.

Resources for PBL

If you are interested in implementing PBL in your classroom, there are several resources available to support your journey:

- The Buck Institute for Education (BIE) offers numerous PBL resources, including project ideas, planning tools, and professional development opportunities. Visit their website at `https://www.bie.org` for more information.

- The PBLWorks website (`https://www.pblworks.org`) provides a variety of resources, research-based strategies, and examples of PBL implementation across different grade levels and subject areas.

- The book "Setting the Standard for Project-Based Learning" by John Larmer, John Mergendoller, and Suzie Boss offers practical guidance, examples, and a framework for successful PBL implementation.

- Educator communities and social media platforms, such as Twitter and Facebook, provide spaces for educators to connect, collaborate, and share PBL ideas and experiences. Joining these communities can offer valuable insights and support.

Conclusion

Problem-Based Learning (PBL) is a student-centered and inquiry-based teaching approach that fosters critical thinking, collaborative skills, and real-world relevance. By engaging in authentic problem-solving, students develop a deeper understanding of concepts, actively apply knowledge, and cultivate lifelong learning skills. While implementing PBL comes with its challenges, employing effective strategies and resources can enhance the learning experience and outcomes. Incorporating PBL into your classroom can revolutionize the way students learn and prepare them for success in the 21st century. So, why not embrace the power of PBL and empower your students to become confident problem solvers and lifelong learners? Let the journey begin!

Cooperative Learning

Cooperative learning is a teaching and learning approach that emphasizes collaboration and active participation among students in order to maximize their learning outcomes. In a cooperative learning environment, students work together in small groups to achieve common goals while supporting and helping each other. This section will explore the principles, strategies, benefits, and challenges of cooperative learning, as well as discuss its role in fostering a positive classroom culture and promoting social-emotional development.

Principles and Strategies of Cooperative Learning

Cooperative learning is rooted in several key principles that guide its implementation in the classroom. These principles are based on the belief that learning is a social activity and that students can benefit greatly from interacting with their peers. Some of the main principles of cooperative learning include:

1. **Positive interdependence:** Students perceive that their success is tied to the success of their groupmates. This encourages them to work together and support each other in achieving common goals.

2. **Individual accountability:** Each student is responsible for their own learning and is held accountable for their contributions to the group. This ensures that every student actively participates and takes ownership of their own learning.

3. **Face-to-face interaction:** Students engage in direct communication and collaboration with their groupmates. This allows for the exchange of ideas, discussion, and the sharing of knowledge and perspectives.

4. **Collaborative skills:** Students develop important social and interpersonal skills such as communication, teamwork, and problem-solving, which are essential for success in school and beyond.

To effectively implement cooperative learning, teachers employ a variety of strategies that promote active engagement and interaction among students. Some common strategies include:

1. **Think-pair-share:** Students think individually about a question or problem, pair up with a partner to discuss their thoughts, and then share their ideas with the whole class. This encourages active participation and fosters deeper understanding through peer discussion.

2. **Jigsaw:** Students are divided into small expert groups, where each group focuses on a specific topic or concept. Afterwards, the expert group members reassemble into new groups, with each member sharing their expertise on the topic. This strategy promotes individual accountability and interdependence, as well as encourages knowledge construction through collaboration.

3. **Group investigations:** Students work in small groups to conduct research, experiments, or problem-solving activities. This allows for the pooling of ideas, resources, and expertise, fostering collaborative learning and critical thinking skills.

4. **Group projects:** Students collaborate in small groups to complete a project or assignment, promoting shared responsibility, decision-making, and problem-solving. This strategy develops teamwork skills and allows for the integration of diverse perspectives.

The choice of cooperative learning strategies should align with the specific learning objectives and needs of the students. By incorporating a variety of strategies, teachers can cater to different learning styles and create a dynamic and engaging cooperative learning environment.

Benefits and Challenges of Cooperative Learning

Cooperative learning has been extensively researched and has shown numerous benefits for students across various academic disciplines. Some of the key benefits include:

1. **Enhanced learning outcomes:** Cooperative learning promotes active engagement, critical thinking, and deep understanding of concepts. It allows students to construct their own knowledge through interaction and collaboration, leading to improved academic achievement.

2. **Social-emotional development:** Cooperative learning provides students with opportunities to develop important social skills such as communication, teamwork, and conflict resolution. It also fosters a sense of belonging, empathy, and positive relationships among students.

3. **Increased motivation and engagement:** Working together in small groups creates a supportive and interactive learning environment that increases students' interest and motivation to learn. It allows for the exploration of different perspectives and promotes a sense of ownership and autonomy in the learning process.

4. **Promotion of diversity and inclusivity:** Cooperative learning encourages the inclusion of diverse voices and perspectives. It values the strengths and contributions of each student, promoting equity and fostering a sense of belonging for all learners.

Despite its numerous benefits, cooperative learning may also present challenges that teachers need to address in order to ensure its successful implementation. Some of the challenges include:

1. **Group dynamics:** Group work can sometimes be challenging due to varying levels of motivation, conflicts, or differences in ability and personality. Teachers need to carefully plan and structure cooperative learning activities to ensure equal participation and create a positive group dynamic.

2. **Individual accountability:** While cooperative learning emphasizes collaboration, it is important to ensure that each student is individually accountable for their learning. Teachers must implement strategies such as group roles, individual assessments, and regular check-ins to promote individual accountability within the group.

3. **Assessment and grading:** Assessing individual student performance in cooperative learning settings can be complex. Teachers need to develop fair and reliable assessment methods that measure both individual and group achievements, while considering the dynamics of group work and the contributions of each student.

4. **Time management:** Cooperative learning activities may require additional time compared to traditional instructional methods. Teachers should carefully plan and allocate sufficient time for group work, while balancing it with other instructional activities to ensure effective time management.

Addressing these challenges requires careful planning, ongoing reflection, and the implementation of appropriate strategies and supports. Collaborative professional development opportunities and sharing of best practices among educators can also be valuable in effectively implementing cooperative learning in the classroom.

Promoting Cooperative Learning in the Classroom

To create a cooperative learning culture in the classroom, teachers can take several steps to promote collaboration and active participation among students. Some strategies include:

1. **Establish clear expectations:** Set clear guidelines and expectations for cooperative learning activities, including rules for group work, discussion norms, and accountability for individual and group performance.

2. **Build a positive classroom community:** Foster a supportive and inclusive classroom environment where students feel safe to take risks, share their ideas, and learn from their peers. Encourage respect, active listening, and empathy among students.

3. **Establish group norms and roles:** Help students understand their roles within the group and establish norms for effective collaboration. Rotate

group roles periodically to give students the opportunity to develop different skills and take on different responsibilities.

4. **Provide scaffolding and support:** Offer necessary support and guidance to students as they engage in cooperative learning activities. This may include modeling effective collaboration, providing prompts or guiding questions, and offering specific feedback on teamwork and communication skills.

5. **Reflect and debrief:** Facilitate regular opportunities for students to reflect on their cooperative learning experiences. This can be done through group discussions, self-reflection activities, or written reflections, where students can share their successes, challenges, and strategies for improvement.

By promoting a cooperative learning culture, teachers can create a classroom environment that fosters active engagement, critical thinking, and positive social interactions.

Cooperative Learning and Technology

Technology can play a significant role in enhancing cooperative learning experiences. Various technological tools and platforms can support communication, collaboration, and knowledge sharing among students. Some examples include:

1. **Online collaborative platforms:** Platforms such as Google Docs, Microsoft Teams, and Padlet enable real-time collaboration and document sharing, allowing students to work together on projects, share ideas, and provide feedback to their peers.

2. **Virtual classrooms:** Learning management systems like Moodle or Canvas provide a virtual space for students to collaborate, access resources, and submit assignments. These platforms also allow for asynchronous communication, making it possible for students to collaborate outside of traditional classroom hours.

3. **Digital storytelling tools:** Tools like Storybird or Book Creator enable students to work collaboratively in creating and sharing digital stories. This allows for the integration of multimedia elements and enhances students' creativity and communication skills.

4. **Video conferencing:** Video conferencing tools, such as Zoom or Microsoft Teams, can facilitate virtual group discussions and presentations, enabling students to collaborate remotely. This is especially valuable for distance or blended learning environments.

5. **Online discussion boards:** Discussion board platforms, like Padlet or Flipgrid, provide a space for students to engage in asynchronous discussions, share their ideas, and respond to their peers' contributions. This promotes active participation and reflection.

It is important for teachers to select appropriate technological tools that align with the learning objectives and promote meaningful collaboration among students. Technology integration should enhance and support cooperative learning, rather than replace or hinder face-to-face interaction.

Conclusion

Cooperative learning offers a powerful approach to engage students in active learning, enhance critical thinking skills, and promote social-emotional development. By creating a supportive and collaborative classroom environment, teachers can foster student ownership of learning, promote meaningful interactions, and prepare students for success in the 21st century. However, the successful implementation of cooperative learning requires careful planning, effective management of group dynamics, and ongoing reflection and adjustment. By embracing cooperative learning and leveraging the potential of technology, educators can create dynamic and inclusive learning environments that empower students to become lifelong learners and active contributors to society.

Now you have explored the principles, strategies, benefits, and challenges of cooperative learning. It is time to reflect on how you can incorporate cooperative learning strategies in your own teaching practice. Consider the specific needs and dynamics of your classroom and explore innovative ways to engage students in collaborative learning experiences. Remember, by fostering a cooperative learning culture, you are not only supporting students' academic growth but also nurturing their social and emotional development.

Advantages and Challenges of Student-Centered Learning

Enhanced Motivation and Engagement

Motivation and engagement are crucial factors in student-centered learning. When students feel motivated and engaged, they are more likely to be active participants in their own learning process, leading to better overall educational outcomes. This section explores the various ways in which student-centered learning enhances motivation and engagement, along with strategies to foster these qualities in the classroom.

Intrinsic and Extrinsic Motivation

Motivation can be categorized as either intrinsic or extrinsic. Intrinsic motivation refers to the internal desire to engage in an activity for its own sake, driven by personal interest, curiosity, or a sense of enjoyment. Extrinsic motivation, on the other hand, involves engaging in an activity to obtain external rewards or avoid punishment.

Student-centered learning places a strong emphasis on fostering intrinsic motivation. By giving students more autonomy and control over their learning, they are more likely to feel a sense of ownership and personal investment in their educational journey. When students have the freedom to choose topics that interest them or have a say in how they demonstrate their learning, their intrinsic motivation is activated.

Choice and Autonomy

One way to enhance motivation and engagement is by providing students with choice and autonomy in their learning. Allowing students to have a say in what they learn, how they learn, and how they demonstrate their understanding can significantly increase their motivation.

For example, instead of assigning a specific research topic to students, teachers can provide a range of options and let students choose the one that interests them the most. This not only taps into students' intrinsic motivation but also promotes a sense of ownership and agency in their learning process. Similarly, allowing students to have a voice in the assessment methods, such as giving them options to create presentations, write essays, or design projects, can increase their motivation to perform well and showcase their abilities.

Real-World Relevance

Another way to enhance motivation and engagement is by making learning relevant to students' lives and the real world. When students understand the practical applications of what they are learning, they are more likely to be motivated to engage with the content.

Integrating real-world examples and scenarios into the curriculum can help students see the value and relevance of their learning. For instance, in a mathematics class, teachers can use real-world problems, such as calculating the cost of groceries or planning a budget, to demonstrate the practical uses of mathematical concepts. This approach not only boosts students' motivation but also helps them develop critical thinking skills and problem-solving abilities that are essential in real-life situations.

Collaborative Learning

Collaborative learning is another effective strategy to enhance motivation and engagement. When students work together in groups or teams, they have the opportunity to actively participate, learn from their peers, and contribute to the collective knowledge.

Group projects, discussions, and problem-solving activities promote a sense of shared responsibility and encourage students to actively engage in the learning process. Working collaboratively also allows students to hear different perspectives and gain new insights, leading to a deeper understanding of the subject matter.

Incorporating Technology

Technology can be a powerful tool to enhance motivation and engagement in student-centered learning environments. Various technological tools and platforms can be leveraged to create interactive and immersive learning experiences.

For example, online platforms and educational apps can provide personalized learning pathways, adaptive feedback, and gamified elements to make learning more engaging. Virtual reality and augmented reality can transport students to virtual worlds, allowing them to explore and interact with complex concepts in a hands-on manner. These technologies not only enhance motivation but also provide opportunities for active learning and problem-solving.

Innovative Teaching Strategies

In addition to the above approaches, teachers can employ innovative teaching strategies to enhance motivation and engagement. For instance, incorporating hands-on activities, field trips, guest speakers, and role-playing exercises can make learning more exciting and relevant to students.

Teachers can also harness the power of storytelling to capture students' attention and trigger their imagination. By weaving narratives and real-life anecdotes into lessons, teachers can create an emotional connection with students, making the learning experience more memorable and engaging.

Caveats and Challenges

While student-centered learning enhances motivation and engagement, it is important to address potential challenges and caveats. Students may have different learning preferences and levels of motivation, requiring teachers to employ varied strategies to cater to individual needs. Additionally, it is essential to consider cultural and socioeconomic factors that may influence students' motivation and engagement.

Furthermore, fostering motivation and engagement is an ongoing process that requires continuous reflection and adaptation. Teachers should regularly assess the effectiveness of their strategies and make adjustments as needed to meet students' changing needs.

Conclusion

Enhancing motivation and engagement is a critical aspect of student-centered learning. By providing choice and autonomy, making learning relevant, fostering collaborative environments, leveraging technology, and employing innovative teaching strategies, teachers can create a classroom environment where students are actively engaged in their own learning. When students feel motivated and engaged, they become active participants in their education, leading to better learning outcomes and a love for lifelong learning.

Improved Critical Thinking and Problem-Solving Skills

Critical thinking and problem-solving skills are fundamental to a student's academic success and future career. In today's rapidly changing world, where information is readily available, students need to be able to think critically, analyze complex problems, and come up with innovative solutions. This section will explore how student-centered learning approaches can enhance critical thinking and problem-solving skills, and provide strategies for teachers to foster these skills in their classrooms.

Developing Critical Thinking Skills

Critical thinking is the ability to objectively analyze and evaluate information, arguments, claims, and assumptions. It involves logical reasoning, evidence-based decision making, and the ability to consider multiple perspectives. Student-centered learning approaches lay the foundation for developing critical thinking skills by engaging students in active learning experiences. Here are some strategies to promote critical thinking:

1. Encourage questioning: Teachers can encourage students to ask questions and critically examine the information presented to them. By asking thought-provoking questions, students learn to think analytically and independently.

2. Problem-solving activities: Engaging students in problem-solving activities helps them develop their critical thinking skills. Teachers can provide real-world scenarios or complex problems that require analysis and evaluation to find solutions.

3. Collaborative learning: Collaborative learning environments promote critical thinking by encouraging students to discuss and debate ideas with their peers. Through these interactions, students gain different perspectives and learn to evaluate and justify their own opinions.

4. Socratic questioning: Utilizing Socratic questioning techniques challenges students to think deeply and critically. By asking open-ended questions that probe for evidence and assumptions, teachers can guide students towards thoughtful and logical reasoning.

Enhancing Problem-Solving Skills

Problem-solving skills are essential for success in various areas of life. Through student-centered learning approaches, teachers can help students develop effective problem-solving techniques. Here are some strategies to enhance problem-solving skills:

1. Real-world problem-solving: Teachers can provide authentic, real-world problems for students to solve. By addressing actual challenges, students understand the relevance of their learning, and develop problem-solving skills that can be applied beyond the classroom.

2. Inquiry-based projects: Inquiry-based projects provide students with opportunities to identify problems, conduct research, and propose solutions. This approach helps students develop critical thinking and problem-solving skills while fostering their curiosity and creativity.

3. Decision-making exercises: Teachers can engage students in decision-making exercises where they have to evaluate different options, consider the pros and cons, and make informed decisions. This helps students develop analytical thinking and problem-solving abilities.

4. Reflection and self-assessment: Teachers can encourage students to reflect on their problem-solving processes and outcomes. Through self-assessment, students can identify areas for improvement, develop metacognitive skills, and refine their problem-solving strategies.

Examples and Resources

To further enhance critical thinking and problem-solving skills, educators can utilize a variety of examples and resources. Here are some examples:

1. Case studies: Case studies present real-world scenarios to students, challenging them to analyze complex situations and propose solutions. They encourage students to think critically and apply their knowledge and skills to solve problems.

2. Simulations and virtual laboratories: Simulations and virtual laboratories provide students with hands-on experiences in problem-solving. They allow students to experiment, make decisions, and observe the outcomes of their actions, fostering critical thinking and problem-solving skills.

3. Online resources: There are numerous online resources available that promote critical thinking and problem-solving skills. Websites, interactive videos, and educational platforms offer engaging activities and exercises to develop these skills.

4. Professional development workshops: Teachers can participate in professional development workshops that focus on enhancing critical thinking and problem-solving skills. These workshops provide educators with new strategies, techniques, and resources to implement in their classrooms.

Unconventional Strategy: Design Thinking

Design thinking is a problem-solving approach that focuses on human-centered design. It encourages students to empathize, define, ideate, prototype, and test solutions to complex problems. This unconventional strategy combines critical thinking, creativity, and collaboration, allowing students to develop innovative solutions and enhance their problem-solving skills.

For example, in a science class, students can use design thinking to solve environmental challenges in their community. They can empathize with different stakeholders, define the problem, brainstorm ideas, create prototypes, and test their solutions. This approach not only develops critical thinking and problem-solving skills but also fosters creativity, collaboration, and empathy.

Exercises

1. Imagine you are a city planner tasked with reducing traffic congestion. Using your critical thinking skills, propose three innovative solutions to this problem.

2. Analyze the impact of social media on society, considering both the positive and negative effects. Use evidence and critical thinking to support your arguments.

3. Create a design thinking project for your students to solve a local community problem. Outline the steps involved and the expected learning outcomes.

4. Reflect on a recent problem you encountered and describe how you used critical thinking and problem-solving skills to overcome it. What were the outcomes of your problem-solving process?

Conclusion

Improved critical thinking and problem-solving skills are vital for students to succeed in their academic and professional lives. By implementing student-centered learning approaches and leveraging strategies like questioning, problem-solving activities, collaboration, and Socratic questioning, teachers can cultivate these essential skills in their students. Furthermore, utilizing examples and resources such as case studies, simulations, online platforms, and professional development workshops, educators can enhance critical thinking and problem-solving abilities. By employing unconventional strategies like design thinking, students can develop innovative solutions to complex problems, fostering creativity, collaboration, and empathy along the way.

Addressing Individual Learning Needs

In the realm of education, every student is unique and has their own set of learning needs. Addressing these individual needs is crucial to ensure that all students have equal opportunities to succeed academically. In this section, we will explore various strategies and approaches to address individual learning needs effectively.

Understanding Individual Learning Needs

Before we delve into the strategies, it is important to understand what individual learning needs entail. Individual learning needs refer to the specific requirements and preferences that students have when it comes to acquiring and processing information. These needs can be influenced by various factors, including cognitive abilities, learning styles, language proficiency, disabilities, cultural backgrounds, and personal interests.

Recognizing and considering these factors is essential for designing instruction that caters to the diverse needs of students. It is important to move away from a one-size-fits-all approach and instead adopt a learner-centered mindset, which requires educators to be proactive and responsive to students' individual learning needs.

Differentiating Instruction

One effective way to address individual learning needs is through differentiated instruction. This instructional approach involves tailoring teaching methods, content, and assessment to meet the diverse needs of students. By considering students' readiness, interests, and learning profiles, educators can create a learning environment that promotes engagement and success.

1. **Adapted Content:** Providing different levels of complexity and depth allows students to access content that is appropriate for their current skill level. For instance, in a mathematics class, teachers can assign different sets of problems based on students' readiness.

2. **Varied Instructional Strategies:** Different students respond to different instructional methods. By incorporating a variety of strategies such as visual aids, hands-on activities, group work, and technology-based resources, educators can accommodate different learning styles and preferences.

3. **Flexible Grouping:** Grouping students flexibly based on their strengths and needs can promote collaboration, enhance peer learning, and provide opportunities for students to support each other. Educators can assign group tasks that allow students to contribute their unique skills and knowledge.

4. **Individualized Assessment:** Assessments should be designed to evaluate students' understanding and mastery of the content. Providing options for students to demonstrate their learning through varied formats such as oral presentations, written reports, or multimedia projects allows for individual strengths and preferences.

Personalized Learning Plans

Another approach to addressing individual learning needs is through the development and implementation of personalized learning plans. Personalized learning plans are tailored to each student's specific learning goals, strengths, challenges, and interests. These plans involve a collaborative effort between educators, students, and sometimes parents, to create a roadmap for learning.

1. **Goal Setting**: Students and educators collaborate to set measurable, attainable, and relevant learning goals. These goals can be academic, social-emotional, or skill-based and provide a focus for individualized instruction.

2. **Progress Monitoring**: Regularly tracking and assessing student progress is crucial to ensure that personalized learning goals are being met. Educators can use a variety of assessment methods, such as ongoing observation, formative assessments, student self-reflection, and portfolios, to gather evidence of learning.

3. **Adaptive Technology**: Technology can play a significant role in facilitating personalized learning plans. Adaptive learning platforms and software can provide students with individualized learning pathways, immediate feedback, and resources tailored to their needs.

4. **Student Agency**: In personalized learning, students have a greater role in decision-making and self-regulation of their learning. Encouraging student agency empowers students to take ownership of their learning, set goals, make choices, and reflect on their progress.

Inclusive Classroom Practices

Creating an inclusive classroom environment is key to effectively addressing individual learning needs. Inclusion ensures that all students, regardless of their abilities or backgrounds, feel welcome, respected, and supported. Here are some strategies for fostering inclusivity:

1. **Universal Design for Learning (UDL)**: UDL is an approach that promotes the design of flexible learning environments and instructional materials to accommodate a wide range of learner variability. By considering diverse needs from the outset, educators can reduce barriers to learning for all students.

2. **Culturally Responsive Teaching**: Recognizing and valuing students' cultural backgrounds is essential for creating an inclusive classroom. Culturally responsive teaching involves incorporating culturally relevant content and perspectives, using diverse teaching strategies, and building strong relationships with students and their communities.

3. Collaborative Partnerships: Collaborating with other professionals, such as special education teachers, therapists, and support staff, can provide additional resources and expertise to meet the individual needs of students. Building strong partnerships with parents and guardians is also crucial for understanding students' background and creating a supportive learning environment.

4. Social-Emotional Support: Addressing students' social-emotional needs is essential for creating a positive classroom climate. Educators can implement strategies such as classroom meetings, restorative practices, and mindfulness exercises to foster emotional well-being and build strong relationships among students.

Conclusion

Addressing individual learning needs is a fundamental aspect of modern education. By employing strategies such as differentiated instruction, personalized learning plans, and inclusive classroom practices, educators can create a learning environment that supports the diverse needs and strengths of all students. Recognizing and catering to individual learning needs not only ensures academic success but also promotes a sense of belonging, equity, and empowerment for every learner.

Promoting Creativity and Innovation

In today's rapidly evolving world, creativity and innovation have become indispensable skills for students. Encouraging creativity and nurturing innovative thinking in the classroom can empower students to think critically, solve problems, and adapt to new challenges. This section explores various strategies and approaches to promote creativity and innovation within the student-centered learning environment.

Understanding Creativity and Innovation

Creativity refers to the ability to generate original ideas or solutions, while innovation involves implementing those ideas to create meaningful change. Both creativity and innovation are essential for success in the 21st century, as they foster adaptability, entrepreneurship, and critical thinking. By encouraging students to think outside the box, explore new perspectives, and embrace risk-taking, educators can cultivate an environment that nurtures creativity and innovation.

Importance of Creativity and Innovation in Education

Creativity and innovation go beyond traditional academic knowledge and facilitate the development of essential skills for the future workforce. By promoting creativity and innovation in education, we equip students with the ability to:

- Solve complex problems: Creative and innovative thinkers can approach problems from multiple angles and devise unique solutions.

- Adapt to change: In a rapidly changing world, creativity and innovation help individuals adapt and thrive in new environments.

- Think critically: Creative thinking involves questioning assumptions, analyzing information, and evaluating different perspectives to make informed decisions.

- Collaborate effectively: Creativity and innovation enhance collaboration by encouraging students to value diverse opinions and work together towards a common goal.

Strategies for Promoting Creativity and Innovation

1. **Encourage open-ended questions and curiosity:** Pose thought-provoking questions that do not have a single correct answer. This encourages students to explore different possibilities, think critically, and develop creative solutions.

2. **Foster an inclusive and supportive classroom environment:** Create a safe space where students feel comfortable expressing their ideas without fear of judgment. Encourage active participation and value diverse perspectives.

3. **Provide opportunities for hands-on learning:** Engage students in activities that require them to apply their knowledge and skills in practical ways. This can involve experimenting, designing, or creating tangible products.

4. **Promote interdisciplinary learning:** Encourage students to make connections between different subject areas and explore how they intersect. This helps them see the big picture and develop a holistic understanding of complex issues.

5. **Offer autonomy and freedom in learning:** Give students the freedom to choose topics of interest or design their own projects. Allowing them to pursue their passions fosters intrinsic motivation and stimulates creative thinking.

6. **Provide time for reflection and revision:** Creativity often requires iteration and refinement. Build regular reflection and revision opportunities into students' learning process, allowing them to improve their ideas and solutions over time.

ADVANTAGES AND CHALLENGES OF STUDENT-CENTERED LEARNING

Integrating Technology to Enhance Creativity and Innovation

Digital tools and technologies can amplify creativity and innovation in the classroom. Here are some ways to leverage technology:

1. **Digital creation tools:** Provide access to various digital creation tools, such as graphic design software, video editing tools, and coding platforms. These tools empower students to express their ideas in different formats and explore new means of communication.

2. **Online collaboration platforms:** Use online platforms that facilitate collaboration, such as virtual whiteboards or project management tools. These platforms enable students to work together, share ideas, and provide feedback in real-time.

3. **Virtual reality (VR) and augmented reality (AR):** VR and AR technologies offer immersive experiences that can enhance creativity and innovation. Students can explore virtual environments, design 3D models, or simulate scenarios to solve complex problems.

4. **Gamification:** Gamify learning experiences by incorporating game elements into educational activities. This approach motivates students, fosters creativity, and encourages innovation through challenges, rewards, and friendly competition.

Real-World Examples

To better understand how promoting creativity and innovation can translate into real-world applications, here are a few examples:

1. **Design thinking challenges:** Assign students a design thinking challenge, where they have to identify a problem, brainstorm solutions, and create prototypes. This hands-on approach fosters creative problem-solving skills.

2. **Entrepreneurship projects:** Encourage students to develop their own business ideas and create a business plan. This project-based approach cultivates innovation, critical thinking, and collaboration skills.

3. **Invention competitions:** Participating in invention competitions such as science fairs or innovation challenges provides students with an opportunity to showcase their creative ideas and receive feedback from experts.

Resources and Further Reading

- "Creative Schools: The Grassroots Revolution That's Transforming Education" by Sir Ken Robinson - "Innovator's Mindset: Empower Learning, Unleash Talent, and Lead a Culture of Creativity" by George Couros - TED Talks: "Do Schools Kill

Creativity?" by Sir Ken Robinson, "Embrace the Shake" by Phil Hansen, and "The Surprising Habits of Original Thinkers" by Adam Grant.

Conclusion

Promoting creativity and innovation in education is vital for preparing students for the challenges of the future. By incorporating strategies that encourage open-mindedness, collaboration, and the use of technology, educators can foster creativity, innovation, and critical thinking skills. Empowering students to explore their creativity and embrace innovative ideas will not only benefit their academic success but also equip them with essential skills for life beyond the classroom.

Challenges in Implementation

Implementing student-centered learning in the classroom can bring about numerous benefits for both students and teachers. However, it is not without its challenges. In this section, we will discuss some of the key challenges that educators may face when trying to implement student-centered learning and explore strategies for overcoming them.

1. **Resistance to Change:** One of the major challenges in implementing student-centered learning is the resistance to change from teachers, administrators, and even students themselves. Traditional teaching methods have been ingrained in the education system for a long time, and transitioning to a student-centered approach requires a shift in mindset and pedagogy. Many teachers may be apprehensive about giving up control and allowing students to take charge of their own learning.

To overcome this challenge, it is crucial to provide professional development opportunities for teachers to learn about student-centered instructional strategies and their benefits. Offering workshops, training sessions, and ongoing support can help teachers understand the value of student-centered learning and gain confidence in implementing it in their classrooms.

2. **Lack of Resources:** Another challenge in implementing student-centered learning is the availability and access to resources. Student-centered learning often requires a wide range of resources, including technology, manipulatives, and materials for project-based activities. However, not all schools have the necessary resources to support this approach.

To address this challenge, it is essential to seek creative solutions and leverage existing resources. Collaborating with other teachers, sharing resources, and seeking external partnerships can help overcome resource constraints. Additionally, using open educational resources (OER) and free online tools can provide cost-effective alternatives.

3. **Time Constraints:** Time constraints are a significant challenge in implementing student-centered learning. Student-centered activities often require more time for inquiry, discovery, and collaborative work. In a traditional teaching model where teachers need to cover a set curriculum within a specific timeframe, finding time for student-centered learning can be challenging.

To address this, teachers can integrate student-centered activities strategically into the curriculum. By identifying key concepts and skills that lend themselves well to student-centered approaches, teachers can ensure that they make the most of the available time. It is also important to prioritize deep learning and critical thinking over superficial coverage of content.

4. **Assessment and Evaluation:** Assessing student learning in a student-centered environment can be more complex than traditional assessment methods. Student-centered learning focuses on individual growth, collaboration, and the development of higher-order thinking skills, which may not align well with standardized testing and traditional grading systems.

To overcome this challenge, teachers can utilize a variety of assessment strategies. Performance-based assessments, self-assessments, portfolios, and rubrics can provide a more comprehensive and holistic understanding of student learning. It is important to align assessments with the learning goals and objectives of student-centered activities.

5. **Classroom Management:** Student-centered learning often involves greater student autonomy, active engagement, and collaborative work. While these aspects can greatly enhance learning, they can also pose challenges in terms of classroom management. Teachers may struggle with maintaining discipline, managing group dynamics, and ensuring that all students are actively participating.

To address this challenge, teachers need to establish clear expectations, rules, and procedures from the beginning. Providing guidance on effective collaboration, establishing routines for managing group work, and fostering a positive classroom culture can help manage these issues. It is important to create an inclusive and supportive learning environment where all students feel valued and engaged.

In summary, implementing student-centered learning comes with its own set of challenges. However, with careful planning, ongoing professional development, collaboration, and creative problem-solving, these challenges can be overcome. The benefits of student-centered learning such as increased student engagement, critical thinking, and personalized learning experiences make it worth the effort. By embracing these challenges as opportunities for growth, teachers can create transformative learning environments that empower students and prepare them for the future.

Strategies for Overcoming Challenges

Implementing student-centered learning approaches can bring numerous benefits to education, but it is not without its challenges. In this section, we will discuss some strategies for overcoming these challenges and ensuring the successful implementation of student-centered learning in the classroom.

1. **Providing Professional Development:** One of the key strategies for overcoming challenges in student-centered learning is to provide teachers with professional development opportunities. Teachers need support and resources to understand the principles and practices of student-centered learning. They need training on how to effectively facilitate collaborative activities, personalize instruction, and integrate technology. By investing in professional development programs, schools can equip teachers with the necessary skills and knowledge to implement student-centered approaches effectively.

2. **Fostering a Collaborative Culture:** Collaboration plays a significant role in student-centered learning. However, creating a collaborative culture can be a challenge if teachers and students are not accustomed to working collectively. Schools can address this challenge by promoting collaboration through various means, such as establishing professional learning communities, providing opportunities for collaborative planning and reflection, and encouraging teachers to share best practices. Building a collaborative culture will help create an environment where student-centered learning can thrive.

3. **Addressing Curriculum and Assessment Challenges:** Traditional curricula and assessments may not align perfectly with student-centered learning. To overcome this challenge, schools should review and revise curricular materials to ensure they are aligned with the principles of student-centered learning. This may involve restructuring the curriculum to provide more flexibility and choice for students, creating authentic and meaningful assessments that reflect students' knowledge and skills, and incorporating innovative assessment practices, such as portfolios or project-based assessments. By aligning curricula and assessments with student-centered approaches, schools can better support and evaluate student learning.

4. **Creating a Supportive Learning Environment:** Student-centered learning requires a supportive and safe learning environment. Schools can create such an environment by fostering positive relationships between teachers and students, promoting a growth mindset, and providing differentiated support for individual

student needs. Teachers should strive to create a classroom atmosphere where students feel comfortable expressing their ideas, taking risks, and collaborating with their peers. A supportive learning environment is crucial for student engagement and motivation, which are the cornerstones of student-centered learning.

5. **Engaging Parents and the Community**: Involving parents and the community can be a powerful strategy for overcoming challenges in student-centered learning. Schools can actively engage parents by sharing information about the benefits of student-centered approaches and involving them in the decision-making process. Parents can be invited to participate in workshops, classroom activities, and school events that showcase student-centered learning. Community partnerships can also enhance student-centered learning by providing real-world connections and resources for students. By fostering strong relationships with parents and the community, schools can create a supportive network that complements student-centered learning efforts.

Remember, implementing student-centered learning approaches requires a shift in mindset and pedagogical practices. Challenges will inevitably arise, but with the right strategies and support, these challenges can be overcome. By providing professional development, fostering a collaborative culture, addressing curriculum and assessment challenges, creating a supportive learning environment, and engaging parents and the community, schools can successfully implement student-centered learning and revolutionize education.

Engaging Parents and the Community

Engaging parents and the community is essential for creating a supportive and collaborative learning environment. When parents are actively involved in their child's education, students tend to perform better academically, exhibit positive behavior, and have higher motivation levels. In this section, we will explore strategies and approaches to effectively engage parents and the community in the educational process.

Importance of Parent and Community Engagement

Parent and community engagement plays a crucial role in student success. It fosters a sense of belonging and connection between the home, school, and community. When parents actively participate in their child's education, they can provide valuable insights, support academic goals, and reinforce positive values and behaviors. Additionally, community partnerships provide resources, expertise, and authentic learning opportunities that enhance student learning experiences.

Building Positive Relationships with Parents

Building positive relationships with parents is key to creating strong home-school partnerships. Teachers can start with the following strategies:

1. Regular Communication: Maintaining open and regular communication channels helps keep parents informed about their child's progress, upcoming events, and classroom activities. Teachers can use a variety of communication tools such as newsletters, emails, phone calls, or even social media platforms.

2. Welcoming Environment: Teachers can create a welcoming and inclusive environment during parent-teacher conferences, school events, and classroom visits. This helps parents feel comfortable and encourages their active participation.

3. Active Listening: Actively listening to parents' concerns, questions, and ideas demonstrates respect and shows that their opinions are valued. Teachers can hold one-on-one conversations with parents, conduct surveys, or organize focus groups to gather feedback on their child's education.

4. Parent Education Workshops: Conducting parent education workshops on various topics, such as supporting literacy development or understanding social-emotional needs, can empower parents to actively engage in their child's education.

5. Celebrating Diversity: Recognizing and celebrating the diverse backgrounds, cultures, and languages of families creates a sense of inclusivity and promotes mutual respect between teachers, students, and parents.

Collaborative Decision-Making

Involving parents in decision-making processes helps ensure their voices are heard and their perspectives are considered. Teachers can engage parents in the following ways:

1. Parent Advisory Committees: Establishing parent advisory committees allows parents to actively participate in school-level decision-making processes. These committees can be involved in curriculum development, school policies, or strategic planning.

2. Parent Surveys and Feedback: Regularly seeking input from parents through surveys or feedback forms can provide valuable insights and perspectives on various educational initiatives or changes.

3. Parent Representatives: Designating parent representatives in parent-teacher associations or school councils can ensure that parents have a formal channel to voice their opinions and concerns.

4. Parent Volunteer Opportunities: Providing opportunities for parents to volunteer in the classroom or school events can foster a sense of ownership and involvement in their child's education.

Community Partnerships

Engaging the community as educational partners can enrich students' learning experiences and provide valuable resources. Teachers can establish community partnerships through the following approaches:

1. Business and Industry Collaboration: Collaborating with local businesses or industry experts can expose students to real-world applications of classroom learning. Guest speakers or mentorship programs can offer valuable insights and career guidance.

2. Service Learning Projects: Engaging students in service learning projects that address community needs fosters a sense of civic responsibility and allows students to apply their learning in meaningful ways.

3. Community Events and Resources: Actively participating in community events, such as local festivals or workshops, helps establish connections between the school and the community. Utilizing local resources, such as libraries or museums, can also enhance learning opportunities.

4. Parent Workshops: Collaborating with community organizations to conduct parent workshops on relevant topics, such as health and wellness or financial literacy, can support parents in their role as educators.

Challenges and Solutions

Engaging parents and the community may present certain challenges. Some possible challenges include language barriers, diverse cultural expectations, or lack of available resources. However, addressing these challenges can lead to more effective engagement. Here are some solutions:

1. Language Support: Providing translation services or bilingual staff can help overcome language barriers and ensure effective communication with parents.

2. Cultural Sensitivity: Developing cultural competence among teachers and promoting inclusivity can help bridge cultural gaps and ensure that all families feel valued and respected.

3. Outreach and Accessibility: Making school events and resources accessible to all parents, including those with limited resources or transportation, can increase participation and engagement.

4. Collaboration with Community Organizations: Partnering with community organizations or local agencies can provide additional support for addressing barriers or challenges faced by families.

Conclusion

Engaging parents and the community is crucial for creating a holistic and supportive educational environment. By building positive relationships, involving parents in decision-making, and establishing community partnerships, educators can enhance student learning experiences and foster a sense of shared responsibility for education. Overcoming challenges through language support, cultural sensitivity, outreach, and collaboration ensures that all families feel included and valued. By working together, parents, educators, and the community can contribute to the success and well-being of students.

Professional Development for Student-Centered Teaching

Professional development plays a crucial role in supporting teachers as they transition to student-centered teaching methods. Recognizing that the traditional role of a teacher is gradually evolving to that of a facilitator and guide, it becomes imperative to provide teachers with the necessary skills, knowledge, and resources to effectively implement student-centered approaches in the classroom. This section explores the importance of professional development for student-centered teaching, strategies for effective professional development, and the role of collaboration and ongoing support for teachers.

Importance of Professional Development

Professional development serves as a platform for teachers to enhance their teaching skills, expand their knowledge base, and stay updated with the latest research and best practices in education. It is essential for teachers to develop a deep understanding of student-centered learning principles, as well as the strategies and instructional models associated with it.

Student-centered teaching requires a shift in mindset, pedagogical approaches, and classroom dynamics. Teachers need to be equipped with the knowledge and skills to effectively implement strategies such as personalized learning, differentiated instruction, and project-based learning. Professional development helps teachers gain the necessary knowledge, confidence, and expertise needed to create a student-centered learning environment conducive to meaningful engagement and academic success.

Strategies for Effective Professional Development

To ensure that professional development for student-centered teaching is effective, it should be designed in a way that enables teachers to reflect on their current practices, acquire new skills, and apply them in the classroom. Here are some strategies for effective professional development:

1. **Needs Assessment:** Conduct a needs assessment to identify the specific areas where teachers require support and development. This can be done through surveys, classroom observations, and discussions with teachers.

2. **Collaborative Learning Communities:** Foster collaborative learning communities where teachers can share experiences, ideas, and resources. Regular meetings, discussions, and workshops can be organized to facilitate collaboration and the exchange of knowledge among teachers.

3. **Job-Embedded Learning:** Provide opportunities for job-embedded learning, where teachers can apply their newly acquired knowledge and skills in their everyday classroom practice. This can be done through coaching, mentoring, and peer observation.

4. **Modeling and Demonstration:** Use modeling and demonstration to show teachers how student-centered strategies can be implemented in the classroom. This can be done through classroom visits, video recordings, or simulations.

5. **Hands-on Workshops:** Conduct hands-on workshops where teachers can actively engage in learning and practice new instructional strategies. These workshops should provide teachers with opportunities to collaborate, reflect, and receive feedback.

6. **Technology Integration:** Integrate technology into professional development activities to familiarize teachers with the tools and resources that can support student-centered learning. This can include training on using learning management systems, online collaboration tools, and educational software.

7. **Ongoing Support and Reflection:** Provide ongoing support and opportunities for reflection. This can include follow-up workshops, coaching sessions, and collaborative learning communities where teachers can continuously refine and improve their practice.

Collaboration and Ongoing Support

Collaboration and ongoing support are critical components of effective professional development for student-centered teaching. A collaborative culture within the school encourages teachers to share ideas, resources, and challenges, leading to collective growth and improvement. Ongoing support ensures that teachers receive the necessary guidance, feedback, and resources to implement student-centered strategies effectively.

To foster collaboration and ongoing support, schools can:

- Establish professional learning communities where teachers can meet regularly to discuss student-centered teaching practices, share successes and challenges, and collaborate on curriculum development and assessment strategies.

- Encourage mentoring and coaching relationships between experienced and novice teachers. This promotes the exchange of knowledge and provides new teachers with the support and guidance they need to implement student-centered approaches.

- Provide teachers with access to a variety of resources, such as books, articles, websites, and online communities, that offer ongoing support and professional development opportunities.

- Create opportunities for teachers to observe each other's classrooms and engage in collaborative planning and reflection. This allows for the sharing of effective practices and the identification of areas for growth and improvement.

- Allocate dedicated time for professional development, collaboration, and reflection within the school schedule. This demonstrates the school's commitment to teacher growth and ensures that professional development is prioritized and valued.

Collaboration and ongoing support not only enhance the effectiveness of professional development but also create a culture of continuous improvement, promoting the long-term sustainability of student-centered teaching practices.

Conclusion

Professional development is essential for teachers to successfully implement student-centered teaching methods. By offering support, resources, and ongoing collaboration, schools can empower teachers to embrace and excel in student-centered approaches. Effective professional development helps teachers acquire the necessary knowledge and skills, build confidence, and create a community of practice where they can continuously learn, reflect, and refine their teaching strategies. Ultimately, investing in professional development for student-centered teaching enables teachers to create engaging, meaningful, and impactful learning experiences for their students.

Assessing Student Learning in Student-Centered Environments

Assessing student learning in student-centered environments is a crucial aspect of ensuring the effectiveness of this educational approach. Student-centered learning emphasizes the active engagement of students in their own learning process, promoting autonomy, collaboration, and critical thinking. Therefore, assessment methods in student-centered environments should align with these principles and provide meaningful feedback to both students and teachers. This section will explore various assessment strategies and tools that can be used in student-centered classrooms.

Formative Assessment

Formative assessment plays a central role in enhancing student learning in student-centered environments. It involves gathering information about students' understanding and progress throughout the learning process, allowing teachers to modify instruction accordingly. Here are some formative assessment strategies that can be used:

1. **Observations:** Teachers can observe students' engagement, participation, and problem-solving skills during activities and discussions to assess their understanding and learning progress.//
2. **Questioning:** Asking open-ended questions can help elicit students' thinking, promote reflection, and assess their understanding of concepts and ideas.
3. **Think-Pair-Share:** This strategy involves students working individually (think), discussing their ideas with a partner (pair), and sharing their

thoughts with the whole class (share). It allows teachers to assess students' understanding and the diversity of perspectives.

4. **Exit Tickets:** At the end of a lesson or class, students can provide brief written responses or complete a short online questionnaire to summarize what they have learned. This provides valuable feedback for teachers to adjust their instruction.

5. **Peer Feedback:** Encouraging students to provide feedback to their peers promotes collaboration and self-reflection. It allows students to evaluate their own work against criteria and learn from others' perspectives.

These formative assessment strategies provide ongoing feedback to both students and teachers, enabling instructional adjustments and informing the next steps in the learning process.

Summative Assessment

While formative assessment focuses on the ongoing learning process, summative assessment evaluates students' achievement at the end of a unit, course, or project. In student-centered environments, summative assessment should also align with the key principles of autonomy, collaboration, and critical thinking. Here are some summative assessment methods suitable for student-centered classrooms:

1. **Performance-Based Assessments:** These assessments require students to demonstrate their understanding and skills through real-world tasks, such as presentations, projects, portfolios, or performances. They allow students to apply their knowledge in authentic contexts and showcase their abilities.

2. **Authentic Assessments:** Authentic assessments simulate real-world situations and problems, providing students with challenges that require higher-order thinking and problem-solving skills. Examples include case studies, simulations, and group projects.

3. **Rubrics:** Rubrics provide clear criteria and expectations for student performance. They are particularly useful in evaluating complex projects or performances and help students understand how their work will be assessed.

4. **Self-Assessment and Reflection:** In student-centered environments, students should be actively involved in assessing their own learning. This encourages metacognition, self-reflection, and self-regulation skills.

Students can use checklists, journals, or reflection prompts to evaluate their work and set goals for improvement.

By incorporating these summative assessment methods into student-centered classrooms, teachers can gain valuable insights into students' achievement and provide meaningful feedback on their progress.

Technology-Enhanced Assessment

Technology can significantly enhance the assessment process in student-centered environments. Here are some technology tools and platforms that can be effectively used for assessment:

1. **Online Quizzes and Surveys:** Online platforms enable teachers to create and administer quizzes and surveys easily. These tools provide immediate feedback, allowing students to track their progress and providing teachers with instant data for analysis.

2. **Digital Portfolios:** Students can collect and showcase their work, including projects, papers, and multimedia presentations, in digital portfolios. Digital portfolios enable easy sharing, reflection, and feedback from teachers and peers.

3. **Collaborative Document Editing:** Tools like Google Docs enable students to work collaboratively on documents, facilitating peer feedback and assessment. Teachers can monitor the editing process and provide guidance as needed.

4. **Data Visualization Tools:** Analyzing and visualizing data can help both teachers and students make sense of complex information. Tools like spreadsheets or graphing software enable students to interpret and present data effectively.

Integrating technology into assessment practices not only enhances efficiency but also provides opportunities for personalized feedback and self-directed learning.

Evaluating the Impact of Student-Centered Learning

Evaluating the impact of student-centered learning is essential to understand its effectiveness and make informed decisions about instructional practices. Here are some evaluation methods that can be used:

1. **Standardized Tests:** While not the primary measure of student-centered learning, standardized tests can provide insights into students' overall academic achievement and growth. However, it is important to consider the limitations of relying solely on standardized tests.

2. **Surveys and Questionnaires:** Gathering feedback from students, teachers, and parents through surveys and questionnaires can provide valuable insights into the perceived benefits and challenges of student-centered approaches. It allows for continuous improvement and adjustment of instructional practices.

3. **Qualitative Research Methods:** Qualitative research methods, such as interviews or focus groups, can offer in-depth understanding of the experiences, perceptions, and outcomes of student-centered learning. They allow for the exploration of complex aspects that quantitative methods may not capture.

4. **Data Analysis:** Analyzing various data sources, such as student work, observations, and test scores, can provide a comprehensive picture of students' progress and achievement. Data analysis techniques can help identify patterns, trends, and areas for improvement.

It is crucial to use a combination of evaluation methods to gain a holistic understanding of the impact of student-centered learning. Continuous evaluation and reflection enable educators to refine their practices and ensure effective implementation of student-centered approaches.

In conclusion, assessing student learning in student-centered environments requires the use of diverse and dynamic assessment strategies that align with the principles of autonomy, collaboration, and critical thinking. Formative and summative assessments, as well as technology-enhanced assessment methods, provide valuable feedback to students and teachers, informing instructional decisions and promoting continuous improvement. Evaluating the impact of student-centered learning involves a combination of assessment data, surveys, qualitative research methods, and data analysis techniques. By employing a comprehensive assessment and evaluation framework, educators can effectively support student learning and growth in student-centered classrooms.

Evaluating the Impact of Student-Centered Learning

Evaluating the impact of student-centered learning is crucial for educators and policymakers to determine its effectiveness and make informed decisions regarding its implementation. By assessing the outcomes and benefits of student-centered learning, educational institutions can strive for continuous improvement and provide evidence-based practices.

Importance of Evaluation

Evaluation is an essential step in the educational process as it allows us to measure the effectiveness and outcomes of instructional strategies. When it comes to student-centered learning, evaluation helps answer important questions such as:

- Does student-centered learning improve academic performance?
- Does it enhance student motivation and engagement?
- Does it foster critical thinking and problem-solving skills?
- Does it address individual learning needs and promote personalized learning?
- Does it prepare students for future challenges and opportunities?

By addressing these questions, evaluation provides valuable insights into the impact of student-centered learning and helps identify areas for improvement.

Evaluation Methods

To evaluate the impact of student-centered learning, educators and researchers employ various evaluation methods. Here are some commonly used methods:

1. **Quantitative Measures:** Quantitative methods involve collecting and analyzing numerical data to assess the impact of student-centered learning. These methods often include standardized tests, pre and post-tests, surveys, and statistical analysis. For example, researchers may compare the academic performance of students who have experienced student-centered learning with those who haven't to determine its impact on learning outcomes.

2. **Qualitative Measures:** Qualitative methods involve collecting non-numerical data such as observations, interviews, and open-ended survey responses to gain in-depth insights into the impact of student-centered learning. These methods focus on understanding the experiences, perceptions, and reflections of students, teachers, and parents. For example, interviews can provide valuable information about how student-centered learning has positively influenced students' motivation and engagement.

3. **Mixed Methods Approach:** A combination of quantitative and qualitative methods can provide a comprehensive evaluation of student-centered learning. This approach allows researchers to examine both the statistical evidence and the rich narratives surrounding the impact of student-centered learning. By employing a mixed methods approach, educators and researchers can explore the complex dynamics and nuances of student-centered learning in a more holistic manner.

Considerations for Evaluation

When evaluating the impact of student-centered learning, there are some considerations that need to be taken into account:

- **Baseline Assessment:** To measure the impact of student-centered learning, it is essential to establish a baseline assessment of students' initial abilities and performance before implementing student-centered approaches. This allows for a comparison between the outcomes of student-centered learning and traditional instructional methods.

- **Longitudinal Studies:** Evaluating the impact of student-centered learning should not be limited to short-term assessments. Longitudinal studies that track students' progress over an extended period provide a more comprehensive understanding of the long-term effects of student-centered learning.

- **Contextual Factors:** The impact of student-centered learning can vary depending on various contextual factors such as student demographics, school environment, and available resources. Evaluations should consider these factors to gain a deeper understanding of the impact and effectiveness of student-centered learning.

- **Multiple Stakeholders:** Evaluating the impact of student-centered learning should involve multiple stakeholders, including students, teachers, parents, and administrators. Each stakeholder group can provide unique perspectives on the impact of student-centered learning, allowing for a more comprehensive evaluation.

- **Continuous Improvement:** The evaluation of student-centered learning should not be seen as a one-time process. It should be an ongoing and iterative process that informs and drives continuous improvement. By regularly evaluating the impact and making necessary adjustments, educators can enhance the effectiveness of student-centered learning practices.

Challenges and Limitations

Evaluating the impact of student-centered learning can pose several challenges and limitations:

- **Measurement Issues:** Assessing the impact of student-centered learning requires reliable and valid measures. However, finding appropriate instruments that capture the multidimensional nature of student-centered learning can be challenging.

- **Complexity of Causality:** Isolating the impact of student-centered learning from other factors influencing student outcomes can be difficult. Student success is influenced by various factors, including socio-economic status, prior knowledge, and teaching quality. Untangling the causal effects of student-centered learning from these factors is a complex task.

- **Subjectivity:** Evaluating the impact of student-centered learning often involves subjective measures such as student self-assessments or teacher observations. Subjectivity introduces some degree of bias and can impact the reliability of the evaluation.

- **Time and Resources:** Conducting rigorous evaluations of student-centered learning requires significant time, expertise, and resources. Many educational institutions may struggle to allocate sufficient resources for evaluation purposes.

- **Resistance to Change:** The implementation of student-centered learning may face resistance from stakeholders who are accustomed to traditional instructional methods. This resistance can hinder the evaluation process and limit the collection of comprehensive data.

Despite these challenges, evaluating the impact of student-centered learning remains essential to foster evidence-based practices and drive educational improvement.

Conclusion

Evaluating the impact of student-centered learning plays a crucial role in understanding its effectiveness and making informed decisions regarding its implementation. By employing various evaluation methods, considering contextual factors, involving multiple stakeholders, and striving for continuous improvement, educators can determine the outcomes and benefits of student-centered learning. While challenges exist, evaluation provides valuable insights that can enhance instructional practices and support the creation of student-centered learning environments. Ultimately, evaluation empowers educational institutions to leverage the power of student-centered learning and maximize its impact on student success.

Technology and Student-Centered Learning

Blended Learning

Blended learning is an innovative approach to education that combines traditional face-to-face instruction with online learning activities. It aims to create a flexible and personalized learning experience for students by integrating technology into the classroom. In this section, we will explore the principles, benefits, challenges, and implementation strategies of blended learning.

Principles of Blended Learning

At the core of blended learning is the idea of leveraging the strengths of both face-to-face and online instruction. The following principles guide the design and implementation of blended learning:

1. **Flexible Learning Environments**: Blended learning allows students to learn at their own pace and in a variety of settings. It provides a balance between structured classroom instruction and self-directed online learning.

2. **Personalized Instruction**: Blended learning provides opportunities for individualized instruction based on each student's needs and learning preferences. Online learning platforms can offer adaptive content and assessments to cater to the unique needs of each learner.

3. **Active Learning**: Blended learning encourages active participation and engagement. It promotes hands-on activities, collaborative projects, and discussions, both in the classroom and online.

4. **Data-Driven Instruction:** Blended learning makes use of technology to collect and analyze data on student performance. This data can inform instructional decisions, allowing teachers to tailor their instruction to meet the needs of each student.

Benefits of Blended Learning

Blended learning offers numerous advantages for both students and teachers. Some of the key benefits include:

1. **Increased Engagement:** Blended learning provides opportunities for interactive and multimedia-rich learning experiences, which can enhance student engagement and motivation.

2. **Flexible Learning Opportunities:** Blended learning allows students to access learning materials and resources anytime and anywhere. This flexibility accommodates different learning styles and schedules.

3. **Individualized Instruction:** Blended learning facilitates personalized instruction, allowing students to progress at their own pace and receive targeted interventions when needed.

4. **Improved Learning Outcomes:** Research has shown that blended learning can lead to improved learning outcomes, including higher achievement scores and better retention of knowledge.

5. **Efficient Use of Instructional Time:** Blended learning can optimize instructional time by offloading certain activities, such as content delivery and practice exercises, to online platforms. This gives teachers more time for in-depth discussions and individualized support.

Challenges of Blended Learning

While blended learning offers many benefits, it is not without challenges. Educators must be aware of these challenges and proactively address them. Some of the common challenges include:

1. **Technological Infrastructure:** Blended learning requires reliable access to technology and the internet. Ensuring that all students have access to the necessary hardware and connectivity can be a challenge in some schools or districts.

2. **Teacher Training and Support:** Teachers need to be trained on how to effectively integrate technology into their instruction. Ongoing professional development and support are essential for successful implementation of blended learning.

3. **Course Design and Selection**: Designing and selecting appropriate online learning materials can be time-consuming and challenging. Ensuring the quality and alignment of online resources with the curriculum requires careful consideration.

4. **Student Readiness and Digital Literacy**: Blended learning assumes that students have the necessary digital literacy skills to navigate online platforms and resources. Some students may require additional support to develop these skills.

5. **Maintaining Student Engagement**: The online components of blended learning can sometimes lead to reduced face-to-face interactions. Teachers need to actively promote collaboration and interaction among students to maintain engagement.

Implementation Strategies

To implement successful blended learning, educators can follow these strategies:

1. **Define Learning Objectives**: Clearly define the learning objectives for the blended learning experience. Determine how online and face-to-face components will support these objectives.

2. **Select Technology Tools**: Choose the appropriate technology tools that align with the learning objectives and suit the needs of both teachers and students. Consider factors such as ease of use, compatibility, and support.

3. **Design Course Content**: Develop or select online learning materials that align with the curriculum. Ensure that they are engaging, interactive, and provide opportunities for active learning.

4. **Create a Schedule**: Establish a schedule that outlines when and how the online and face-to-face components will be integrated. Provide clear guidelines to students on how to access and submit online assignments.

5. **Prepare Teachers**: Provide teachers with professional development opportunities to build their technology skills and instructional strategies for blended learning. Encourage collaboration and sharing of best practices among teachers.

6. **Monitor and Assess**: Regularly monitor student progress and provide timely feedback. Use data from online platforms to inform instructional decisions and identify areas for improvement.

7. **Reflect and Improve**: Continuously evaluate the effectiveness of blended learning. Seek feedback from students, teachers, and parents to make necessary adjustments and improvements.

Case Study: Blended Learning in a High School Science Class

To illustrate the benefits of blended learning, let's consider a case study of a high school science class. The teacher uses a blended learning approach to enhance student understanding of complex scientific concepts.

In this case, the teacher begins the unit by assigning an online module that introduces the foundational concepts. Students are encouraged to explore interactive simulations and videos to gain a solid understanding of the topic. They can progress through the module at their own pace, revisiting difficult concepts as needed.

After completing the online module, students come to the classroom for hands-on experiments, group discussions, and demonstrations. The teacher facilitates deeper discussions and provides individualized support to address misconceptions and reinforce key concepts.

Throughout the unit, students engage in online discussions, collaborative projects, and quizzes to reinforce their learning. The teacher collects data from the online platform to monitor student progress and identify areas for intervention.

At the end of the unit, students demonstrate their understanding through a project-based assessment, where they apply their knowledge to a real-world problem. The teacher assesses their performance using rubrics that align with the unit's learning objectives.

This case study showcases how blended learning can provide a more holistic and engaging learning experience for students. By combining online resources with face-to-face activities, students can deepen their understanding and develop critical thinking skills.

Additional Resources

For further exploration of blended learning, here are some recommended resources:

1. *Blended: Using Disruptive Innovation to Improve Schools* by Michael B. Horn and Heather Staker.

2. *The Blended Learning Blueprint for Elementary Teachers: How to Integrate Technology in the Classroom* by Amber Teamann.

3. *Blended Learning in Action: A Practical Guide Toward Sustainable Change* by Catlin R. Tucker, Tiffany Wycoff, and Jason T. Green.

These resources provide valuable insights, practical tips, and case studies to help educators implement blended learning effectively.

Flipped Classroom

The flipped classroom is an innovative approach to teaching that reverses the traditional learning model. In a flipped classroom, the typical lecture and homework components are swapped. Students are exposed to the lecture content outside of class time through pre-recorded videos or other resources, allowing them to learn at their own pace and review the material as needed. Class time is then dedicated to applying the knowledge through collaborative activities, problem-solving, and discussions facilitated by the teacher.

Principles of Flipped Classroom

The flipped classroom is based on several key principles. First and foremost, it recognizes that students learn in different ways and at different paces. By providing access to lecture materials outside of class, students have the opportunity to engage with the content in a way that best suits their individual learning style.

Another important principle is active learning. In a traditional classroom, students passively receive information during lectures, limiting their engagement and understanding. In a flipped classroom, students actively participate in applying their knowledge, working together with peers, and engaging in critical thinking activities.

The flipped classroom also promotes the idea of student autonomy and ownership of learning. Students take control of their learning journey by accessing lecture materials, reviewing them as needed, and actively engaging in class activities. This approach fosters self-directed learning skills, which are essential for lifelong learning.

Benefits of Flipped Classroom

The flipped classroom offers several benefits for both students and teachers. By shifting the lecture component outside of class, students have more time for collaborative and interactive activities during class time. This promotes deeper understanding of the material, as students can actively engage with the content through discussions, problem-solving, and hands-on experiments.

In a flipped classroom, students also have the opportunity to personalize their learning experience. They can revisit lecture materials at their own pace, pause and rewind videos, and delve deeper into topics of interest. This flexibility accommodates different learning styles and allows students to take ownership of their learning.

Moreover, the flipped classroom encourages student-teacher interaction. With more time available in class, teachers can provide individualized support, address specific questions or misconceptions, and guide students in their learning process. This personalized attention helps foster a supportive and engaging learning environment.

From the teacher's perspective, the flipped classroom allows for more effective use of class time. Instead of spending valuable class time simply delivering lectures, teachers can focus on facilitating discussions, providing guidance, and assessing students' understanding in real-time. This enables them to adapt their teaching strategies based on students' needs and actively promote deeper learning.

Challenges and Solutions

Implementing a flipped classroom approach can present some challenges. One of the main challenges is ensuring that all students access the pre-recorded lectures or resources outside of class. Not all students have equal access to technology or the internet at home. To address this, teachers can offer alternatives, such as providing printed materials or creating offline access to videos through USB drives or DVDs.

Another challenge is maintaining students' engagement with the pre-recorded materials. Students may be tempted to skip or only partially watch the videos. To overcome this challenge, teachers can introduce interactive elements in the videos, such as embedded questions or quizzes, to ensure students are actively engaging with the content.

Additionally, the flipped classroom may require a shift in mindset for both teachers and students. Students need to take responsibility for their learning and be proactive in accessing and reviewing the materials. Teachers need to adapt their instructional strategies to facilitate collaborative activities and provide support when needed.

To address these challenges, it is essential to establish clear expectations and routines from the start. Teachers can provide guidelines on accessing and reviewing the materials, set deadlines for watching the videos, and create a supportive classroom environment where students feel comfortable asking questions and seeking assistance.

Examples of Flipped Classroom Activities

The flipped classroom approach allows for a wide range of activities that promote active and collaborative learning. Here are a few examples:

1. Group discussions: In class, students can engage in group discussions to share their understanding of the lecture content, ask questions, and deepen their knowledge through peer interactions.

2. Problem-solving activities: Students can work in teams to solve real-world problems related to the lecture topic. This encourages critical thinking, application of knowledge, and collaboration.

3. Hands-on experiments: Class time can be dedicated to conducting experiments, simulations, or other hands-on activities that reinforce the concepts covered in the pre-recorded lectures.

4. Debates or role-playing: Students can engage in debates or role-playing activities to explore different perspectives and develop critical thinking skills.

Resources for Flipped Classroom

There are several resources available to support teachers in implementing the flipped classroom approach. Here are a few examples:

1. Video creation tools: Teachers can use various video creation tools such as Screencast-O-Matic, Camtasia, or OBS Studio to record their lectures or create interactive video lessons.

2. Learning management systems (LMS): Platforms like Google Classroom, Moodle, or Canvas provide features for organizing and delivering pre-recorded lectures, tracking student progress, and facilitating online discussions.

3. Open educational resources (OER): Teachers can leverage OER platforms like Khan Academy, OpenStax, or TED-Ed, which provide a vast collection of pre-recorded lessons and resources across different subjects.

4. Collaboration tools: Online collaboration tools like Google Docs, Padlet, or Microsoft Teams can empower students to collaborate on projects and share their work with peers.

Caveats and Considerations

While the flipped classroom approach offers numerous advantages, it is important to consider some caveats and potential challenges. Not all students may embrace the shift in learning model, and some may struggle with the increased responsibility and self-direction required.

Teachers must also carefully design and select the pre-recorded lecture content to ensure its quality and relevance. It is crucial to balance the length and complexity of the materials, as well as provide additional resources or support for students who need further clarification.

Furthermore, the flipped classroom is not a one-size-fits-all approach. It works best when carefully aligned with the learning goals, students' needs, and the subject matter. Teachers should be mindful of adapting and refining their approach to fit the unique dynamics of their classroom.

Conclusion

The flipped classroom is a transformative educational method that allows for a more personalized and active learning experience. By shifting the lecture component outside of class, students have the opportunity to engage with content at their own pace, while class time can be dedicated to collaborative and application activities. The flipped classroom promotes student autonomy, enhances engagement, and fosters deeper understanding. By overcoming challenges and leveraging the available resources, teachers can effectively implement the flipped classroom and create a dynamic and impactful learning environment for their students.

Personalized Learning Platforms

Personalized learning platforms are educational tools that adapt to the needs and preferences of individual students, providing them with customized learning experiences. These platforms utilize technology to deliver targeted instruction, track progress, and offer personalized feedback, allowing students to learn at their own pace and in their own style. In this section, we will explore the principles behind personalized learning platforms, their benefits, challenges, and some examples of popular platforms.

Principles of Personalized Learning Platforms

Personalized learning platforms are built upon several key principles:

1. **Individualized Instruction**: Personalized learning platforms provide individualized instruction that is tailored to each student's unique learning needs. This allows students to progress at their own pace, focusing on areas where they need more support and moving ahead in areas where they demonstrate proficiency.

2. **Adaptive Learning**: These platforms use adaptive learning algorithms to dynamically adjust the content and difficulty level based on the student's performance and progress. This ensures that the material is neither too easy nor too challenging, optimizing the learning experience for each student.

3. **Data-Driven Insights:** Personalized learning platforms collect and analyze data on student performance, engagement, and preferences. This data is used to generate insights that inform instructional decisions, allowing teachers to better understand each student's strengths, weaknesses, and learning patterns.

4. **Differentiated Content and Resources:** These platforms offer a wide range of learning materials, resources, and activities to cater to diverse learning styles and preferences. This includes interactive multimedia, simulations, virtual labs, and other engaging content that promotes active learning and deepens conceptual understanding.

5. **Continuous Feedback and Assessment:** Personalized learning platforms provide continuous feedback and assessment through quizzes, exercises, and other interactive activities. This allows students to monitor their own progress and receive immediate feedback, enabling them to identify areas that require further practice or review.

Benefits of Personalized Learning Platforms

Personalized learning platforms offer several advantages over traditional one-size-fits-all instructional approaches:

- **Higher Engagement and Motivation:** By tailoring the learning experience to each student's needs and interests, personalized learning platforms enhance engagement and motivation. Students are more likely to be actively involved in their learning and take ownership of their educational journey.

- **Improved Learning Outcomes:** Research suggests that personalized learning can lead to improved learning outcomes. By adapting the instruction to match individual student needs, these platforms can facilitate deeper understanding, critical thinking, and problem-solving skills.

- **Flexibility and Self-Pacing:** Personalized learning platforms afford students the flexibility to learn at their own pace. Students can spend more time on challenging concepts and move quickly through familiar material, increasing efficiency and accommodating individual learning preferences.

- **Enhanced Teacher-Student Interactions:** With personalized learning platforms, teachers can spend more one-on-one time with students, providing targeted support and guidance. This promotes stronger teacher-student relationships and allows teachers to focus on higher-order instructional tasks.

- **Data-Informed Instruction:** Personalized learning platforms generate valuable data on student performance, allowing teachers to make data-informed instructional decisions. Teachers can identify learning gaps, track progress, and tailor instruction accordingly, ensuring that students receive the support they need.

Challenges in Implementing Personalized Learning Platforms

Despite the benefits they offer, personalized learning platforms also present certain challenges that must be addressed:

- **Technology Infrastructure:** Implementing personalized learning platforms requires a reliable and robust technology infrastructure. Schools must ensure that they have sufficient devices, internet access, and technical support to effectively integrate these platforms into the learning environment.

- **Professional Development:** Teachers need appropriate training and professional development to effectively use personalized learning platforms. They must be equipped with the necessary skills and knowledge to leverage the platform's features and interpret student data.

- **Equitable Access:** Personalized learning platforms can exacerbate existing inequities if not implemented thoughtfully. Schools must ensure that all students have equitable access to technology and digital resources, bridging the digital divide and addressing potential disparities.

- **Data Privacy and Security:** As personalized learning platforms collect sensitive student data, ensuring data privacy and security is paramount. Schools must have robust policies and protocols in place to protect student information and comply with relevant data protection regulations.

Example Personalized Learning Platforms

There are several popular personalized learning platforms that schools and educators are using worldwide. Here are a few examples:

- **Khan Academy:** Khan Academy is a widely recognized personalized learning platform that offers a vast library of video lessons, interactive exercises, and progress tracking features. It covers a wide range of subjects and grade levels, allowing students to learn at their own pace.

- **Duolingo:** Duolingo is a personalized learning platform that focuses on language learning. It offers a gamified approach to language acquisition, providing personalized exercises, immediate feedback, and adaptive assessments to help learners improve their language skills.

- **IXL:** IXL is an adaptive learning platform that provides individualized practice and targeted instruction in math, language arts, science, and social studies. It offers a comprehensive curriculum with interactive activities, real-time feedback, and progress tracking.

- **DreamBox Learning:** DreamBox Learning is a personalized math learning platform for elementary and middle school students. It offers adaptive math instruction, personalized lessons, and interactive games to build conceptual understanding and procedural fluency.

These platforms, along with numerous others, demonstrate the potential of personalized learning in providing tailored educational experiences for students.

Conclusion

Personalized learning platforms leverage technology to provide customized learning experiences tailored to the needs, preferences, and pace of individual students. They offer several benefits, including increased engagement, improved learning outcomes, flexibility, and data-informed instruction. However, implementing personalized learning platforms comes with challenges, such as technology infrastructure, professional development, equitable access, and data privacy. By addressing these challenges and leveraging the power of personalized learning platforms, educators can create more effective and engaging learning environments that meet the diverse needs of their students.

Gamification in Education

Gamification is the process of incorporating game elements into non-game contexts to enhance motivation, engagement, and learning outcomes. In the realm of education, gamification has gained significant attention for its potential to transform traditional teaching and learning methods. By integrating game-based elements, such as competition, rewards, challenges, and progress tracking, into the learning experience, gamification aims to make education more interactive, enjoyable, and effective.

Principles of Gamification in Education

The principles underlying gamification in education revolve around creating a meaningful and immersive learning environment. Here are some key principles:

1. **Clear goals and objectives:** Gamification sets clear goals and objectives, providing learners with a sense of purpose and direction. By defining specific learning outcomes and milestones, learners know what they need to achieve and can track their progress.

2. **Rewards and feedback:** Gamification introduces rewards and feedback mechanisms to incentivize learners and provide instant feedback on their performance. Rewards can be intrinsic, such as badges and achievements, or extrinsic, such as points and leaderboards. Feedback helps learners understand their strengths and areas for improvement.

3. **Challenge and progression:** Gamification introduces challenges of varying difficulty levels and allows learners to progress through levels or stages, providing a sense of accomplishment and mastery. This element keeps learners engaged and motivated to overcome obstacles and reach higher levels of achievement.

4. **Competition and collaboration:** Gamification enables learners to compete with others, fostering healthy competition and a drive for improvement. It also encourages collaboration and teamwork, allowing learners to work together towards common goals.

Application of Gamification in Education

Gamification can be applied across different educational settings and subjects, catering to various age groups and learning styles. Here are a few examples:

1. **Language Learning:** Gamification can be used to enhance language learning by incorporating interactive language challenges, vocabulary quizzes, role-playing games, and virtual language exchanges. Learners can earn points, unlock levels, and receive rewards for their progress and achievements in language proficiency.

2. **Mathematics and Science:** Gamification can make abstract concepts in mathematics and science more engaging and accessible. For example, learners can solve math puzzles, engage in virtual science experiments, and participate in interactive simulations that provide immediate feedback and rewards for correct answers.

3. **History and Social Studies:** Gamification can bring history and social studies to life by immersing learners in virtual historical scenarios and role-playing games. By making history interactive and allowing learners to make choices and

experience the consequences, gamification enhances understanding, critical thinking, and empathy.

4. **Physical Education:** Gamification can be used to promote physical activity and healthy lifestyle choices. Fitness apps and wearable devices can track progress, set goals, and provide rewards for achieving fitness milestones. This element of gamification encourages physical activity and reinforces healthy habits.

Benefits of Gamification in Education

Gamification offers several benefits in an educational context:

1. **Increased motivation and engagement:** By making learning interactive, challenging, and rewarding, gamification increases learner motivation and engagement. Learners are more likely to be actively involved in the learning process and persist in their efforts to achieve their goals.

2. **Enhanced learning outcomes:** Gamification fosters deeper learning by providing immediate feedback, reinforcing knowledge retention, and promoting higher-order thinking skills. It encourages learners to explore and apply concepts in meaningful and practical ways.

3. **Personalized learning experiences:** Gamification allows for personalized learning experiences by adapting to individual learner needs and preferences. Learners can progress at their own pace, receive tailored feedback, and engage with content that aligns with their interests.

4. **Promotion of collaboration and teamwork:** Gamification can promote collaboration and teamwork by incorporating multiplayer games and challenges. Learners can collaborate with peers, share knowledge, and work together towards common goals, thereby developing social and communication skills.

Challenges and Considerations

While gamification offers significant potential for education, there are also challenges and considerations to take into account:

1. **Directing focus on learning objectives:** It is essential to ensure that the game elements in gamification align with the learning objectives and do not distract from the educational content. The emphasis should always be on meaningful learning and not solely on gaming aspects.

2. **Avoiding extrinsic motivation reliance:** While rewards and points can initially motivate learners, it is crucial to encourage intrinsic motivation by focusing on the inherent value and relevance of the learning content. Overreliance on extrinsic rewards may undermine long-term engagement.

3. **Balancing competition and collaboration:** Incorporating competition can drive motivation, but it should be balanced with collaboration to promote a supportive and inclusive learning environment. Students should feel encouraged and supported rather than discouraged or left behind.

4. **Equity and accessibility considerations:** Gamification tools should be inclusive and accessible to all learners, considering factors such as student abilities, resources, and technological limitations. It is crucial to ensure that gamification does not exacerbate existing educational inequities.

Examples of Gamification Tools

Here are some examples of gamification tools and platforms that can be used in an educational setting:

1. **Kahoot!:** Kahoot! is a popular gamification platform that allows educators to create quizzes, surveys, and discussions with interactive elements. It engages learners in a competitive and fun learning environment.

2. **Classcraft:** Classcraft is a gamification platform that transforms classrooms into collaborative role-playing games. It encourages teamwork, sets goals, and enables educators to track students' progress.

3. **Duolingo:** Duolingo is a language learning app that incorporates gamification elements like leveling up, earning points, and competing with friends. It offers a playful and engaging way to learn languages.

4. **Minecraft:** Minecraft, a popular sandbox game, can be used in education to create immersive virtual learning environments. Educators can design interactive lessons and activities within the game world.

In conclusion, gamification in education offers exciting possibilities for transforming the learning experience. By integrating game elements, educators can enhance motivation, engagement, and learning outcomes. However, it is important to ensure that gamification aligns with learning objectives, promotes collaboration, and considers equity and accessibility. With the right implementation and thoughtful design, gamification can revolutionize education by making it more interactive, enjoyable, and effective.

Artificial Intelligence in Education

Artificial Intelligence (AI) has gained significant attention in various industries, and education is no exception. The integration of AI technologies in education has the potential to transform the way students learn and teachers teach. In this section, we will explore the applications and benefits of AI in education, as well as the challenges that arise with its implementation.

Understanding Artificial Intelligence

Before delving into the specific applications of AI in education, it is essential to have a clear understanding of what AI is. AI refers to the development of intelligent machines that can perform tasks that typically require human intelligence. These tasks include learning, reasoning, problem-solving, perception, and language understanding.

Machine Learning (ML) is a subfield of AI that focuses on enabling machines to learn from data and improve their performance without being explicitly programmed. ML algorithms can detect patterns, make predictions, and generate insights from vast amounts of data. Natural Language Processing (NLP) is another subfield of AI that enables machines to understand and interact with human language.

Applications of Artificial Intelligence in Education

1. Intelligent Tutoring Systems: AI can be utilized to develop intelligent tutoring systems that provide personalized learning experiences to students. These systems analyze students' performance, identify areas of improvement, and provide targeted feedback and guidance. By adapting the instructional content and pace to individual students' needs, intelligent tutoring systems can enhance learning outcomes.

2. Adaptive Learning Platforms: AI-powered adaptive learning platforms use data analytics and machine learning algorithms to personalize the learning experience. These platforms assess students' knowledge and skills and provide tailored content and activities to address their specific needs. Adaptive learning platforms can track students' progress, identify learning gaps, and suggest targeted resources to support their learning journey.

3. Automated Grading and Feedback: AI can automate the grading process, allowing educators to save time and provide faster feedback to students. Automated grading systems use machine learning algorithms to evaluate answers based on predefined criteria and provide immediate scores and feedback. This enables students to receive timely feedback and facilitates the effective monitoring of their progress.

4. Intelligent Content Creation: AI technologies can assist in the creation of educational content. Natural Language Generation (NLG) algorithms can generate written content, such as explanations, summaries, and even essays. These

algorithms can analyze data and transform it into coherent and comprehensible language, supporting educators in creating high-quality resources.

Benefits of Artificial Intelligence in Education

The integration of AI in education offers several benefits:

1. Personalized Learning: AI technologies empower educators to provide personalized learning experiences to students, catering to their specific needs and learning styles. This individualized approach enhances student engagement, motivation, and overall learning outcomes.

2. Data-Driven Decision Making: AI enables the collection and analysis of vast amounts of data, providing valuable insights into student performance, learning patterns, and areas of improvement. Educators can use this data to make informed decisions and develop evidence-based instructional strategies.

3. Enhanced Collaboration: AI technologies facilitate collaboration and knowledge sharing among students. Intelligent tutoring systems and adaptive learning platforms can foster collaborative learning environments, allowing students to work together on projects and share resources.

Challenges of Artificial Intelligence in Education

While the potential of AI in education is promising, several challenges need to be addressed:

1. Ethical Considerations: As AI technologies continue to advance, ethical concerns arise. Issues such as data privacy, algorithmic bias, and consent must be carefully considered and addressed to ensure the ethical use of AI in education.

2. Teacher-Student Relationship: The integration of AI in education raises questions about the role of teachers and the impact it may have on the teacher-student relationship. Educators need to find a balance between technology and human interaction, ensuring that AI serves as a tool to support teaching, rather than replace it.

Conclusion

Artificial Intelligence has the potential to revolutionize education by providing personalized learning experiences, automating routine tasks, and enhancing collaboration. However, the successful integration of AI in education requires careful consideration of ethical issues and the maintenance of a strong teacher-student relationship. By harnessing the power of AI, we can create more effective and engaging learning environments, preparing students for the challenges of the future.

Virtual Reality in Education

Virtual Reality (VR) is a rapidly evolving technology that has the potential to revolutionize education. By creating immersive and interactive virtual environments, VR offers students a unique and engaging learning experience that enhances their understanding and retention of knowledge. In this section, we will explore the principles of VR, its applications in education, and the benefits it brings to the learning process.

Principles of Virtual Reality

Virtual Reality is based on the principle of creating a computer-generated environment that simulates a real or imaginary world. This environment can be experienced through a variety of devices, such as headsets or goggles, that track the user's movements and display the virtual environment in a 3D format. The user can interact with the environment using controllers or other input devices, allowing them to manipulate objects and navigate within the virtual space.

The success of VR lies in its ability to create a sense of presence, where the user feels fully immersed and engaged in the virtual environment. This is achieved through a combination of visual, auditory, and haptic feedback, which stimulates the user's senses and tricks their brain into perceiving the virtual world as real.

Applications in Education

Virtual Reality has a wide range of applications in education, from primary schools to universities and professional training programs. Here are some examples of how VR can be used in different educational contexts:

- **Science and Exploration:** VR can transport students to distant locations, such as the bottom of the ocean or outer space, allowing them to explore and study phenomena that are otherwise inaccessible. For example, students can virtually dissect a human body or observe the behavior of animals in their natural habitats.

- **Historical and Cultural Immersion:** VR can recreate historical events, ancient civilizations, and cultural landmarks, enabling students to experience and interact with history in a more vivid and engaging way. They can visit ancient Rome, witness the signing of important historical documents, or explore famous artworks in virtual museums.

- **Language Learning:** VR provides a stimulating environment for language learning, allowing students to practice their language skills in realistic scenarios. They can interact with virtual native speakers, engage in conversations, and navigate virtual cities to improve their language fluency.

- **Simulations and Training:** VR is particularly useful for training in fields that require hands-on experience, such as medicine, engineering, and aviation. By using VR simulations, students can practice complex procedures, simulate emergency situations, and develop critical skills in a safe and controlled environment.

- **Special Education:** VR can be a valuable tool for students with special needs, providing a multisensory and personalized learning experience. It can help improve spatial awareness, sensory integration, and social skills through interactive and engaging virtual scenarios.

Benefits of Virtual Reality in Education

Virtual Reality offers several benefits that enhance the learning process and improve educational outcomes for students. Here are some of the key advantages of using VR in education:

- **Immersive and Engaging Learning Experience:** VR provides a highly immersive and engaging learning experience that captures students' attention and improves their focus. This heightened level of engagement leads to better information retention and understanding of complex concepts.

- **Active and Experiential Learning:** VR allows students to actively participate in the learning process by interacting with objects and exploring virtual environments. This hands-on approach fosters experiential learning, enabling students to apply their knowledge in practical and meaningful ways.

- **Cultural and Global Perspective:** VR can bridge geographical and cultural barriers, exposing students to diverse perspectives and experiences. It promotes empathy and cultural understanding by allowing students to virtually visit different countries, experience foreign cultures, and interact with people from around the world.

- **Learning Personalization and Adaptivity:** VR can adapt to the individual needs and learning styles of students. It can provide personalized feedback, scaffold learning experiences, and adapt the difficulty level based on the learner's progress, ensuring a customized and tailored learning journey.

- **Safe and Cost-Effective Training:** VR simulations offer a safe and controlled environment for training purposes, reducing the risks associated with real-world practice. It eliminates the need for expensive equipment or field trips, making it a cost-effective solution for practical training in various disciplines.

Challenges and Considerations

While Virtual Reality holds great potential for education, there are also challenges and considerations that need to be addressed:

- **Access and Affordability:** VR equipment can be costly, making it difficult for some educational institutions to implement VR programs. Ensuring equitable access to VR technology and providing affordable solutions is crucial to prevent the digital divide.

- **Technical Requirements and Infrastructure:** The effective use of VR in education relies on robust technical infrastructure, including high-speed internet connections and powerful computers. Educational institutions need to invest in the necessary hardware and software to support VR applications.

- **Content Creation and Curriculum Integration:** Developing high-quality VR content and integrating it into the curriculum requires significant planning and collaboration between educators and content developers. Educators need training and support to effectively incorporate VR experiences into their teaching practices.

- **Health and Safety Considerations:** Prolonged use of VR headsets may cause discomfort or health issues for some individuals, such as eye strain, motion sickness, or disorientation. Educators should implement guidelines for safe and responsible use of VR and ensure students take regular breaks during VR sessions.

- **Ethical and Privacy Concerns:** As with any technology, there are ethical considerations and privacy concerns associated with the use of VR in education. Educational institutions must ensure the protection of students' privacy and adhere to ethical guidelines when collecting data or creating virtual environments.

Case Study: Using Virtual Reality for Science Education

To illustrate the potential of VR in education, let us consider a case study of using VR in science education. In a high school biology class, students are learning about the human anatomy. Instead of relying solely on textbooks and diagrams, the teacher introduces a VR experience that allows students to navigate through a virtual human body.

Equipped with VR headsets and controllers, students can explore different systems and organs in an immersive 3D environment. They can visualize the intricate details of the circulatory system, observe the beating of the heart from different angles, and interact with various organs to understand their functions.

The VR experience offers a hands-on and interactive learning opportunity, enabling students to grasp complex concepts with ease. They can dissect virtual organs, observe the effects of different diseases, and even simulate medical procedures. This experiential learning approach not only improves knowledge retention but also cultivates students' curiosity and critical thinking skills.

By integrating VR into science education, students develop a deeper understanding of the subject matter and gain practical insights into the human body. This immersive learning experience sparks their interest in the field of medicine, inspiring them to pursue further studies or careers in healthcare.

Resources and Tools

Here are some resources and tools to explore further about Virtual Reality in education:

- **Google Expeditions:** A platform that offers immersive virtual field trips for students, allowing them to explore different locations and landmarks.

- **Nearpod VR:** A tool that combines VR with interactive lessons, quizzes, and multimedia content, providing a comprehensive learning experience.

- **Mozilla Hubs:** A platform for creating and sharing virtual spaces, where educators can design their own VR experiences and simulations.

- **Viveport:** An online platform that offers a wide range of educational VR experiences and applications for various subjects.

- **VRTY:** A platform that enables educators to create their own VR content and interactive lessons without coding skills.

In conclusion, Virtual Reality has the potential to transform education by providing immersive and engaging learning experiences. Through its applications in various disciplines, VR enhances student engagement, promotes active learning, and enables personalized and experiential learning journeys. However, careful consideration of the challenges and ethical considerations is necessary to ensure the effective and responsible use of VR in education. By embracing this transformative technology, educators can unlock new possibilities and empower students to explore, create, and learn in ways never before possible.

Augmented Reality in Education

Augmented reality (AR) is a technology that blends virtual elements with the real world. It enhances the perception of reality by superimposing computer-generated information, such as images, videos, or 3D models, onto the user's view of the physical environment. In recent years, AR has gained significant attention in the field of education due to its potential to create immersive and interactive learning experiences.

Principles and Benefits of Augmented Reality in Education

AR in education is based on the principles of situated cognition and constructivism. Situated cognition emphasizes the importance of learning in context, where the environment plays a crucial role in shaping knowledge and understanding. Constructivism posits that learners actively construct knowledge by connecting new information with their existing mental models. AR aligns with these principles by providing learners with contextualized and interactive experiences, enabling them to explore and manipulate virtual objects in real-world settings.

One of the key benefits of AR in education is its ability to enhance visualization and spatial understanding. Through AR, abstract concepts can be visualized and represented in a tangible manner, making them more comprehensible for learners. For example, in subjects like biology or anatomy, AR can overlay virtual 3D models of cells or organs onto physical specimens, allowing students to examine them from various angles and explore their internal structures.

AR also promotes engagement and motivation by creating immersive and interactive learning environments. By blending virtual elements with real-world contexts, AR engages multiple senses and captures learners' attention. This active participation increases motivation and promotes deeper learning. For instance, in history lessons, students can use AR to visit historical sites virtually, interact with historical figures, and witness key events, making history come alive and fostering a deeper understanding.

Applications of Augmented Reality in Education

1. *Science and STEM Education*

AR can revolutionize science education by providing learners with hands-on experiences and simulations. In physics, students can use AR to conduct virtual experiments, visualize abstract concepts like electromagnetic fields, or explore the solar system by overlaying planet models onto the real sky. In chemistry, AR can enable students to visualize molecular structures in 3D or perform virtual chemical reactions.

2. *Language Learning*

AR can enhance language learning by providing immersive language experiences. Users can point their mobile devices at objects, and the AR system can recognize and label those objects with their corresponding translations in real-time. This way, learners can easily associate new vocabulary with real-world objects, making language acquisition more contextual and meaningful.

3. *Art and Design Education*

AR can be a powerful tool in art and design education, enabling students to create and interact with virtual artworks in physical spaces. For example, in architecture, students can use AR to visualize 3D building models in real environments or simulate the impact of different lighting conditions on interior spaces. In fine arts, AR can extend traditional artworks by overlaying digital content, such as animations or explanations, on physical paintings or sculptures.

Challenges and Considerations

Despite its numerous benefits, the integration of AR in education comes with a few challenges that need to be addressed:

1. *Access to Technology*

AR requires devices with built-in cameras, sensors, and processing power, such as smartphones or tablets. Ensuring equitable access to these devices for all students can be a challenge, especially in resource-constrained environments. Educators and institutions need to consider strategies to provide access to AR technology for all learners.

2. *Content Development*

Creating high-quality educational AR content requires expertise in both subject matter and AR development. Educators and developers need to work together to design and develop content that aligns with curriculum objectives and engages learners effectively. Collaboration between educators, designers, and developers is essential to ensure the creation of meaningful AR experiences.

3. *Teacher Training and Support*

Integrating AR into teaching practices requires teachers to have a solid understanding of the technology itself and how to leverage it for educational purposes. Professional development programs should be provided to support teachers in developing the necessary skills and pedagogical strategies to effectively integrate AR into their classrooms.

4. *Ethical and Privacy Concerns*

As with any technology, the use of AR in education raises concerns about data privacy, security, and ethical considerations. Educators and policymakers need to establish guidelines and best practices to protect students' privacy and ensure responsible use of AR technology in educational settings.

Conclusion

Augmented reality holds tremendous potential to transform education by providing immersive and interactive learning experiences. By blending virtual elements with the real world, AR enhances visualization, promotes engagement, and fosters contextualized learning. Although challenges exist, addressing issues related to access, content development, teacher training, and ethical considerations can pave the way for successful integration of AR in education. By embracing this emerging technology, educators can tap into innovative and effective teaching methods that enhance student learning and prepare them for the future.

Mobile Learning

Mobile learning, also known as m-learning, is a form of learning that utilizes mobile devices, such as smartphones and tablets, to enhance the learning experience. With the widespread integration of technology in education, mobile learning has gained popularity due to its accessibility, flexibility, and convenience. In this section, we will explore the principles, benefits, challenges, and strategies of mobile learning in educational settings.

Principles of Mobile Learning

Mobile learning is built on several key principles that guide its implementation and effectiveness. These principles include:

1. **Ubiquitous access:** Mobile devices offer students the opportunity to access learning materials anytime and anywhere, ensuring a seamless learning experience beyond traditional classroom settings.

2. **Personalization:** Mobile learning can be tailored to individual student needs, allowing for a personalized learning experience. Students can choose their own pace, style, and content, fostering engagement and motivation.

3. **Interactivity:** Mobile devices provide a platform for interactive learning experiences, including multimedia content, quizzes, and educational apps. This interactivity fosters active engagement and deeper understanding of the subject matter.

4. **Collaboration:** Mobile learning facilitates collaboration among students and teachers, enabling the sharing of ideas, resources, and feedback. Collaborative learning enhances critical thinking and problem-solving skills.

Benefits of Mobile Learning

Mobile learning offers numerous benefits that enhance the learning process and outcomes. Some of these benefits include:

1. **Flexibility:** Mobile learning allows students to learn at their own pace and convenience. They can access learning materials on the go, making learning more flexible and adaptable to individual schedules.

2. **Engagement:** Mobile devices provide interactive and multimedia-rich content, making learning more engaging and compelling. This helps in capturing students' interest and motivating them to actively participate in the learning process.

3. **Accessibility:** Mobile learning provides equal access to educational resources for students from diverse backgrounds and geographical locations. It eliminates barriers to education and promotes inclusivity.

4. **Collaboration:** Mobile learning platforms often include collaborative tools that promote teamwork, communication, and peer-to-peer learning. Students can connect with peers and teachers, fostering a sense of community and support.

5. **Real-world application:** Mobile learning can facilitate real-world application of knowledge through simulations, virtual experiments, and interactive case studies. This bridges the gap between theory and practice, enabling a deeper understanding of concepts.

Challenges of Mobile Learning

While mobile learning presents numerous benefits, it also comes with certain challenges that need to be addressed. Some of these challenges include:

1. **Device compatibility**: Mobile learning requires devices with compatible operating systems and internet connectivity. Ensuring that all students have access to suitable devices and network connections can be a logistical challenge.

2. **Teacher training**: Teachers need adequate training and support to effectively integrate mobile learning into their instructional practices. They need to be familiar with various educational apps, platforms, and pedagogical strategies to optimize mobile learning experiences.

3. **Digital divide**: Not all students have equal access to mobile devices and internet connectivity. The digital divide can further exacerbate existing educational disparities, limiting the effectiveness of mobile learning in reaching all students.

4. **Distractions**: Mobile devices can be a source of distraction for students, as they may be tempted to engage in non-educational activities during learning sessions. Proper monitoring and guidance are necessary to ensure productive use of mobile devices.

Strategies for Effective Mobile Learning

To ensure the successful implementation of mobile learning, educators can employ various strategies. Some of these strategies include:

1. **Appropriate app selection**: Educators should carefully select educational apps that align with the curriculum and learning objectives. The chosen apps should be interactive, engaging, and offer valuable content and activities.

2. **Integration with classroom activities**: Mobile learning should be seamlessly integrated into classroom activities to enhance the learning experience. Teachers can design lessons that integrate mobile learning apps, encourage collaborative learning, and promote active engagement.

3. **Setting clear guidelines**: Establishing clear guidelines and expectations regarding mobile device usage during learning sessions is crucial. This helps minimize distractions and ensures that students are focused on educational activities.

4. **Providing technical support**: Educators should provide technical support to students to address any issues related to device compatibility, app usage, and connectivity. This helps minimize technical barriers and ensures a smooth mobile learning experience.

5. **Promoting digital citizenship**: Educators can promote responsible use of mobile devices by teaching students about digital citizenship. This includes discussing online safety, privacy, and ethical behavior, fostering a responsible and respectful digital presence.

Examples of Mobile Learning

To illustrate the potential of mobile learning, let's consider a few examples:

1. **Language learning**: Mobile language learning apps provide interactive exercises, vocabulary drills, and pronunciation guides. Students can use these apps to practice their language skills anytime and anywhere, making language learning more accessible and engaging.

2. **Science experiments**: Mobile devices can be used to conduct virtual science experiments through simulation apps. Students can explore and manipulate virtual laboratory setups, enhancing their understanding of scientific concepts and experimental procedures.

3. **Geography exploration**: Mobile learning apps that utilize augmented reality can transport students to different geographical locations virtually. They can explore landmarks, historical sites, and cultures, making geography learning more immersive and interactive.

4. **Mathematics tutorials**: Mobile apps that offer step-by-step math tutorials and practice exercises can help students understand complex mathematical concepts. These apps provide interactive visuals and feedback, enabling students to learn and practice mathematical skills at their own pace.

Resources for Mobile Learning

There are numerous resources available to support mobile learning in educational settings. Some notable resources include:

1. **Educational app stores**: Both Apple App Store and Google Play Store have dedicated sections for educational apps. Educators can explore these stores to find apps relevant to their subject areas and grade levels.

2. **Online communities and forums**: Online communities and forums, such as Edutopia and TeachThought, provide valuable insights, resources, and discussion forums for educators interested in mobile learning.

3. **Research papers and journals**: Academic journals and research papers offer in-depth analysis and evidence-based practices for integrating mobile learning into educational settings. Some notable journals include the Journal of Educational

Technology and Society and the Journal of Mobile Learning and Organizational Change.

4. **Professional development opportunities:** Online platforms like Coursera, Udemy, and EdX offer professional development courses and certifications for educators interested in mobile learning. These courses provide valuable insights, strategies, and best practices for effective implementation.

Conclusion

Mobile learning is a promising approach that leverages the ubiquity and accessibility of mobile devices to enhance the learning experience. By following the principles of mobile learning and addressing the associated challenges, educators can create engaging, personalized, and interactive learning environments. Integrating mobile learning into educational practices empowers students to take ownership of their learning, fosters collaboration and creativity, and promotes lifelong learning skills. With the multitude of resources and strategies available, educators can embrace mobile learning to transform education and meet the diverse needs of contemporary learners.

Chapter 2: Inquiry-Based Learning

Principles and Process of Inquiry-Based Learning

Asking Questions and Posing Problems

Inquiry-based learning is a powerful educational approach that places students at the center of the learning process. One of the key principles of inquiry-based learning is the act of asking questions and posing problems. By encouraging students to ask questions and frame problems, teachers provide them with opportunities to investigate, explore, and construct their own knowledge.

Importance of Asking Questions

Asking questions is a fundamental aspect of human curiosity and is crucial for intellectual growth and development. When students ask questions, they demonstrate a desire to understand the world around them and engage in critical thinking. It promotes active learning and allows students to take ownership of their learning experiences.

Types of Questions

When it comes to inquiry-based learning, questions can be classified into different types based on their cognitive complexity. Here are a few common types of questions:

- **Recall Questions:** These questions require students to retrieve information from memory. They are typically used to assess understanding of facts and concepts.

- **Understanding Questions:** These questions require students to demonstrate comprehension of the material. They may involve explaining concepts, interpreting data, or summarizing information.

- **Application Questions:** These questions require students to apply their knowledge and understanding to solve real or simulated problems. They often involve the transfer of learning to new contexts.

- **Analysis Questions:** These questions require students to break down information, identify patterns, and make connections between different ideas or concepts.

- **Evaluation Questions:** These questions require students to make judgments and provide evidence to support their opinions. They encourage critical thinking and reflection.

- **Synthesis Questions:** These questions require students to integrate information from different sources or perspectives to create something new. They involve creativity and higher-order thinking.

By using a combination of these question types, educators can guide students through a structured inquiry process that fosters deep understanding and skill development.

Posing Problems

Inquiry-based learning also involves posing problems for students to solve. A well-posed problem is one that is open-ended, authentic, and intellectually challenging. It requires students to think critically, gather and analyze information, make decisions, and communicate their findings.

Here are some characteristics of well-posed problems:

- **Relevance:** Problems should be meaningful and connected to students' lives and interests. They should align with real-world challenges, making the learning experience more authentic and engaging.

- **Complexity:** Problems should be intellectually challenging, requiring students to apply multiple strategies, think deeply, and make connections between different concepts or disciplines.

- **Open-endedness:** Problems should not have a single correct solution. They should allow for multiple approaches and interpretations, promoting creativity and divergent thinking.

- **Opportunity for Exploration:** Problems should offer opportunities for students to investigate, gather information, and develop solutions. They should encourage students to think critically and engage in hands-on activities.

By posing well-structured problems, educators can stimulate curiosity, promote problem-solving skills, and enhance students' ability to apply knowledge to real-world situations.

Example Scenario

To illustrate the importance of asking questions and posing problems in inquiry-based learning, let's consider a scenario in a high school science class:

The teacher presents the students with a simple experiment: growing plants under different light conditions. The students are tasked with designing an experiment to investigate how different colors of light affect plant growth.

The students begin by asking questions:

- How does light affect plant growth?

- Are there specific colors of light that plants need for photosynthesis?

- How can we measure plant growth accurately?

Based on their questions, the students then move on to pose problems:

- How can we design an experiment to test the effect of different colors of light on plant growth?

- What variables do we need to control to ensure a fair experiment?

- How can we collect and analyze data to draw meaningful conclusions?

With these questions and problems in mind, the students start planning their experiment, considering variables, designing procedures, and creating data collection methods. Throughout the process, the teacher guides and supports the students, encouraging critical thinking and providing resources for further exploration.

By engaging with the inquiry process, the students not only gain a deeper understanding of plant growth and light, but they also develop valuable skills such as problem-solving, critical thinking, and collaboration.

Additional Resources and Tools

Inquiry-based learning relies on a variety of resources and tools to support the asking of questions and posing of problems. Here are a few examples:

- **Online research databases:** Provide access to a wide range of academic journals, articles, and research papers that can help students in the process of asking questions and finding solutions to complex problems.

- **Collaborative platforms:** Enable students to work together, share ideas, and solve problems in a collaborative and interactive online environment. Examples include Google Docs, Padlet, and Wikis.

- **Data collection tools:** Allow students to collect and analyze data, such as sensors for measuring temperature, pH, or light intensity. These tools can support students' investigations and help them draw evidence-based conclusions.

- **Online simulations and virtual laboratories:** Provide virtual environments where students can conduct experiments, explore scientific concepts, and solve problems without the need for physical resources. Examples include PhET Simulations and Molecular Workbench.

By leveraging these resources and tools, educators can enhance the quality of inquiry-based learning experiences and empower students to ask meaningful questions and pose challenging problems.

Conclusion

Asking questions and posing problems are fundamental aspects of inquiry-based learning. They promote active engagement, critical thinking, and deep understanding. By nurturing students' curiosity and challenging them with well-structured problems, educators can create a learning environment that fosters intellectual growth and supports the development of essential skills. So let's encourage questioning and problem-posing, and embrace the power of inquiry-based learning.

Conducting Investigations

Conducting investigations is a crucial component of inquiry-based learning. It allows students to actively explore and gather information, develop critical thinking skills, and construct their own knowledge and understanding. In this section, we will explore the principles and process of conducting investigations, as well as provide strategies and examples for effective implementation.

Principles of Conducting Investigations

Conducting investigations is based on several fundamental principles that guide the process and ensure its effectiveness. These principles are as follows:

1. **Asking Questions:** The first step in conducting investigations is to encourage students to ask meaningful questions. Questions serve as the driving force behind inquiry, helping students identify problems, gaps in knowledge, or areas of interest that they want to explore further.

2. **Developing Hypotheses:** Once the questions have been identified, students can develop hypotheses or educated guesses to answer their questions. Hypotheses provide a framework for conducting investigations and guide students' efforts in collecting and analyzing data.

3. **Designing Experiments:** After formulating hypotheses, students need to design experiments or investigations to test their hypotheses. This involves planning and organizing procedures, identifying variables, and selecting appropriate tools and materials.

4. **Collecting Data:** Students then collect data through various methods such as observations, measurements, surveys, or experiments. It is essential to ensure the data collected is accurate, reliable, and relevant to the investigation.

5. **Analyzing Data:** Once the data is gathered, students analyze and interpret it to draw conclusions. This may involve organizing data into tables or graphs, identifying patterns or trends, and making connections between variables.

6. **Drawing Conclusions:** Based on the analysis of the data, students draw conclusions that either support or refute their hypotheses. Conclusions should be based on evidence and logical reasoning.

7. **Communicating Findings:** Finally, students communicate their findings in a clear and concise manner. This may involve creating presentations, writing reports, or engaging in discussions with peers or the wider community.

Process of Conducting Investigations

Conducting investigations involves a systematic process that allows students to engage in inquiry-based learning effectively. The process can be broken down into the following steps:

1. **Identify a Question**: Students start by identifying a question or problem they want to investigate. The question should be meaningful, relevant, and aligned with the learning objectives.

2. **Develop a Hypothesis**: Once the question is identified, students formulate a hypothesis that provides a potential answer or explanation. The hypothesis should be testable and based on prior knowledge or observations.

3. **Design an Investigation**: In this step, students design an investigation to test their hypothesis. They plan and organize the procedures, determine the variables to be measured, and select appropriate tools and materials.

4. **Collect and Record Data**: Students collect relevant data using the chosen methods and record their observations or measurements accurately. It is important to document the data in a systematic and organized manner.

5. **Analyze the Data**: Once the data is collected, students analyze it to look for patterns, trends, or relationships. They may use mathematical calculations, statistical analysis, or visual representations like graphs or charts.

6. **Draw Conclusions**: Based on the analysis of the data, students draw conclusions that address the initial question or problem. The conclusions should be supported by evidence and logical reasoning.

7. **Communicate Findings**: Lastly, students communicate their findings to others. This may involve creating a presentation, writing a report, or engaging in a class discussion. Effective communication helps students reflect on their learning and receive feedback from others.

Example: Investigating the Effect of Fertilizers on Plant Growth

To illustrate the process of conducting investigations, let's consider an example where students investigate the effect of different fertilizers on plant growth. The steps involved in this investigation are as follows:

1. **Identify a Question**: The students may ask, "How do different types of fertilizers affect the growth of plants?"

2. **Develop a Hypothesis:** Based on their prior knowledge, the students may hypothesize that plants treated with fertilizer will grow taller and healthier compared to those without fertilizer.

3. **Design an Investigation:** The students plan an investigation where they divide a group of plants into several groups and assign each group a different fertilizer (e.g., organic, synthetic, no fertilizer).

4. **Collect and Record Data:** The students carefully measure and record the height, number of leaves, and overall health of the plants over a period of time.

5. **Analyze the Data:** Students analyze the collected data by comparing the growth and health of plants across the different fertilizer groups. They may create bar graphs or line graphs to visually represent the data.

6. **Draw Conclusions:** Based on the analysis, students draw conclusions about the effect of fertilizers on plant growth. They may find that plants treated with organic fertilizer showed the highest growth and health.

7. **Communicate Findings:** Finally, students communicate their findings by presenting their data and conclusions to their classmates or writing a report. They may discuss the limitations of their investigation and suggest areas for further research.

Resources and Tips for Conducting Investigations

To support students in conducting effective investigations, here are some additional resources and tips:

- **Science Kits and Supplies:** Utilize science kits, laboratory equipment, and other supplies to enhance the investigative process. These resources provide students with hands-on experiences and ensure safety during experiments.

- **Research and Reference Materials:** Encourage students to use research articles, books, or reliable online sources to gather information, understand concepts, and develop their investigative skills.

- **Collaboration and Peer Feedback:** Foster a collaborative learning environment where students can work together, share ideas, and provide constructive feedback to improve their investigations.

- **Teacher Guidance:** Provide guidance, support, and feedback throughout the investigation process. Help students develop clear research questions, design appropriate experiments, and interpret their findings accurately.

- **Real-World Connections:** Connect the investigations to real-world contexts and contemporary issues to help students see the relevance and impact of their findings.

- **Reflection and Self-Evaluation:** Encourage students to reflect on their investigation process, their learning experiences, and their growth as critical thinkers. Self-evaluation can promote metacognition and improve future investigations.

Caveats and Precautions

When conducting investigations, it is important to consider the following caveats and precautions:

- **Ethical Considerations:** Make sure students understand and adhere to ethical guidelines, especially when conducting research involving human participants or animals. Emphasize the importance of respect, informed consent, and welfare.

- **Safety Measures:** Prioritize safety during experiments by providing necessary safety equipment, proper guidance, and clear instructions. Encourage students to follow safety protocols and report any potential risks or accidents.

- **Research Validity:** Help students understand the limitations and potential biases in their investigations. Discuss factors that may affect the validity of their findings, such as sample size, control variables, or external influences.

Further Exploration

To deepen students' understanding of conducting investigations, consider the following exercises:

1. Design an investigation to explore the effects of different light intensities on plant growth.

2. Analyze a research study and evaluate the strengths and weaknesses of the investigative process.

3. Conduct a survey or interview to investigate people's attitudes towards renewable energy sources.

4. Investigate the relationship between exercise and heart rate by measuring heart rate before, during, and after physical activity.

5. Research and discuss the ethical issues related to animal testing in scientific investigations. Explore alternative methods or strategies to minimize animal use.

By engaging in these exercises, students can develop their skills in conducting investigations, critical thinking, and scientific inquiry.

In conclusion, conducting investigations is an essential aspect of inquiry-based learning. By following the principles and process outlined in this section, students can explore, investigate, and construct meaningful knowledge. Through carefully designed investigations, students can develop critical thinking, problem-solving, and communication skills necessary for their academic success and future endeavors.

Constructing Knowledge and Meaning

Inquiry-based learning is a teaching approach that emphasizes the importance of students actively constructing their knowledge and meaning through the process of inquiry. This section will explore the principles and process of constructing knowledge and meaning in inquiry-based learning, as well as provide examples and strategies for facilitating this process effectively.

Principles of Constructing Knowledge and Meaning

The process of constructing knowledge and meaning involves several key principles that guide students in their learning journey. These principles are fundamental to inquiry-based learning and provide a framework for students to explore, investigate, and make connections with the concepts being taught. Let's explore these principles in more detail:

1. **Asking Questions and Posing Problems:** This principle emphasizes the importance of curiosity and inquiry in the learning process. Students are encouraged to ask questions, pose problems, and identify areas of interest or gaps in their understanding. By initiating their inquiries, students take ownership of their learning and develop a deeper understanding of the subject matter.

2. **Conducting Investigations:** This principle involves students actively engaging in investigations to gather data, analyze information, and draw conclusions. Students may conduct experiments, gather primary and secondary sources, or use simulations and models to explore concepts and test hypotheses. Through these investigations, students develop critical thinking and problem-solving skills.

3. **Constructing Knowledge and Meaning:** The central principle of constructing knowledge and meaning emphasizes the active role of students in building their understanding of the subject matter. Students organize and synthesize information, make connections between new and prior knowledge, and construct their own meaning through deep reflection and critical analysis.

4. **Communicating and Reflecting on Learning:** This principle highlights the importance of effective communication and reflection in the learning process. Students are encouraged to articulate their ideas, ask for feedback, and engage in dialogue with their peers and teachers. By reflecting on their learning experiences, students deepen their understanding and develop metacognitive skills.

5. **Collaborative Inquiry:** Collaboration is an essential element of constructing knowledge and meaning. Students work together in groups or teams to explore complex problems, share ideas, negotiate meaning, and co-construct knowledge. Collaborative inquiry fosters mutual respect, enhances communication skills, and promotes a sense of collective responsibility for learning.

Strategies for Facilitating Constructing Knowledge and Meaning

Facilitating the process of constructing knowledge and meaning requires intentional strategies and instructional practices. Here are some effective strategies that educators can utilize to support students in their learning journey:

- **Activate Prior Knowledge:** Before diving into new content, activate students' prior knowledge related to the topic. This helps students make connections between what they already know and the new information they will encounter, fostering a sense of relevance and facilitating the construction of knowledge.

- **Provide Authentic Contexts:** Present real-world contexts and authentic problems that students can relate to. Authentic contexts encourage students to engage in meaningful learning experiences and apply their knowledge and skills to solve practical problems. This promotes the construction of knowledge and meaning that has real-world significance.

- **Encourage Reflection and Metacognition:** Provide regular opportunities for students to reflect on their learning process and think metacognitively about their thinking. Encourage them to consider how they constructed their understanding, what strategies they used, and what they learned from the experience. Reflection and metacognition enhance the construction of deep and meaningful knowledge.

- **Promote Discussions and Collaboration:** Foster a collaborative learning environment where students can engage in discussions, share their ideas, and learn from one another. Encourage students to explain their thinking, ask probing questions, and challenge each other respectfully. Collaboration promotes the construction of knowledge through the exploration of multiple perspectives and the negotiation of meaning.

- **Provide Scaffolding and Support:** Offer appropriate scaffolding and support to help students navigate complex concepts and tasks. Scaffolding can take the form of graphic organizers, guiding questions, visual aids, or simplified examples. Gradually release responsibility to students as they develop their understanding and become more independent in constructing knowledge and meaning.

Example: Constructing Knowledge and Meaning in Science Education

To illustrate the process of constructing knowledge and meaning in inquiry-based learning, let's consider a science education example. Imagine a middle school class studying the concept of photosynthesis. Here's how the process might unfold:

1. **Asking Questions and Posing Problems:** The teacher begins by asking students a series of questions to elicit their prior knowledge and generate curiosity. Students generate questions about photosynthesis, such as "What is photosynthesis?" or "How does photosynthesis occur?"

2. **Conducting Investigations:** Students conduct investigations to explore photosynthesis in action. They may set up experiments to observe the role of

light, water, and carbon dioxide in the process. They gather data, make observations, and analyze their findings.

3. **Constructing Knowledge and Meaning:** Students construct their understanding of photosynthesis by organizing and synthesizing the information gathered from their investigations. They connect the dots between light, water, carbon dioxide, and glucose production, deepening their understanding of the process.

4. **Communicating and Reflecting on Learning:** Students share their findings and reflections with their peers through presentations, group discussions, or written reports. They reflect on their learning process, identify challenges they encountered, and discuss the significance of their findings.

5. **Collaborative Inquiry:** Throughout the process, students work collaboratively in small groups, sharing ideas, discussing their findings, and supporting each other's learning. They engage in dialogue, challenge each other's assumptions, and collectively construct knowledge and meaning.

Resources and Further Reading

To deepen your understanding of constructing knowledge and meaning in inquiry-based learning, here are some recommended resources:

- *Inquiry-Based Learning: Designing Instruction to Promote Higher-Level Thinking* by John L. Barell
- *How We Think: A Theory of Inquiry-Based Learning* by John Dewey
- *Engaging Students in Learning: An Inquiry-Based Approach* by Judith L. Irvin et al.

Additionally, explore online platforms and resources that provide practical strategies and examples of constructing knowledge and meaning in inquiry-based learning. These resources can inspire educators and provide helpful insights into implementing effective instructional practices.

Exercises

To reinforce your understanding of constructing knowledge and meaning, here are some exercises to try:

1. Choose a topic of interest and formulate questions that could guide an inquiry-based learning approach. Reflect on why these questions are valuable and how they could facilitate the construction of knowledge and meaning.

2. Design an inquiry-based learning activity for a specific subject and grade level. Consider how you would activate prior knowledge, provide authentic contexts, promote reflection and collaboration, and scaffold students' learning.

3. Reflect on a recent learning experience you had where you actively constructed knowledge and meaning. What strategies or principles of inquiry-based learning were evident in this experience? How did this approach enhance your understanding?

Remember, constructing knowledge and meaning is at the core of inquiry-based learning. By engaging in active inquiry, students become active participants in their learning journey, leading to deeper understanding, critical thinking, and the ability to apply knowledge in meaningful ways.

Communicating and Reflecting on Learning

Effective communication and reflection play vital roles in the learning process. They allow students to articulate their thoughts, engage in critical thinking, and make connections between concepts. In this section, we will explore the importance of communication and reflection in learning, along with practical strategies for incorporating these skills into the classroom.

Importance of Communication

Communication is a fundamental skill that enables students to express their ideas, listen to others, and participate actively in the learning community. It encompasses both verbal and non-verbal forms of expression. When students communicate effectively, they can clarify their understanding, ask questions, and seek feedback. Additionally, communication skills are essential for collaboration, problem-solving, and building relationships.

To foster effective communication, teachers should create a supportive and inclusive classroom environment. They can encourage open discussions, provide opportunities for collaborative work, and model good communication skills. Teachers should also emphasize active listening, empathy, and respect for diverse perspectives. By cultivating a culture of effective communication, students can develop their communication skills and become confident and articulate learners.

Strategies for Promoting Communication

To promote effective communication in the classroom, teachers can employ a range of strategies. One effective strategy is the use of structured discussions, such as Socratic seminars or fishbowl discussions. These discussions provide students with a framework for expressing their ideas, engaging with others' perspectives, and practicing active listening. Teachers can also use think-pair-share activities, where students think individually, discuss in pairs, and then share their ideas with the whole class. This strategy allows students to refine their thoughts and gain different viewpoints.

Another strategy is the use of technology tools that facilitate communication. Online discussion boards or chat platforms can extend classroom conversations beyond the physical space, allowing students to engage in asynchronous discussions and express their thoughts in writing. Teachers can also make use of video conferencing tools to connect students from different locations, providing opportunities for collaboration and communication.

To foster reflection and metacognition, teachers can incorporate regular opportunities for students to reflect on their learning experiences. This can take the form of reflective writing prompts, exit slips, or class discussions. By reflecting on their learning, students can identify their strengths and areas for growth, make connections between concepts, and deepen their understanding. Teachers can provide guidance and support by asking probing questions and encouraging students to think critically about their learning process.

Encouraging Meaningful Reflection

Meaningful reflection requires students to go beyond surface-level thinking and engage in critical analysis of their learning experiences. To encourage meaningful reflection, teachers can guide students through a structured reflection process. This process can involve asking students to identify their learning goals, assess their progress, and consider strategies for improvement. Teachers can also provide prompts or guiding questions to prompt deeper reflection.

In addition to individual reflection, collaborative reflection activities can also be valuable. Group discussions or peer feedback sessions allow students to share their perspectives, learn from each other, and gain new insights. Collaborative reflection promotes a sense of community and collective learning, as students build upon each other's ideas and provide support and feedback.

To make reflection a continuous part of the learning process, teachers can incorporate regular reflection checkpoints throughout a unit or project. For example, students can be asked to reflect on their understanding at the beginning and end of a lesson, or they can engage in periodic journaling or portfolio creation to track their progress over time. By integrating reflection into the learning process, students develop metacognitive skills and become more self-directed learners.

Real-World Applications and Examples

Effective communication and reflection are essential skills in various real-world contexts. For example, in professional settings, effective communication is crucial for collaboration, presenting ideas, and building relationships with colleagues and clients. Reflective practice is also widely used in professions such as teaching, healthcare, and business, where individuals reflect on their experiences to enhance their skills and decision-making.

In science, communication and reflection are integral to the scientific process. Scientists must effectively communicate their research findings to peers through publications and presentations. They also engage in reflection to critically analyze their data, methodologies, and conclusions, ensuring the integrity and validity of their work.

In an example from mathematics, communication and reflection are important for problem-solving. When students work on math problems, they need to communicate their reasoning and strategies clearly. They also reflect on their problem-solving approaches, analyzing their mistakes and seeking alternative solutions.

Resources for Further Exploration

To further explore the topic of communication and reflection in learning, the following resources may be helpful:

- *Classroom Discussions: Using Math Talk to Help Students Learn* by Suzanne H. Chapin, Catherine O'Connor, and Nancy Canavan Anderson

- *Teaching for Learning: 101 Intentionally Designed Educational Activities to Put Students on the Path to Success* by Jillian McDonald and Zachary Goodell

- *Visible Learning for Teachers: Maximizing Impact on Learning* by John Hattie

- *Enhancing Learning Through Formative Assessment and Feedback* by Dylan Wiliam
- *Becoming a Reflective Teacher* by Robert J. Marzano and Tina Boogren

These resources provide practical strategies, research-based insights, and case studies to support teachers in promoting effective communication and reflection in the classroom.

Conclusion

Communication and reflection are essential skills for students to develop as they navigate the learning process. By promoting effective communication and providing opportunities for reflection, teachers can empower students to express their ideas, engage critically with content, and become active participants in their own learning. Through a combination of structured discussions, technology integration, and reflective practices, educators can create vibrant and collaborative learning environments that foster student success.

Collaborative Inquiry

Collaborative inquiry is a powerful learning approach that involves students working together in groups or teams to explore and investigate complex problems or questions. It is an active and engaging process that encourages students to develop critical thinking skills, problem-solving abilities, and effective communication and collaboration skills. In this section, we will explore the principles and benefits of collaborative inquiry, as well as strategies for implementing and assessing it in the classroom.

Principles of Collaborative Inquiry

Collaborative inquiry is based on several key principles that guide the process and ensure its effectiveness. These principles include:

- **Shared responsibility:** In collaborative inquiry, all group members share the responsibility for the learning process. Each member contributes their ideas, perspectives, and strengths to the group, fostering a sense of ownership and empowerment.

- **Active participation:** Collaborative inquiry requires active participation from all group members. They are actively involved in posing questions, conducting research, analyzing data, and generating solutions. This active engagement promotes deeper understanding and critical thinking.

- **Respectful and inclusive communication:** Effective communication is essential in collaborative inquiry. Group members must listen actively, express their ideas respectfully, and consider diverse viewpoints. Creating a safe and inclusive environment encourages open discussion and fosters a sense of belonging.

- **Collaborative problem-solving:** Collaborative inquiry involves tackling authentic and complex problems or questions. It requires group members to work together to analyze the problem, generate possible solutions, and refine their ideas through discussion and debate. This collaborative problem-solving approach encourages creative and collaborative thinking.

- **Reflection and metacognition:** Throughout the collaborative inquiry process, students are encouraged to reflect on their learning experiences. They think about their thinking (metacognition), identify their strengths and areas for improvement, and set goals for further learning. This reflective practice enhances self-awareness and promotes lifelong learning.

Implementing Collaborative Inquiry in the Classroom

To implement collaborative inquiry in the classroom, teachers can follow these strategies:

- **Designing meaningful tasks:** Teachers should create authentic and challenging tasks that require students to collaborate and engage in inquiry. These tasks should align with the curriculum, be relevant to students' lives, and promote deep understanding and critical thinking.

- **Group formation:** Careful consideration should be given to group formation. Teachers can create heterogeneous groups based on students' diverse abilities and backgrounds. Mixing students with different strengths and perspectives encourages collaborative problem-solving and fosters cooperative learning.

- **Establishing norms and expectations:** Teachers should establish clear norms and expectations for collaborative inquiry. These include guidelines for respectful communication, active participation, and shared responsibility. Students should understand the importance of collaboration and the value of each group member's contributions.

- **Providing guidance and support:** Teachers play a crucial role in facilitating collaborative inquiry. They provide guidance and support, ensuring that students stay on track, understand the inquiry process, and develop the necessary skills. Teachers can use questioning techniques to prompt students' thinking and scaffold their learning.

- **Promoting reflection and feedback:** Reflection is an integral part of collaborative inquiry. Teachers can encourage students to reflect on their learning experiences, evaluate their group dynamics, and identify areas of improvement. Providing timely and constructive feedback helps students refine their thinking and enhance their collaborative skills.

- **Using suitable technologies:** Technology can support collaborative inquiry by providing tools for communication, information sharing, and data analysis. Online collaboration platforms, such as Google Docs or Padlet, facilitate group work and allow students to collaborate beyond the confines of the classroom.

Assessing Collaborative Inquiry

Assessing collaborative inquiry involves evaluating both individual and group performance. Here are some assessment strategies:

- **Observation and documentation:** Teachers can observe students' interactions and document their contributions during collaborative inquiry. This allows them to assess individual participation, communication skills, and ability to work effectively in a team.

- **Peer assessment:** Peer assessment involves students evaluating their group members' contributions. This allows them to develop self-assessment and evaluation skills, as well as provide feedback to their peers. Rubrics or checklists can be used to guide peer assessments.

- **Portfolios or journals:** Students can maintain portfolios or journals to document their learning journey in collaborative inquiry. These can include reflections, examples of their work, and evidence of their growth and development.

- **Presentations or demonstrations:** Students can present their findings, solutions, or projects to the class or to a broader audience. This assesses their ability to communicate their ideas effectively and showcase their learning.

- **Assessment of final products:** The final products of collaborative inquiry, such as reports, presentations, or digital artifacts, can be assessed using rubrics or criteria that align with the learning objectives. This ensures that the assessment focuses on the intended outcomes.

Example: Collaborative Inquiry in Science

Let's consider an example of collaborative inquiry in a science class. The teacher poses the question, "How does pollution affect the local ecosystem?" Students are divided into groups and tasked with conducting research, collecting data, and analyzing the impact of different types of pollution on the local environment.

The groups collaborate to design experiments, collect samples, and analyze the data. They engage in discussions, share their findings, and collectively develop solutions to minimize pollution. Throughout the process, the teacher provides guidance, asks probing questions, and encourages reflection.

As a culminating activity, each group presents their findings to the class. They showcase their data, explain their experimental design, and propose ways to mitigate pollution in the local ecosystem. The class engages in a lively discussion, providing feedback and asking questions.

Through this collaborative inquiry, students not only develop a deeper understanding of the impact of pollution but also enhance their critical thinking, communication, and problem-solving skills. They learn the value of collaboration and appreciate the diverse perspectives and ideas within their group.

Resources for Collaborative Inquiry

Here are some resources that can assist in implementing collaborative inquiry in the classroom:

- The Critical Thinking Consortium: This organization provides resources and professional development opportunities to support inquiry-based learning and critical thinking skills (https://tc2.ca).

- Edutopia: Edutopia offers articles, videos, and classroom examples of collaborative learning and inquiry-based instruction (https://www.edutopia.org).

- National Geographic Education: National Geographic Education provides resources and activities to promote collaborative inquiry in various subject areas, including science and geography (https://www.nationalgeographic.org/education).

- Project-Based Learning: A resource by Edutopia offering guidance and examples for implementing project-based learning, which aligns well with collaborative inquiry (https://www.edutopia.org/project-based-learning).

Conclusion

Collaborative inquiry offers a dynamic and effective way to engage students in deep learning, critical thinking, and meaningful collaboration. By fostering shared responsibility, active participation, respectful communication, collaborative problem-solving, and reflection, it equips students with essential skills for success in the 21st century. As educators, we have the opportunity to create rich learning experiences that cultivate these skills and empower students to become lifelong learners and contributors to their communities.

Inquiry-Based Learning Models

Problem-Based Learning

Problem-based learning (PBL) is an instructional approach that engages students in solving real-world problems as a way to promote critical thinking, problem-solving skills, and deep understanding of the subject matter. This section will explore the principles and process of PBL, its benefits and challenges, the role of teachers in facilitating PBL, and strategies for assessing and evaluating PBL.

Principles and Process of Problem-Based Learning

PBL is based on several key principles that guide the learning process:

1. **Authentic problems:** PBL involves presenting students with authentic, complex, and open-ended problems that require analysis, synthesis, and evaluation. These problems are often derived from real-world situations, allowing students to see the relevance and applicability of what they learn.

2. **Student-centered inquiry:** PBL places students at the center of the learning process, encouraging them to actively explore and construct their knowledge through inquiry. Students are responsible for identifying their learning needs, setting goals, and seeking resources to solve the problem.

INQUIRY-BASED LEARNING MODELS

3. **Collaboration:** PBL emphasizes collaborative learning, fostering teamwork, communication, and social interaction. Students work in small groups to brainstorm ideas, share perspectives, and collectively generate solutions to the problem.

4. **Facilitator's role:** The role of the teacher in PBL is that of a facilitator or guide rather than a traditional instructor. The teacher provides support, guidance, and feedback to help students navigate the problem-solving process and develop their critical thinking skills.

5. **Reflection and metacognition:** PBL encourages students to reflect on their learning experience and think metacognitively about their problem-solving strategies. Through self-assessment and reflection, students deepen their understanding, identify areas of growth, and develop problem-solving skills that transfer to other contexts.

The process of PBL typically involves the following steps:

1. **Problem presentation:** The teacher presents the problem to the students, providing sufficient context and background information. The problem should be authentic, meaningful, and aligned with the learning objectives.

2. **Brainstorming and hypothesis generation:** Students engage in brainstorming activities to generate ideas, hypotheses, or possible approaches to solving the problem. This step encourages creativity, critical thinking, and divergent perspectives.

3. **Investigation and research:** Students conduct independent investigations and research to gather information, explore different perspectives, and deepen their understanding of the problem. They analyze data, review literature, and consult with experts or other resources.

4. **Collaborative problem-solving:** Students work together in small groups to discuss their findings, share insights, and develop solutions to the problem. This collaborative process promotes teamwork, communication skills, and the negotiation of ideas.

5. **Reflection and evaluation:** After developing their solutions, students reflect on their problem-solving process, evaluate the effectiveness of their solutions, and consider alternative approaches or improvements. This step encourages metacognition and critical reflection.

6. **Presentation and communication:** Finally, students present their findings, solutions, and recommendations to their peers, teachers, or an authentic audience. This step develops oral communication skills and allows for feedback and discussion.

Advantages and Challenges of Problem-Based Learning

PBL offers several benefits for students' learning and development:

1. **Enhanced critical thinking skills:** PBL nurtures students' ability to think critically, analyze complex problems, and make informed decisions. By engaging in problem-solving activities, students learn to think deeply, evaluate evidence, and justify their reasoning.

2. **Authentic learning experiences:** PBL connects students to real-world problems, allowing them to apply their knowledge and skills in meaningful contexts. This authenticity increases motivation, engagement, and the transferability of learning to future situations.

3. **Collaborative skills and social interaction:** Through collaboration in PBL, students develop interpersonal skills, such as communication, teamwork, and negotiation. They learn to appreciate diverse perspectives, resolve conflicts, and work effectively in a team.

4. **Intrinsic motivation and ownership:** PBL taps into students' intrinsic motivation by giving them autonomy and ownership over their learning. Students experience a sense of responsibility and pride in their work, leading to higher engagement and perseverance.

5. **Problem-solving and transferability:** PBL equips students with problem-solving skills that can be applied in various domains and disciplines. Students learn to think creatively, adapt solutions to different contexts, and approach new challenges with confidence.

Despite its advantages, PBL also presents some challenges:

1. **Time management:** PBL requires careful planning and time management to ensure that students have enough time to engage in the problem-solving process. Teachers must balance the time spent on investigations, group work, and reflection.

2. **Assessment complexity:** Assessing PBL can be challenging due to its open-ended nature and the multiple dimensions of learning involved. Teachers need to design assessment strategies that capture students' depth of understanding, critical thinking skills, and collaborative abilities.

3. **Teacher role transition:** Adopting a facilitator role can be a significant shift for teachers accustomed to a more traditional instructional approach. Teachers may need professional development and support to effectively facilitate PBL and provide meaningful feedback to students.

4. **Group dynamics:** Collaboration in PBL relies on effective group dynamics and interpersonal skills. Managing group conflicts, ensuring equitable participation, and fostering a positive learning environment can be demanding for both students and teachers.

The Role of Teachers in Problem-Based Learning

In PBL, the teacher's role shifts from a content disseminator to a facilitator of learning. The teacher plays a crucial role in guiding and supporting students throughout the problem-solving process. Here are some key responsibilities of teachers in PBL:

1. **Designing problems:** Teachers need to design or select authentic problems that align with the curriculum and learning objectives. The problems should be challenging yet achievable, stimulating students' curiosity and promoting deep learning.

2. **Creating a supportive learning environment:** Teachers establish a safe and supportive learning environment where students feel comfortable taking risks, asking questions, and sharing their ideas. They foster a culture of respect, collaboration, and academic rigor.

3. **Providing guidance and feedback:** Teachers provide guidance and feedback to students as they engage in problem-solving activities. They offer support in the form of scaffolding, question prompts, resources, and constructive feedback to help students overcome challenges and deepen their understanding.

4. **Facilitating group work:** Teachers facilitate group work by establishing clear expectations and roles for group members. They help students navigate group dynamics, resolve conflicts, and ensure equitable participation.

Teachers encourage effective communication and collaboration among group members.

5. **Promoting metacognition**: Teachers prompt students to reflect on their problem-solving processes, evaluate the effectiveness of their strategies, and make connections to prior knowledge. They encourage students to think metacognitively about their learning and provide opportunities for self-assessment.

6. **Assessing student learning**: Teachers design assessments that align with the learning objectives and capture the depth of students' understanding. They evaluate not only the final product or solution but also the process, critical thinking skills, collaboration, and reflection involved in problem-solving.

Assessing and Evaluating Problem-Based Learning

Assessment in PBL aims to evaluate students' understanding, critical thinking skills, collaboration, and problem-solving abilities. Here are some strategies for assessing and evaluating PBL:

1. **Rubrics and criteria**: Teachers can develop rubrics and scoring criteria that outline the expectations for the final product or solution. The rubrics should encompass the depth of understanding, critical thinking, communication, and collaboration involved in the problem-solving process.

2. **Portfolios**: Portfolios allow students to compile evidence of their learning journey in PBL. The portfolios can include reflections, research notes, drafts, peer evaluations, and the final product. Students can demonstrate their growth, metacognition, and mastery of content through the portfolio.

3. **Presentations and discussions**: Presentations and discussions provide students with opportunities to showcase their understanding, communicate their ideas, and receive peer feedback. Teachers can assess students' oral communication skills, clarity of thinking, and ability to articulate their problem-solving strategies.

4. **Self-assessment and reflection**: Students can engage in self-assessment and reflection activities to evaluate their problem-solving processes and outcomes. They can use self-assessment checklists, journaling, or structured reflection prompts to critically analyze their strengths, areas for growth, and next steps.

5. **Peer assessment:** Peer assessment allows students to provide feedback, evaluate each other's work, and engage in critical dialogue. This process develops their evaluative skills, communication skills, and promotes a culture of constructive feedback and reflection.

6. **Formative assessment:** Formative assessment strategies, such as quizzes, concept maps, or classroom discussions, can be used to gauge students' understanding, clarify misconceptions, and provide timely feedback during the problem-solving process. Formative assessment guides instructional decisions and supports student learning.

7. **Reflection and evaluation:** Teachers can facilitate reflective discussions or provide prompts for students to evaluate their learning experience in PBL. This process allows students to think metacognitively about their growth, the effectiveness of their problem-solving strategies, and the impact of their solutions.

Example: Problem-Based Learning in Biology

To illustrate the application of PBL, let us consider a scenario in a high school biology class. The problem presented to the students is as follows:

"Your local community is experiencing a decline in the bee population, which is essential for pollination and maintaining biodiversity. The community is concerned about the potential consequences of this decline. Your task is to investigate the causes of the decline and propose measures to address the issue."

In response to this problem, students form small groups and engage in the following activities:

1. **Brainstorming and hypothesis generation:** Students brainstorm potential factors contributing to the decline of bees, such as habitat loss, pesticide use, climate change, and disease. They develop hypotheses about the most significant factors and their interrelationships.

2. **Investigation and research:** Students conduct research to gather information about the factors they identified. They consult scientific articles, environmental reports, and interviews with local experts. They analyze data related to bee populations and their decline.

3. **Collaborative problem-solving:** Students work together to analyze their findings and develop strategies to address the issue. They discuss the

feasibility and effectiveness of different measures, considering the ecological, economic, and social implications.

4. **Reflection and evaluation:** After proposing their solutions, students reflect on their problem-solving process. They evaluate the evidence they gathered, the quality of their reasoning, and the potential impact of their solutions. They consider alternative perspectives and strategies.

5. **Presentation and communication:** Finally, students present their findings and recommendations to their peers, the teacher, and members of the community. They explain their analysis, propose measures, and engage in a discussion about the issue and potential solutions.

Through this PBL experience, students deepen their understanding of biology concepts related to ecosystems, interdependencies, and sustainability. They develop critical thinking skills, collaboration skills, and awareness of real-world environmental issues. This problem also fosters a sense of responsibility and engagement in addressing local community concerns.

Resources for Problem-Based Learning

For teachers interested in implementing PBL, there are various resources available. Some notable resources include:

- **BIE (Buck Institute for Education):** BIE provides a wealth of resources, including project ideas, professional development materials, and sample rubrics for PBL implementation across various subjects and grade levels. Their website (https://www.bie.org/) offers a comprehensive collection of resources and access to a supportive community of educators.

- **PBLWorks:** Formerly known as the Buck Institute for Education, PBLWorks offers research-based professional development, coaching, and resources to help schools and districts implement effective PBL. Their website (https://www.pblworks.org/) provides access to project ideas, curriculum materials, and articles on PBL best practices.

- **Edutopia:** Edutopia, a website by the George Lucas Educational Foundation, offers a range of articles, videos, and resource guides on PBL. Educators can find inspiration, strategies, and examples of PBL in action across diverse subjects and grade levels. The website (https://www.edutopia.org/) is a valuable source of information and ideas.

- **Online communities:** Online communities, such as social media groups or dedicated platforms, provide spaces for educators to collaborate, share ideas, and seek support in implementing PBL. Platforms like Twitter and Facebook have groups dedicated to PBL, where teachers can connect with like-minded educators and access a wide range of resources.

Caveats and Considerations

When implementing PBL, teachers should consider the following caveats:

1. **Balance with other instructional strategies:** PBL is not a one-size-fits-all approach and may not be suitable for all topics or objectives. Teachers should consider the balance between PBL and other instructional strategies to ensure a comprehensive and well-rounded learning experience.

2. **Scaffolding and support:** PBL requires scaffolding and support to help students navigate the problem-solving process effectively. Teachers should provide necessary guidance, resources, and checkpoints to ensure that students do not feel overwhelmed or lost.

3. **Equitable participation:** Teachers should be mindful of equitable participation within groups and address any potential issues related to dominance or exclusion. Promoting inclusive discussions and fostering a supportive environment for all students is crucial.

4. **Transparent assessment criteria:** Clearly communicating assessment criteria and expectations to students is important to ensure fairness and clarity. Rubrics and scoring guides should be shared in advance, allowing students to understand what is expected of them.

5. **Reflection and metacognition:** Teachers should provide structured opportunities for students to reflect on their learning experiences and think metacognitively about their problem-solving strategies. This reflection enhances the transferability of skills and helps students become increasingly self-directed learners.

Overall, Problem-Based Learning offers a student-centered, authentic approach to education. By engaging students in solving real-world problems, PBL promotes critical thinking, collaboration, and deep understanding. With careful planning, support, and assessment strategies, teachers can effectively implement PBL and create meaningful learning experiences for their students.

Project-Based Learning

Project-Based Learning (PBL) is a student-centered approach to teaching and learning that emphasizes active, hands-on experiences. In this section, we will explore the principles and process of PBL, the role of teachers, different project-based learning models, and the benefits of implementing PBL in the classroom.

Principles and Process of Project-Based Learning

At its core, PBL involves students working on a project that engages them in solving real-world problems or answering complex questions. The following principles guide the implementation of PBL:

1. **Relevance:** Projects should be meaningful and relevant to students' lives. By tackling authentic problems or issues, students understand the purpose behind their learning and become intrinsically motivated.

2. **Inquiry:** PBL encourages students to ask questions and explore a topic in-depth. Through inquiry, students develop critical thinking and problem-solving skills.

3. **Collaboration:** PBL fosters collaboration and teamwork. Students work together to brainstorm ideas, delegate tasks, and achieve common goals. Collaboration enhances communication, interpersonal skills, and the ability to work effectively in groups.

4. **Authenticity:** Projects should mirror the real world. By simulating real-life scenarios, students gain practical skills and develop a deeper understanding of the subject matter.

5. **Reflection:** Regular reflection allows students to evaluate their progress, identify areas for improvement, and assess their learning outcomes. Reflection also helps students make connections between their project experiences and broader concepts or theories.

The process of PBL typically involves the following steps:

1. **Identify a driving question or problem:** A driving question or problem is the foundation of a project. It should be open-ended, engaging, and encourage student inquiry.

2. **Plan and research:** Students plan their project, identify resources, and conduct research to gain a deep understanding of the topic.

3. **Create a project plan:** Students develop a project plan, outlining the steps they will take to complete the project and the roles and responsibilities of each team member.

4. **Implement the project:** Students engage in hands-on activities, collect data, create products, or design solutions. They collaborate, make decisions, and solve problems throughout the project.

5. **Present and reflect:** Students present their work to an authentic audience, such as their peers, teachers, or community members. They reflect on their learning journey, evaluate their work, and receive feedback.

Project-Based Learning Models

There are different models of PBL, each with its own unique characteristics. Let's explore some of the commonly used project-based learning models:

1. **Problem-Based Learning (PBL):** In this model, students work on solving a specific problem or challenge. They identify and analyze the problem, research possible solutions, and develop and implement a solution.

2. **Case-Based Learning (CBL):** CBL involves presenting students with a real or simulated case that represents a problem or situation. Students analyze the case, propose solutions or actions, and evaluate the outcomes.

3. **Service-Learning:** Service-learning combines academic learning with community service. Students identify community needs, design projects to address those needs, and reflect on their experiences while serving the community.

4. **Project-Based Learning in Different Subjects:** PBL can be implemented across various subjects, allowing students to apply their knowledge and skills in a relevant context. For example, in science, students can design and conduct experiments, while in history, they can create documentaries or museum exhibits.

5. **Interdisciplinary Project-Based Learning:** This model involves integrating multiple subjects or disciplines into a single project. Interdisciplinary projects promote the application of knowledge and skills across different domains, fostering holistic learning.

The Role of Teachers in Project-Based Learning

Teachers play a crucial role in facilitating PBL experiences. They act as guides, mentors, and facilitators throughout the project. Some key roles of teachers in PBL include:

1. **Designing and scaffolding the project**: Teachers design projects that align with curriculum goals and provide appropriate scaffolding to support student learning.

2. **Facilitating student learning**: Teachers create a supportive learning environment and provide guidance as students work on their projects. They monitor progress, offer feedback, and help students overcome challenges.

3. **Promoting collaboration and communication**: Teachers foster teamwork, encourage effective communication, and facilitate collaboration among students. They promote a positive classroom culture that values respect, active listening, and open dialogue.

4. **Building subject knowledge**: Teachers ensure students have the necessary subject knowledge and skills to undertake their projects. They provide direct instruction, offer resources, and facilitate discussions to support student learning.

5. **Assessing student learning**: Teachers use various formative and summative assessment strategies to evaluate both the process and outcomes of student projects. They provide feedback that helps students improve their work and demonstrate their learning.

Benefits of Project-Based Learning

Implementing PBL in the classroom offers numerous benefits to students. Here are some key advantages of project-based learning:

1. **Deep understanding**: PBL promotes a deeper understanding of concepts and skills by connecting them to real-world applications. Students see the relevance of their learning and are motivated to explore and analyze topics more comprehensively.

2. **Critical thinking and problem-solving skills**: PBL requires students to engage in complex problem-solving, think critically, and make informed

INQUIRY-BASED LEARNING MODELS

decisions. Students learn to analyze information, evaluate alternative solutions, and apply their knowledge to solve authentic problems.

3. **Collaboration and communication:** PBL emphasizes collaboration, allowing students to work together, share ideas, and communicate effectively. These skills are essential in the 21st-century workplace where teamwork and effective communication are highly valued.

4. **Autonomy and self-direction:** PBL encourages learner autonomy and self-direction. Students take responsibility for their learning, make decisions, and manage their project timeline and tasks.

5. **Motivation and engagement:** PBL is inherently motivating as it taps into students' interests and passions. By engaging in authentic and meaningful projects, students become more invested in their learning.

Implementation Strategies and Considerations

Implementing PBL effectively requires careful planning and consideration. Here are some strategies and considerations for successful PBL implementation:

1. **Start with a clear driving question:** A well-crafted driving question generates curiosity and sets the stage for the entire project. It should be open-ended, challenging, and relevant to students' lives.

2. **Provide scaffolding and support:** Gradually release responsibility to students as they gain mastery. Teachers can provide scaffolding through initial instruction, guiding questions, templates, and resources.

3. **Create an inclusive learning environment:** Consider students' diverse learning needs, interests, and backgrounds when designing and implementing projects. Foster an inclusive classroom environment where all students feel valued and supported.

4. **Foster reflection and metacognition:** Regular reflection helps students make connections, identify their learning progress, and set goals for improvement. Reflection can take the form of journal writing, group discussions, or presentations.

5. **Encourage student voice and choice:** Allow students to have a say in project topics, approaches, and products. Giving students ownership of their learning enhances motivation and creativity.

6. **Provide opportunities for self-assessment and peer feedback:** Encourage students to assess their progress, reflect on their learning, and provide feedback to their peers. This fosters metacognition and the development of evaluation skills.

Resources

There are various resources available for teachers interested in implementing project-based learning:

- **PBLWorks:** PBLWorks (formerly known as the Buck Institute for Education) offers a wide range of resources, including project ideas, planning tools, and professional development opportunities. Their website (www.pblworks.org) is a valuable starting point.

- **Edutopia:** Edutopia (www.edutopia.org) is an online platform that provides articles, videos, and case studies on innovative teaching practices, including project-based learning. It features a diverse collection of resources for teachers at all levels.

- **National Education Association (NEA):** The NEA (www.nea.org) offers valuable guidance and resources on project-based learning. Their website includes articles, lesson plans, and classroom materials related to PBL.

- **Professional Learning Networks (PLNs):** Joining online communities and PLNs focused on PBL allows educators to connect with like-minded individuals, share ideas, and access a wealth of resources. Platforms like Twitter and LinkedIn offer a plethora of PBL-focused groups and hashtags.

Conclusion

Project-Based Learning is a powerful approach that transforms the learning experience for students. By engaging in authentic, hands-on projects, students develop important skills, deepen their understanding of subject matter, and become active participants in their own education. With careful planning and thoughtful implementation, teachers can harness the potential of PBL to create meaningful and impactful learning experiences for their students. So why not embark on a project-based learning journey and empower your students to become lifelong learners and agents of change?

Case-Based Learning

Case-based learning is a student-centered instructional approach that focuses on the analysis and application of real-world cases to develop critical thinking, problem-solving, and decision-making skills. In this approach, students are presented with authentic and complex cases that reflect the challenges and complexities of professional practice. They then work individually or in groups to analyze these cases, identify the key issues, and propose plausible solutions based on their understanding of the subject matter.

Principles and Process of Case-Based Learning

Case-based learning is founded on several key principles that guide its implementation. These principles include:

1. **Authenticity:** Cases should reflect the realities of professional practice, mirroring the complexity and uncertainty that practitioners face in their everyday work. This authenticity helps to develop students' ability to navigate real-world challenges.

2. **Active Learning:** Case-based learning promotes active engagement and participation, as students are actively involved in analyzing and solving problems. This active involvement enhances their understanding of the content and improves retention.

3. **Problem-Oriented:** The focus of case-based learning is on problem-solving. Students are encouraged to identify and define problems, gather relevant information, analyze the situation, and propose feasible solutions. This approach helps develop critical thinking and decision-making skills.

The process of case-based learning involves several stages:

1. **Case Selection:** Educators choose cases that align with the learning objectives and provide meaningful opportunities for students to apply their knowledge and skills. The cases should be authentic, relevant, and challenging.

2. **Preparation:** Students are provided with the necessary background information related to the case, including relevant concepts, theories, and principles. This prepares them for the analysis and solution of the case.

3. **Case Analysis:** Students work individually or in groups to analyze the case, identify the key issues, and gather additional information as needed. They apply their knowledge and problem-solving skills to develop a deep understanding of the case.

4. **Discussion and Debate:** Students engage in rich discussions and debates, sharing their perspectives and analysis of the case. This collaborative learning environment promotes the exchange of ideas and the development of different problem-solving strategies.

5. **Solution Proposal:** Students propose feasible solutions to the case based on their analysis and understanding. They articulate their rationale, considering the potential consequences and ethical implications of their proposed solutions.

6. **Reflection:** Students reflect on their learning experience and evaluate the strengths and weaknesses of their proposed solutions. They identify areas for improvement and further learning.

Advantages and Challenges of Case-Based Learning

Case-based learning offers several advantages for students and educators.

Advantages

- **Real-world Relevance:** Cases reflect real-world situations, making the learning experience more meaningful and applicable to students' future professional practice.

- **Active Engagement:** Students are actively engaged in analyzing and solving problems, promoting deeper understanding and retention of knowledge.

- **Critical Thinking Skills:** Case-based learning develops students' critical thinking skills by requiring them to analyze complex situations, identify pertinent information, and propose well-reasoned solutions.

- **Collaborative Learning:** The collaborative nature of case-based learning encourages students to work together, share ideas, and construct knowledge collectively.

- **Holistic Perspective:** Cases often present multidimensional problems that require students to consider various factors and perspectives when developing solutions, promoting a holistic understanding of the subject matter.

Challenges

- **Time Constraints:** Case-based learning can be time-consuming as students need sufficient time to analyze and discuss complex cases. This may be a challenge in courses with tight schedules.

- **Assessment:** Assessing students' performance in case-based learning can be challenging due to the subjective nature of evaluating problem-solving skills and the multiple valid solutions that can arise.

- **Student Resistance:** Some students may initially find case-based learning unfamiliar or uncomfortable due to the level of uncertainty and open-endedness involved. Educators need to provide support and guidance to help students navigate through this process.

Implementing Case-Based Learning

The successful implementation of case-based learning requires careful planning and consideration of various factors. Here are some strategies to facilitate the effective implementation of case-based learning:

- **Clear Learning Objectives:** Clearly define the learning objectives, outlining the specific knowledge, skills, and attitudes students are expected to acquire through case-based learning.

- **Gradual Complexity:** Start with simpler cases and gradually increase the complexity as students become more proficient in analyzing and solving cases. This scaffolding approach supports students' development of problem-solving skills.

- **Guided Inquiry:** Provide guidance and structure to students' case analysis, especially in the initial stages. This can be done through the provision of guiding questions and prompts that help direct their thinking.

- **Facilitator Role:** The role of the educator is as a facilitator rather than a directive instructor. The educator guides discussions, supports students' analysis, and encourages critical thinking and reflection.

- **Technology Integration:** Utilize technology tools, such as virtual simulations or online collaboration platforms, to enhance the case-based learning experience. These tools can provide students with immersive and interactive learning opportunities.

Example Case-Based Learning Scenario

Let's consider an example scenario to illustrate the application of case-based learning in a biology class. The case revolves around the issue of antibiotic resistance, a growing concern in modern healthcare.

Case Scenario: A patient presents with a severe infection caused by a drug-resistant bacteria strain. Students are provided with the patient's medical history, laboratory reports, and relevant research articles. They are asked to analyze the case and propose a treatment plan for the patient.

Case Analysis: Students analyze the patient's medical history and laboratory reports to understand the severity of the infection and the factors contributing to antibiotic resistance. They identify the key issues, such as the appropriate choice of antibiotics and strategies to prevent further resistance.

Discussion and Debate: Students engage in group discussions to share their analysis and proposed treatment plans. They debate the merits of different antibiotics, considering factors such as efficacy, potential side effects, and the risk of further resistance development.

Solution Proposal: Each group presents their proposed treatment plan, highlighting the rationale behind their choices. They consider the patient's individual circumstances, such as allergies or comorbidities, and discuss potential ethical dilemmas that may arise.

Reflection: After the presentations, students reflect on the learning process, discussing the strengths and weaknesses of their proposed solutions and considering alternative approaches. They identify areas for improvement, such as the need for further research or a more comprehensive understanding of antibiotic resistance mechanisms.

Resources for Case-Based Learning

There are various resources available to support the implementation of case-based learning:

- **Case Libraries and Databases:** Online platforms, such as Harvard Business Publishing or the National Center for Case Study Teaching in Science, provide a wide range of case studies across disciplines.

- **Educational Journals:** Journals focused on case-based learning, such as the Journal of Case Studies in Education, publish articles and case studies that educators can adapt for their own teaching context.

- **Professional Networks:** Professional networks and communities of practice, such as the Case Method Teaching Group, offer opportunities to connect with educators experienced in case-based learning and share resources.

- **Technology Tools:** Technology tools like interactive simulations, virtual laboratories, and online discussion platforms can enhance the case-based learning experience and provide students with additional resources for analysis and solution development.

Caveats and Considerations

When implementing case-based learning, educators should consider the following caveats and considerations:

- **Time Management:** Adequate time must be allocated for students to engage in case analysis, discussions, and reflection. This helps ensure a thorough understanding of the case and the development of critical thinking skills.

- **Resource Availability:** Cases should be carefully selected to ensure access to relevant resources, such as research articles or industry reports, to support students' analysis and solution development.

- **Classroom Dynamics:** Group dynamics may influence the effectiveness of case-based learning. Educators should establish clear guidelines and foster a collaborative learning environment where all students actively participate and contribute to the case analysis.

- **Assessment Alignment:** The assessment should align with the learning objectives and focus on evaluating students' problem-solving skills, critical thinking abilities, and effective communication of their analysis and proposed solutions.

Conclusion

Case-based learning is a powerful instructional approach that engages students in authentic problem-solving experiences. By analyzing and proposing solutions to complex real-world cases, students develop critical thinking, problem-solving, and decision-making skills that are essential for their future professional practice. Through careful planning, thoughtful implementation, and continuous reflection, educators can create engaging and meaningful case-based learning experiences for their students.

Service-Learning

Service-learning is an educational approach that combines classroom instruction with meaningful community service. It is a powerful tool that allows students to apply academic knowledge and critical thinking skills to address real-world problems and make a positive impact in their communities. In this section, we will explore the principles, benefits, implementation strategies, and evaluation methods of service-learning.

Principles of Service-Learning

Service-learning is based on the following key principles:

1. Service: Service-learning involves actively engaging students in practical activities that meet genuine community needs. Service projects can range from environmental conservation to working with marginalized populations or assisting local nonprofit organizations.

2. Learning: Service-learning integrates academic learning objectives with the service experience. Students not only gain hands-on experience but also deepen their understanding of the subject matter, develop critical thinking and problem-solving skills, and reflect on their experiences.

3. Reciprocity: Service-learning fosters reciprocal relationships between students and the community. Students contribute their skills and knowledge to make a difference in the community while also learning from the people they serve, gaining cultural competence, and developing empathy and social responsibility.

4. Reflection: Reflection is a crucial component of service-learning. Students are encouraged to reflect on their service experiences, connect them to academic content, and critically analyze their own assumptions, biases, and societal structures. Reflection promotes deeper learning and personal growth.

Benefits of Service-Learning

Service-learning offers a range of benefits for both students and communities:

1. Academic Growth: Service-learning brings academic content to life, making it more relevant and meaningful for students. It enhances their understanding of complex concepts by applying them to real-world problems. Service-learning also improves research, writing, communication, and problem-solving skills.

2. Personal Development: Through service-learning, students develop important life skills such as leadership, teamwork, empathy, and cultural competence. They also gain a sense of responsibility, self-confidence, and an understanding of social issues.

3. Civic Engagement: Service-learning fosters active citizenship by encouraging students to be actively involved in their communities. It promotes a sense of social responsibility and empowers students to become agents of positive change.

4. Community Impact: Service-learning addresses community needs and promotes social justice. Students' service projects can have a tangible impact on the community, improving the lives of individuals and contributing to a more just and equitable society.

Implementing Service-Learning

To implement service-learning effectively, educators can follow these strategies:

1. Identify Learning Objectives: Clearly define the academic learning objectives that will be integrated into the service-learning experience. Align the service projects with these objectives to ensure that students are meeting both academic and service goals.

2. Establish Community Partnerships: Collaborate with community organizations, nonprofit groups, or government agencies to identify meaningful service opportunities. Establish partnerships to ensure that the service projects align with community needs and provide authentic learning experiences.

3. Pre-Service Preparation: Provide students with pre-service training to prepare them for their service roles. This training can include orientation to the community issue, cultural sensitivity, ethical considerations, and necessary skills or knowledge related to the project.

4. Reflection Activities: Incorporate structured reflection activities throughout the service-learning experience. Provide time for individual and group reflection, discussions, and journaling. Encourage students to connect their service experiences with academic content and personal growth.

5. Assessment and Evaluation: Develop clear assessment criteria to evaluate student learning and the impact of the service projects. Assess both academic performance and the quality of the service provided. Use a combination of self-assessment, peer assessment, and teacher evaluation methods.

Evaluation Methods

To assess the effectiveness of service-learning and continuously improve the process, various evaluation methods can be applied:

1. Pre-and Post-Service Surveys: Use surveys to gather information on students' knowledge, attitudes, and skills before and after the service-learning

experience. This data can help measure growth in academic content, personal development, and civic engagement.

2. Reflection Papers and Journals: Review students' reflection papers and journals to gain insights into their learning experiences, critical thinking skills, and personal growth. Look for evidence of connections made between service activities and academic content.

3. Community Feedback: Seek feedback from community partners or organizations that students served. Assess their satisfaction with the service provided and the impact of students' work on the community.

4. Student Presentations or Exhibitions: Provide students with an opportunity to present their service projects or exhibit their work to the community, parents, and peers. This allows for public sharing of learning experiences and impact, fostering a sense of pride and accomplishment.

5. Teacher Observation and Feedback: Observe students' engagement in service activities, their interactions with community members, and their reflection processes. Offer constructive feedback to support their learning and growth.

Example: Service-Learning in Environmental Science

Imagine a high school environmental science class that decides to engage in service-learning to address water pollution in a local river. Students could partner with a local environmental organization and conduct regular water quality testing at different points along the river. They would collect samples, analyze them using scientific methods, and identify potential sources of pollution.

Throughout the project, students would learn about various water quality indicators, pollution prevention strategies, and relevant environmental laws. They would reflect on their findings, discuss possible solutions, and present their research to the local community and authorities.

Through this service-learning experience, students would not only deepen their understanding of environmental science but also develop research skills, critical thinking abilities, and a sense of environmental stewardship. The project would have a tangible impact on the community by raising awareness of water pollution issues and contributing to efforts towards cleaner waterways.

Resources for Service-Learning

Here are some resources that can support educators in implementing service-learning:

1. National Service-Learning Clearinghouse: Provides a wealth of information, resources, and examples of service-learning activities across different subjects and grade levels. (Website: www.servicelearning.org)

2. Learn and Serve America: Offers tools, guides, and funding opportunities for service-learning initiatives. (Website: www.learnandserve.gov)

3. The International Association for Service-Learning and Community Engagement (IARSLCE): Provides research and resources related to service-learning and community engagement. (Website: www.researchslce.org)

4. Service Learning in Higher Education: Engaging Students in Social Change by Patti Clayton, Robert Bringle, and Julie Hatcher: A comprehensive guidebook for educators interested in service-learning at the college level.

Caveats and Challenges

While service-learning can be highly beneficial, there are challenges to consider:

1. Time Constraints: Integrating service-learning into the curriculum requires careful planning and time management. Ensure that there is sufficient time allocated for both learning objectives and meaningful service activities.

2. Risk Management: In certain service projects, there may be physical or emotional risks involved. Educators should conduct a risk assessment and put necessary safety measures in place to protect students.

3. Ethical Considerations: Service-learning may involve working with vulnerable populations or addressing sensitive community issues. Educators should address ethical considerations such as cultural competence, confidentiality, and informed consent.

4. Assessing Learning Objectives: Assessing the learning outcomes of service-learning can be challenging. Develop clear assessment criteria that measure both academic content and the quality of service provided.

Despite these challenges, service-learning has the potential to transform students' learning experiences, nurture civic engagement, and create positive change in communities. By combining academic knowledge with meaningful service, service-learning equips students with the skills, values, and perspectives necessary for becoming active and responsible citizens.

In conclusion, service-learning is a powerful approach that integrates academic learning with community service. It enhances students' academic growth, personal development, and civic engagement. Implementing service-learning requires careful planning, community partnerships, and robust evaluation methods. By embracing service-learning, educators can foster deep learning, empathy, and a commitment to social justice in their students.

The Role of Teachers in Inquiry-Based Learning

Inquiry-based learning is a student-centered approach to education that emphasizes active learning, critical thinking, and problem-solving skills. In this approach, teachers play a crucial role in facilitating the learning process and guiding students towards meaningful inquiries. The role of teachers in inquiry-based learning goes beyond being mere instructors; they become facilitators, mentors, and guides. This section will explore the various responsibilities and strategies that teachers should consider when implementing inquiry-based learning in their classrooms.

Facilitating the Learning Process

One of the primary roles of teachers in inquiry-based learning is to facilitate the learning process. Teachers create a supportive environment where students feel safe to express their ideas, ask questions, and explore different possibilities. They encourage curiosity and guide students towards relevant and meaningful inquiries.

To facilitate the learning process effectively, teachers should:

- Introduce the topic or problem that will drive the inquiry, providing a clear purpose and context for the investigation.

- Scaffold learning by providing necessary background information, resources, and guidance.

- Ask open-ended questions to stimulate critical thinking and encourage students to formulate their own questions.

- Help students develop research skills, including finding and evaluating reliable sources of information.

- Provide opportunities for reflection and metacognition, encouraging students to think about their thinking and learning processes.

- Foster collaboration among students, promoting discussions, debates, and the sharing of ideas.

By effectively facilitating the learning process, teachers can create a rich and engaging inquiry-based learning environment.

Mentoring and Guiding Students

Inquiry-based learning requires teachers to take on the role of mentors and guides. Teachers support students in their inquiry process by providing guidance, feedback, and encouragement. They help students develop the necessary skills to navigate through the challenges and complexities of their inquiries.

To effectively mentor and guide students, teachers should:

- Provide individualized support based on each student's needs, abilities, and interests.

- Help students set goals and develop action plans to guide their inquiries.

- Monitor students' progress and provide timely and constructive feedback.

- Encourage students to ask for help when needed and provide guidance to overcome obstacles.

- Foster a growth mindset, emphasizing the value of effort, perseverance, and resilience.

- Model inquiry skills and attitudes, demonstrating curiosity, open-mindedness, and a willingness to learn.

By acting as mentors and guides, teachers can nurture students' curiosity, creativity, and critical thinking skills.

Creating a Supportive Learning Environment

Teachers play a crucial role in creating a supportive learning environment that promotes inquiry-based learning. The classroom environment should be designed to encourage exploration, collaboration, and risk-taking. Teachers should establish a culture of trust and respect, where students feel comfortable sharing their ideas and taking intellectual risks.

To create a supportive learning environment, teachers should:

- Foster a positive classroom climate, where all students feel valued and included.

- Cultivate a sense of community, promoting cooperation and teamwork among students.

- Provide resources and materials that support inquiry-based learning, such as books, journals, technology tools, and manipulatives.

- Arrange the physical space to facilitate collaboration, group work, and hands-on activities.

- Encourage students to take ownership of their learning, promoting self-regulation and autonomy.

- Celebrate and recognize students' achievements and contributions to the learning community.

By creating a supportive learning environment, teachers can enhance students' engagement, motivation, and overall learning outcomes.

Challenges and Strategies

Implementing inquiry-based learning in the classroom can pose several challenges for teachers. Some common challenges include:

- Balancing inquiry and curriculum requirements: Teachers need to find a balance between students' inquiries and the curriculum objectives. They should integrate inquiry-based learning into the existing curriculum while ensuring that essential content and skills are covered.

- Managing time: Inquiry-based learning can be time-consuming, and teachers need to manage time effectively to cover all required topics. They should plan and allocate time strategically, considering the complexity of the inquiry and the students' needs.

- Evaluating student learning: Traditional assessment methods may not fully capture students' learning in inquiry-based environments. Teachers should explore innovative assessment strategies that align with the inquiry process, such as portfolios, presentations, and self-assessments.

- Addressing diverse student needs: Students come to the classroom with different backgrounds, experiences, and abilities. Teachers should design inquiries that are accessible and meaningful for all students, considering their diverse needs and providing appropriate support.

To overcome these challenges, teachers can employ various strategies:

- Collaborate with colleagues: Teachers can collaborate with colleagues to share experiences, resources, and strategies for implementing inquiry-based learning.

- Seek professional development: Engaging in professional development opportunities, such as workshops, courses, and conferences, can enhance teachers' knowledge and skills in inquiry-based learning.

- Use technology tools: Technology tools can support inquiry-based learning by providing access to information, facilitating communication and collaboration, and enabling multimedia presentations.

- Reflect and adapt: Teachers should regularly reflect on their practice, seeking feedback from students and colleagues, and making adjustments as necessary to improve the implementation of inquiry-based learning.

In conclusion, the role of teachers in inquiry-based learning is crucial. They act as facilitators, mentors, and guides, fostering a supportive learning environment and promoting students' engagement, critical thinking, and problem-solving skills. By effectively implementing inquiry-based learning and addressing the associated challenges, teachers can create transformative learning experiences for their students.

Facilitating Inquiry-Based Learning in Different Subjects

Inquiry-based learning is a student-centered approach that encourages learners to ask questions, investigate problems, and construct knowledge through active engagement and collaboration. This approach can be integrated effectively across various subjects, promoting deep understanding and critical thinking skills. In this section, we will explore how inquiry-based learning can be facilitated in different subjects, highlighting specific strategies, examples, and resources for each discipline.

Science

Science is a subject that naturally lends itself to inquiry-based learning. By encouraging students to ask scientific questions, design experiments, and analyze data, teachers can foster a deep understanding of scientific concepts and processes. Here are some strategies for facilitating inquiry-based learning in science:

- **Designing experiments:** Provide opportunities for students to design and conduct their own experiments. This could involve formulating hypotheses, planning procedures, and collecting data. For example, students can investigate the effect of different fertilizers on plant growth or analyze the factors that affect the rate of a chemical reaction.

- **Analyzing real-world data:** Engage students by presenting them with real-world data sets that require analysis and interpretation. This could involve analyzing the impact of climate change on biodiversity or studying the patterns of air pollution in different regions. Encourage students to draw conclusions based on evidence and communicate their findings effectively.

- **Collaborative projects:** Assign collaborative projects that require students to work together to solve scientific problems. For instance, students can investigate the impact of pollution on local ecosystems and propose solutions to mitigate the effects. This not only promotes collaboration but also teaches students about the interdisciplinary nature of scientific research.

- **Fieldwork and outdoor experiments:** Take students outside the classroom to collect data and observe natural phenomena. This could include conducting field surveys to study local flora and fauna or visiting a nearby water body to analyze its water quality. Fieldwork provides students with firsthand experiences and fosters a sense of curiosity and wonder about the natural world.

Social Studies

Inquiry-based learning can also be highly effective in social studies, as it encourages students to explore historical events, analyze primary sources, and critically evaluate different perspectives. Here are some strategies for facilitating inquiry-based learning in social studies:

- **Primary source analysis:** Provide students with authentic primary sources such as historical documents, photographs, and artifacts. Encourage them to analyze these sources and draw conclusions about past events and the people involved. For example, students can examine letters from soldiers in World War II to gain insights into the experiences of individuals during the war.

- **Debates and discussions:** Organize debates and discussions that require students to examine multiple viewpoints on controversial historical issues. This helps them develop critical thinking skills and understand the complexity of historical events. For instance, students can debate the causes of the American Civil War or discuss the impact of colonization on indigenous populations.

- **Simulations and role-playing:** Engage students in simulations and role-playing activities that recreate historical events or decision-making processes. For example, students can simulate a constitutional convention or take on the role of different stakeholders in a negotiation. These activities enhance students' understanding of historical contexts and encourage them to think like historians.

- **Community investigations:** Encourage students to explore local history by conducting interviews, visiting historical sites, or researching community archives. This helps students connect their learning to real-world contexts and develop a sense of historical empathy. For instance, students can interview local elders to document their experiences during significant historical events.

Mathematics

Inquiry-based learning can transform the way students approach mathematics. By engaging them in problem-solving, investigations, and mathematical reasoning, teachers can foster a deep understanding of mathematical concepts. Here are some strategies for facilitating inquiry-based learning in mathematics:

- **Open-ended problem-solving:** Assign open-ended problems that require students to explore different approaches, make conjectures, and justify their reasoning. This promotes critical thinking and creativity in mathematics. For example, students can investigate patterns in Pascal's triangle or explore the concept of infinity.

- **Mathematical investigations:** Guide students in conducting their own mathematical investigations. This could involve formulating questions, collecting and analyzing data, and making mathematical models or predictions. For instance, students can investigate the relationship between the angles of a triangle or explore the concept of probability through data analysis.

- **Real-world applications:** Connect mathematical concepts to real-world contexts to make them more meaningful for students. Provide examples and problems that relate to everyday situations or other subjects. For example, students can analyze data on population growth or explore the mathematics behind music and art.

- **Collaborative problem-solving:** Encourage students to work together to solve complex mathematical problems. This not only fosters collaboration, communication, and teamwork but also exposes students to different problem-solving strategies. For instance, students can engage in mathematical investigations as a group and present their findings collectively.

It is crucial to remember that inquiry-based learning can be adapted to fit the specific needs and requirements of different subjects. By providing students with opportunities to explore, investigate, and reflect, teachers can create engaging learning experiences that promote deep understanding and lifelong learning skills.

Conclusion

Facilitating inquiry-based learning in different subjects requires careful planning, implementation, and support from educators. By incorporating strategies such as designing experiments, analyzing data, engaging in debates, conducting investigations, and solving real-world problems, teachers can foster a culture of inquiry and exploration in the classroom. Furthermore, the integration of technology tools and resources can enhance inquiry-based learning experiences, providing students with additional avenues for research, collaboration, and creativity. By nurturing curiosity, critical thinking, and problem-solving skills, educators can empower students to become lifelong learners and active contributors to their fields of study.

Assessing Inquiry-Based Learning

Assessing inquiry-based learning is crucial to gauge the effectiveness of this teaching approach and to monitor student progress. Traditional methods of assessment may not be suitable for measuring the skills and competencies acquired through inquiry-based learning. In this section, we will explore various strategies and techniques for assessing inquiry-based learning, including both formative and summative assessments.

Formative Assessment

Formative assessment plays a vital role in inquiry-based learning as it provides immediate feedback to students and helps guide their learning process. It allows teachers to identify students' understanding, misconceptions, and areas needing further development. Here are some formative assessment strategies for inquiry-based learning:

1. **Questioning**: Asking open-ended questions can be an effective formative assessment tool. Teachers can use techniques like Socratic questioning to encourage critical thinking, deepen understanding, and prompt reflection.

2. **Think-Pair-Share**: This strategy involves students individually reflecting on a question, discussing their thoughts with a partner, and sharing their ideas with the class. The teacher can monitor the discussions and provide feedback based on students' understanding and reasoning.

3. **Journals and Reflective Writing**: Students can maintain journals or write reflective essays to express their thoughts, ideas, and learning experiences. These written reflections provide insights into students' understanding and help them develop metacognitive skills.

4. **Peer Assessment**: Peer assessment allows students to evaluate and provide feedback on each other's work. It promotes critical thinking, collaboration, and self-reflection. Rubrics or structured feedback frameworks can be provided to guide students' assessment.

5. **Observations and Conversations**: Teachers can observe students' participation, engagement, and interactions during inquiry-based activities. Engaging in conversations with students about their thinking can provide valuable insight into their learning process.

Summative Assessment

Summative assessment is used to evaluate student learning at the end of an inquiry-based learning unit or project. It aims to assess the overall understanding and mastery of the learning objectives. Here are some summative assessment strategies for inquiry-based learning:

1. **Products and Presentations**: Students can showcase their understanding and skills through products or presentations, such as research papers, multimedia presentations, models, or exhibitions. Rubrics can be used to assess the quality of the final products.

2. **Performance Assessments**: Performance assessments involve students solving real-world problems or completing tasks that reflect the application of their learning. For example, in a science inquiry, students could design and conduct experiments, analyze data, and draw conclusions.

3. **Portfolios**: Portfolios provide a collection of students' work over a period of time, demonstrating their progress and growth. Students can curate their best work,

reflections, and evidence of their learning journey. Rubrics or scoring guides can be used to assess portfolios.

4. **Tests and Quizzes:** While traditional tests and quizzes may not align perfectly with the inquiry-based learning approach, they can still be used to assess some aspects of knowledge and understanding. Care should be taken to design questions that gauge critical thinking and problem-solving skills rather than mere recall.

Evaluating the Impact of Inquiry-Based Learning

In addition to assessing individual students' learning, it is essential to evaluate the overall impact of inquiry-based learning as a teaching approach. Here are some ways to evaluate the effectiveness of inquiry-based learning:

1. **Surveys and Questionnaires:** Collecting feedback from students, teachers, and parents through surveys and questionnaires can provide valuable insights into their perception of inquiry-based learning. Questions can focus on engagement, motivation, problem-solving skills, and overall satisfaction with the approach.

2. **Classroom Observations:** Observing inquiry-based lessons in action and noting students' engagement, collaboration, and critical thinking can help evaluate the effectiveness of the approach. Observers can use rubrics or checklists to guide their observations.

3. **Data Analysis:** Analyzing quantitative data, such as test scores or assessments, can provide evidence of the impact of inquiry-based learning on student achievement. Comparing students' performance to their peers in traditional classrooms can help identify potential benefits of the approach.

4. **Action Research:** Teachers can conduct action research studies within their classrooms to assess the impact of inquiry-based learning on student outcomes. They can collect data, analyze the results, and reflect on their teaching practices to make informed decisions about instructional strategies.

It is important to note that assessing and evaluating inquiry-based learning should align with the goals and objectives of the specific learning environment and subject area. Teachers must consider a variety of assessment methods to capture different aspects of students' learning and ensure a comprehensive evaluation of their progress.

By employing these assessment strategies, educators can effectively gauge student understanding, monitor progress, and evaluate the impact of inquiry-based learning on student learning outcomes. This holistic approach to assessment ensures that students are engaged in meaningful learning experiences and have ample opportunities to demonstrate their knowledge and skills.

Evaluating the Impact of Inquiry-Based Learning

Evaluating the impact of inquiry-based learning is essential to determine the effectiveness of this teaching approach and to inform future instructional decisions. It provides valuable insights into student learning outcomes, engagement, and critical thinking skills. In this section, we will explore various methods and strategies for evaluating the impact of inquiry-based learning.

Quantitative Measures

Quantitative measures involve the collection of numerical data to assess the impact of inquiry-based learning. These measures can provide objective evidence of student achievement and growth. Some common quantitative evaluation methods include:

1. **Standardized Tests:** Standardized tests have been widely used to measure student learning outcomes. They provide a benchmark to compare the performance of students who have experienced inquiry-based learning with those who have not. However, it is important to note that standardized tests may not capture the full range of skills and competencies fostered by inquiry-based learning.

2. **Pre- and Post-Assessments:** Pre- and post-assessments are conducted before and after the implementation of inquiry-based learning to measure changes in student knowledge, skills, and attitudes. These assessments can be designed specifically to align with the objectives of the inquiry-based learning activities and can include multiple-choice questions, short answer questions, and performance tasks.

3. **Surveys and Questionnaires:** Surveys and questionnaires can be used to gather data on students' perceptions of their learning experiences. They can assess factors such as engagement, motivation, self-efficacy, and enjoyment of the inquiry-based learning process. Likert-scale rating questions and open-ended questions can provide valuable qualitative insights.

4. **Observations:** Classroom observations can be conducted to assess the implementation of inquiry-based learning strategies. Observers can use rubrics or checklists to document the level of student engagement, collaboration, critical thinking, and problem-solving demonstrated during inquiry-based learning activities.

Qualitative Measures

Qualitative measures are focused on gathering descriptive data to understand the impact of inquiry-based learning. These measures provide rich insights into student learning experiences, perceptions, and the processes they engage in. Some common qualitative evaluation methods include:

1. **Interviews:** Conducting interviews with students can provide in-depth insights into their experiences with inquiry-based learning. Semi-structured interviews allow for open-ended questioning and follow-up probing to explore students' understanding, reflections, and the impact of their learning experiences.

2. **Focus Groups:** Focus groups can facilitate group discussions among students who have experienced inquiry-based learning. This method allows for the exploration of shared experiences, perspectives, and engagement levels. A moderator can guide the discussion to gather valuable insights into the impact of inquiry-based learning on student learning and collaboration.

3. **Journals and Reflections:** Students can maintain journals or reflective logs to document their learning journey throughout the inquiry process. These reflections can provide valuable qualitative data on their thoughts, insights, and metacognitive processes. Analyzing these reflections can reveal how inquiry-based learning has impacted their critical thinking, problem-solving skills, and growth mindset.

4. **Artifacts and Portfolios:** Artifacts and portfolios can showcase students' work products and evidence of their learning progress throughout the inquiry-based learning process. These can include research papers, projects, presentations, and multimedia creations. Analyzing these artifacts helps to evaluate the quality and depth of the learning that has taken place.

Mixed Methods

Using both quantitative and qualitative measures in evaluation allows for a more comprehensive understanding of the impact of inquiry-based learning. Combining different data sources and methods can provide a more robust assessment of student learning outcomes, engagement, and attitudes towards inquiry-based learning. It allows for triangulation of data, thereby enhancing the validity and reliability of evaluation findings.

Considerations and Challenges

When evaluating the impact of inquiry-based learning, there are several considerations and challenges to keep in mind:

- **Contextual Factors:** The impact of inquiry-based learning may be influenced by contextual factors such as school culture, resources, and student characteristics. It is important to consider these factors when interpreting evaluation results.

- **Long-Term Effects:** Evaluating the long-term effects of inquiry-based learning is challenging but crucial. It requires follow-up research to assess the persistence of skills and knowledge gained through inquiry-based learning over time.

- **Ethical Considerations:** When collecting data for evaluation purposes, ethical considerations must be taken into account. Informed consent must be obtained from participants, and data must be anonymized and stored securely to protect privacy.

- **Teacher Professional Development:** Evaluating the impact of inquiry-based learning should also involve assessing the professional development needs of teachers. Providing ongoing support and training can enhance teachers' effectiveness in implementing and facilitating inquiry-based learning.

- **Continuous Improvement:** Evaluation findings should be used to inform continuous improvement of inquiry-based learning practices. By identifying areas of strength and areas for improvement, educators can refine their instructional strategies and curriculum to enhance student learning outcomes.

Example Evaluation Study

To illustrate how the impact of inquiry-based learning can be evaluated, let's consider an example study on the effectiveness of inquiry-based learning in a high school chemistry class. The study aims to assess student learning outcomes and engagement levels through a mixed-methods approach.

Quantitative data collection includes pre- and post-assessments that focus on measuring content knowledge and conceptual understanding in chemistry. Surveys are administered to gather information on students' perceptions of their experiences with inquiry-based learning. Classroom observations using a checklist are conducted to assess student engagement, collaboration, and critical thinking skills during inquiry-based activities.

Qualitative data collection involves interviews with a sample of students to gain insights into their experiences with inquiry-based learning. Additionally, students maintain reflective journals throughout the inquiry process, which provide valuable qualitative data on their metacognitive processes and reflections on their learning experiences.

Data analysis includes quantitative analysis of pre- and post-assessment results to measure the impact on student learning outcomes. Survey responses can be analyzed for common themes and trends related to engagement and motivation. Observational data is used to assess the level of student engagement and collaboration during inquiry-based activities. Interviews and reflective journals are analyzed for emerging themes related to students' thoughts, reflections, and growth mindset.

The evaluation findings will provide insights into the impact of inquiry-based learning on student learning outcomes, engagement, and attitudes towards chemistry. The results will inform future instructional decisions and may lead to modifications in curriculum and instructional practices to further enhance inquiry-based learning in the chemistry classroom.

Resources for Evaluating Inquiry-Based Learning

Here are some additional resources that can aid in the evaluation of inquiry-based learning:

- **American Evaluation Association:** The American Evaluation Association is a professional organization that provides resources, publications, and conferences on evaluation methods and practices (https://www.eval.org).

- **National Science Teachers Association (NSTA):** NSTA offers resources, articles, and journals on evaluating science learning and inquiry-based teaching practices (https://www.nsta.org).

- **Education Development Center (EDC):** EDC provides evaluation tools and resources specifically focused on STEM education and inquiry-based learning (https://www.edc.org).

- **Inquiry-based Learning Research Group (University of Washington):** This research group provides resources and publications on inquiry-based learning evaluation in STEM education (https://www.washington.edu/research/stmt/inquiry-group).

Conclusion

Evaluating the impact of inquiry-based learning is crucial for understanding its effectiveness in promoting student learning outcomes and engagement. By using a combination of quantitative and qualitative measures, educators can gather comprehensive data to inform instructional decisions, improve teaching practices, and enhance student learning experiences. Through thoughtful evaluation, inquiry-based learning can continue to evolve and positively impact education.

Creating a Culture of Inquiry in Schools

Inquiry-based learning has gained immense popularity in recent years due to its effectiveness in promoting critical thinking, problem-solving skills, and deep understanding of concepts. However, for inquiry-based learning to thrive in schools, it is crucial to cultivate a culture that supports and encourages this approach. In this section, we will explore strategies and best practices for creating a culture of inquiry in schools.

Understanding the Importance of Inquiry

Before we delve into creating a culture of inquiry, it is essential to understand why inquiry-based learning is vital for students. By engaging in inquiry, students develop a sense of ownership, curiosity, and active involvement in their learning process. They become active participants in constructing knowledge, rather than passive recipients of information. Moreover, inquiry-based learning helps students develop critical thinking skills, problem-solving abilities, and the capacity to apply knowledge to real-world situations.

Creating a Supportive Environment

To foster a culture of inquiry in schools, it is crucial to create a supportive environment that encourages students to ask questions, explore, and take risks. Here are some strategies to achieve that:

- **Promote a Growth Mindset:** Help students develop a growth mindset by emphasizing that intelligence and abilities can be developed through effort and practice. Encourage a belief in the power of learning from mistakes and the value of persistence.

- **Cultivate a Safe and Respectful Classroom Climate:** Create a classroom culture where students feel safe to ask questions, share their thoughts, and express their ideas without fear of judgment or ridicule. Encourage mutual respect, active listening, and open-mindedness.

- **Model Inquiry:** Model the inquiry process by asking questions, seeking alternative viewpoints, and demonstrating curiosity. Show students that inquiry is a natural part of learning and can be applied in various contexts.

Setting Clear Expectations

Setting clear expectations is crucial for fostering a culture of inquiry. Here are some ways to establish and communicate these expectations:

- **Explicit Teaching of Inquiry Skills:** Teach students the essential skills necessary for successful inquiry-based learning, such as asking meaningful questions, conducting research, analyzing data, and presenting findings. Provide explicit instruction and ongoing guidance on these skills.

- **Developing Inquiry-Based Learning Standards:** Collaborate with colleagues to define inquiry-based learning standards that align with the curriculum. Clearly articulate the skills, knowledge, and dispositions expected from students engaged in inquiry.

- **Incorporating Inquiry in Assessment:** Design assessments that require students to demonstrate their inquiry skills and knowledge. Provide opportunities for self-reflection and peer feedback, emphasizing the importance of the inquiry process rather than just the final product.

Integrated Curriculum Approach

To truly create a culture of inquiry, it is imperative to integrate inquiry-based learning across the curriculum. Here's how:

- **Collaboration Among Teachers:** Foster collaboration among teachers from different subjects to develop interdisciplinary inquiry projects. By working together, teachers can create rich and authentic learning experiences that connect different areas of knowledge.

- **Designing Authentic Learning Experiences:** Design learning experiences that mimic real-world problems and challenges. Create opportunities for students to apply knowledge and skills from various subjects, fostering a holistic understanding of concepts.

- **Supporting Teacher Professional Development:** Provide ongoing professional development opportunities for teachers to enhance their knowledge and skills in inquiry-based learning. Offer workshops, mentoring programs, and collaborative planning time to support teachers in implementing inquiry approaches.

Engaging Stakeholders

Creating a culture of inquiry requires collaboration and support from various stakeholders. Here are some strategies to engage stakeholders:

- **Involving Parents and Guardians:** Educate parents and guardians about the benefits of inquiry-based learning and involve them in the learning process. Share resources, provide regular updates, and encourage open communication between teachers and parents.

- **Forging Partnerships with the Community:** Collaborate with local organizations, experts, and community members to provide authentic learning experiences for students. Engage the community in supporting inquiry projects or mentorship opportunities.

- **Promoting School-wide Events:** Organize school-wide events, exhibitions, or showcases to celebrate inquiry-based learning. Offer opportunities for students to present their projects to the school community, fostering a sense of pride and accomplishment.

Challenges and Solutions

Implementing a culture of inquiry may come with challenges. Here are some common challenges and potential solutions:

- **Time Constraints:** Limited instructional time is a common challenge in schools. To address this, integrate inquiry-based learning into existing lessons or dedicate specific blocks of time for inquiry projects.

- **Assessment Methods:** Assessing inquiry-based learning can be challenging due to its open-ended nature. Employ a variety of assessment methods, such as rubrics, portfolios, and teacher observations, to evaluate the processes and outcomes of student inquiry.

- **Lack of Resources:** Insufficient resources, including materials, technology, or funding, can impede the implementation of inquiry-based learning. Seek grants, partnerships with local organizations, or repurpose existing resources to overcome these challenges.

- **Resistance to Change:** Some teachers, students, or parents may resist the shift towards inquiry-based learning. Provide professional development, share research and success stories, and involve stakeholders in decision-making processes to alleviate resistance.

Conclusion

Creating a culture of inquiry in schools requires intentional effort, collaboration, and ongoing support. By fostering an environment that values questioning, exploration, and critical thinking, we can empower students to become lifelong learners and problem solvers. Through integrated curriculum, clear expectations, and engagement with stakeholders, we can cultivate a culture that embraces the transformative power of inquiry-based learning. So, let's embark on this journey of inquiry together and inspire the next generation of curious minds!

Inquiry-Based Learning and Educational Equity

Inquiry-based learning (IBL) is an approach to education that places the learner at the center of the learning process. It involves engaging students in authentic, real-world problems and encouraging them to ask questions, investigate, and actively construct their knowledge. This student-centered approach fosters curiosity, critical thinking, and problem-solving skills.

IBL not only promotes academic excellence but also holds great potential for promoting educational equity. Educational equity refers to ensuring that all students have access to the resources and opportunities they need to succeed academically, regardless of their background, race, gender, or socioeconomic status.

By adopting IBL practices, teachers can address the diverse needs and backgrounds of their students while promoting equity in the classroom. Here are some key strategies for integrating IBL and promoting educational equity:

1. Cultivate a Culture of Inclusion: Creating an inclusive classroom environment is crucial for promoting equity. Teachers should promote mutual respect, value diversity, and encourage collaboration among students. This can be achieved through activities that foster positive relationships, give voice to all students, and celebrate different perspectives and experiences.

2. Provide Accessible Resources: To ensure equity, it is essential to provide all students with access to resources needed for inquiry-based learning. This includes materials, technology tools, and supportive learning environments. Teachers need to be aware of potential barriers and provide necessary accommodations or alternative resources to meet the diverse needs of their students.

3. Scaffold Learning: In an equitable learning environment, teachers must provide appropriate support and scaffolding to help students engage in inquiry-based learning effectively. This can include providing clear learning objectives, modeling the inquiry process, and providing step-by-step guidance as students develop their questioning, research, and problem-solving skills.

4. Address Social and Cultural Biases: Educational equity also involves addressing biases and stereotypes that may exist in the classroom. Teachers should be mindful of promoting diversity and challenging stereotypes by incorporating diverse perspectives, multicultural resources, and inclusive teaching practices in their instruction.

5. Collaborate with Families and Communities: Educational equity extends beyond the classroom walls. Teachers should actively engage families and communities in the learning process to ensure that all students receive the necessary support to succeed. This can involve involving parents in decision-making, establishing partnerships with community organizations, and leveraging community resources to enhance student learning.

6. Assess for Equity: It is important to design assessments that are fair and inclusive, taking into account the diversity of students' backgrounds and experiences. Teachers should use a variety of formative and summative assessment strategies, including authentic assessments, performance assessments, and alternative forms of assessment, to accurately measure students' learning in an equitable manner.

7. Professional Development: To effectively implement IBL and promote educational equity, ongoing professional development is essential. Teachers should continuously update their knowledge and skills, stay informed about research-based best practices, and collaborate with colleagues to share ideas and experiences.

Inquiry-based learning, when combined with a focus on educational equity, has the potential to transform education by giving all students equal opportunities to develop critical thinking, problem-solving, and communication skills. By implementing the strategies outlined above, educators can create a more inclusive and equitable learning environment where all students thrive.

Technology and Inquiry-Based Learning

Online Research Tools

In today's digital age, online research tools have become essential for students and researchers alike. These tools provide a vast amount of information and resources at our fingertips, enabling us to access knowledge from all over the world. In this section, we will explore some of the most commonly used online research tools and how they can enhance the research process.

Search Engines

Search engines, such as Google and Bing, are the go-to tools for finding information on the internet. They allow users to enter keywords or phrases and retrieve relevant web pages, articles, books, and other resources. However, using search engines effectively requires some techniques to optimize your research process:

- Use specific keywords: Instead of using general terms, be more specific with your search terms to get more accurate results. For example, instead of searching for "history of ancient civilizations," try searching for "Mayan civilization architecture."

- Boolean operators: Use Boolean operators like AND, OR, and NOT to refine your search and include or exclude specific terms. For example, searching for "climate change AND mitigation" will give you results that include both terms.

- Advanced search features: Many search engines offer advanced search options that allow you to filter results by date, domain, file type, and more. Take advantage of these features to narrow down your search results.

Databases

Databases are specialized collections of information that provide access to academic journals, conference proceedings, research reports, and other scholarly resources. Some popular databases include:

- JSTOR: JSTOR is a digital library that provides access to a wide range of academic journals, books, and primary sources. It covers various disciplines, including science, humanities, social sciences, and more.

- PubMed: PubMed is a database maintained by the National Library of Medicine that focuses on biomedical literature. It includes articles from thousands of biomedical journals and provides links to full-text articles and other related resources.

- IEEE Xplore: IEEE Xplore is a digital library that provides access to articles, conference proceedings, standards, and other technical publications in the fields of engineering, computer science, and related disciplines.

When using databases, keep the following tips in mind:

- Refine your search: Use advanced search options provided by databases to narrow down your results. You can filter by publication date, author, keywords, and more.

- Check citation information: Databases often provide citation information for each article, including the author, title, journal, and publication year. This information can help you evaluate the credibility and relevance of the source.

- Access full-text articles: Some databases provide direct access to full-text articles, while others may require a subscription or payment. If you don't have access to a particular article, try searching for it in other databases or consider reaching out to your university or local library for assistance.

Online Libraries

Online libraries are digital repositories of books, journals, and other educational resources. They offer access to a vast collection of literature, including both classic and contemporary works. Here are a few notable online libraries:

- Project Gutenberg: Project Gutenberg is a digital library that offers over 60,000 free eBooks. It includes a wide range of literature, including novels, poems, plays, and non-fiction works, which are available in various formats such as EPUB, MOBI, and PDF.

- Open Library: Open Library is an initiative that aims to provide free access to millions of books. It offers a combination of public domain works and modern titles through partnerships with various libraries and publishers.

- Google Books: Google Books is a vast collection of digitized books from libraries and publishers worldwide. While not all books are available for full view, you can often access a preview or snippets of the content to help with your research.

When using online libraries, keep these points in mind:

- Utilize search features: Online libraries often provide advanced search features that allow you to search by title, author, subject, and more. Take advantage of these features to find the resources you need.

- Check the availability of books: Some online libraries may have limited availability for certain books due to copyright restrictions or licensing agreements. Always check if the book you're looking for is available in full or in part.

- Explore related works: Online libraries often provide recommendations and related works based on your search query. This can be a great way to discover additional resources that are relevant to your topic.

Reference Management Tools

Reference management tools help organize and format citations and bibliography for academic papers and research projects. They simplify the process of collecting, storing, and citing references, saving valuable time and effort. Here are some widely used reference management tools:

- Zotero: Zotero is a free and open-source reference management tool that allows you to collect, organize, cite, and share research materials. It integrates with web browsers, word processors, and other applications to streamline the research process.

- Mendeley: Mendeley is a reference management tool that enables you to discover, store, organize, and annotate research papers. It also offers collaboration features, allowing you to share resources and collaborate with other researchers.

- EndNote: EndNote is a comprehensive reference management tool that helps you collect, organize, and cite references in your research. It offers advanced features like PDF annotation, full-text searching, and compatibility with various citation styles.

When using reference management tools, consider the following tips:

- Import and organize references: Most reference management tools allow you to import references from databases, online libraries, and other sources. Take advantage of this feature to keep your references organized and easily accessible.

- Generate citations and bibliographies: Reference management tools can automatically generate citations and format bibliographies according to various citation styles. Make sure to familiarize yourself with the citation rules and select the appropriate style for your document.

- Collaborate with other researchers: Some reference management tools offer collaboration features that allow you to share references, notes, and annotations with other researchers. This can be particularly useful for group projects or collaborative research efforts.

Online Research Communities and Social Networks

Online research communities and social networks provide platforms for researchers to connect, collaborate, and share their work. These platforms offer opportunities for networking, knowledge exchange, and exposure to new research. Here are a few notable examples:

- ResearchGate: ResearchGate is a social networking site for scientists and researchers. It allows researchers to share their publications, collaborate with others, ask and answer questions, and connect with colleagues in their field of study.

- Academia.edu: Academia.edu is a platform that enables researchers to share and discover research papers. It also provides a forum for researchers to connect with peers and receive feedback on their work.

- LinkedIn: LinkedIn is a professional networking site that can be utilized for research purposes. Researchers can join relevant groups, participate in discussions, and connect with other professionals in their field.

When engaging with online research communities and social networks, consider the following:

- Build a professional profile: Create a comprehensive and up-to-date profile highlighting your research interests, publications, and academic achievements. This will help you connect with like-minded researchers and establish your credibility.

- Participate in discussions: Engage in discussions, forums, and groups related to your research interests. This can provide valuable insights, feedback, and collaborative opportunities.

- Share your work responsibly: When sharing your research, ensure that you comply with copyright laws and respect the intellectual property rights of others. Be cautious about sharing unpublished works or sensitive data.

- Network strategically: Use online research communities and social networks to expand your professional network and collaborate with experts in your field. Be proactive in reaching out to others and building meaningful connections.

Conclusion

Online research tools have revolutionized the way we conduct research, making it more accessible, efficient, and collaborative. From search engines and databases to online libraries and reference management tools, these resources provide unprecedented opportunities for finding, organizing, and citing information. Additionally, engaging with online research communities and social networks can further enrich the research process through networking and knowledge exchange. As technology continues to evolve, it is crucial for researchers and students to stay updated on the latest online research tools and utilize them effectively to enhance their academic endeavors. So, embrace these tools, explore their features, and embark on a remarkable research journey!

Virtual Laboratories

Virtual laboratories have emerged as powerful tools in modern education, enabling students to conduct experiments and simulations in a virtual environment. These computer-based platforms offer a range of benefits and opportunities for students to explore scientific concepts and phenomena in a hands-on and engaging way. In this section, we will explore the principles, advantages, challenges, and examples of virtual laboratories.

Principles of Virtual Laboratories

Virtual laboratories are designed based on the principles of experiential learning, allowing students to actively participate in scientific inquiry and discovery. The following principles guide the development and use of virtual laboratories:

1. **Simulation and experimentation:** Virtual laboratories provide a simulated environment where students can perform experiments, collect data, and observe outcomes. This allows them to explore and analyze complex phenomena that may be otherwise difficult or dangerous to access in a traditional laboratory setting.

2. **Interactivity and engagement:** Virtual laboratories offer interactive interfaces and tools that encourage students to engage with the virtual environment. This interactivity helps students develop critical thinking skills, as they manipulate variables, analyze data, and make connections between concepts.

3. **Real-world context:** Virtual laboratories aim to provide real-world contexts and scenarios to make the learning experience more authentic. By simulating real-life situations, students can understand the relevance and applications of the scientific concepts they are studying.

4. **Collaboration and communication:** Virtual laboratories often incorporate collaborative features that allow students to work together, share data, and discuss findings. This promotes teamwork, communication skills, and the ability to work effectively in a group setting.

5. **Feedback and assessment:** Virtual laboratories provide immediate feedback to students, enabling them to reflect on their actions and improve their understanding. Assessment tools within the virtual environment help teachers evaluate students' performance and identify areas for further support or instruction.

Advantages of Virtual Laboratories

Virtual laboratories offer several advantages compared to traditional laboratory settings:

1. **Accessibility and flexibility:** Virtual laboratories can be accessed anytime and anywhere, allowing students to conduct experiments at their own pace

and convenience. This flexibility is particularly beneficial for distance learning, students with limited access to physical labs, or those with scheduling constraints.

2. **Safety:** Virtual laboratories eliminate the risks associated with handling hazardous materials or conducting experiments that require expensive equipment. Students can explore complex experiments and phenomena without the worry of accidents or damage.

3. **Cost-effectiveness:** Setting up and maintaining physical laboratories can be expensive. Virtual laboratories reduce costs by eliminating the need for physical equipment and consumables. This makes it easier for educational institutions with limited resources to provide quality science education.

4. **Reproducibility and repetition:** Virtual laboratories allow students to repeat experiments and simulations as many times as needed. This enhances their understanding of concepts and provides opportunities for further analysis and exploration.

5. **Enhanced visualization:** Virtual laboratories often incorporate high-quality visuals, animations, and 3D models that help students visualize complex scientific phenomena. This visual representation enhances comprehension and retention of scientific concepts.

6. **Inclusivity:** Virtual laboratories can cater to a wide range of learning styles and abilities. They provide equal opportunities for students with disabilities or limitations, ensuring that they can actively participate in laboratory experiences.

Challenges and Considerations

While virtual laboratories offer numerous advantages, there are also challenges and considerations to keep in mind:

1. **Limited tactile experience:** Virtual laboratories may not fully replicate the tactile experience of handling real equipment or materials. Some experiments, such as those involving precise measurements or delicate techniques, may be better suited for physical laboratories.

2. **Internet connectivity and reliability:** Accessing virtual laboratories requires stable internet connectivity. In areas with limited or unreliable internet

access, students may face difficulties in accessing and utilizing the virtual environment.

3. **Lack of physical experimentation skills:** Virtual laboratories, while providing valuable learning experiences, may not fully develop students' hands-on skills and techniques. Students may still need opportunities to practice in physical laboratories to enhance their practical skills.

4. **Teacher expertise and support:** Effective implementation of virtual laboratories requires teachers with the necessary knowledge and skills to guide students through the virtual experiments. Professional development opportunities and ongoing support are essential for teachers to fully leverage the potential of virtual laboratories.

Examples of Virtual Laboratories

There are numerous virtual laboratory platforms available that cover a wide range of scientific disciplines. Here are a few examples:

- **PhET Interactive Simulations:** PhET provides a collection of free interactive simulations for chemistry, physics, biology, and other subjects. These simulations allow students to explore various scientific concepts through virtual experiments and visualizations.

- **Labster:** Labster offers a virtual laboratory platform for biology, chemistry, and other life science subjects. It provides a catalog of simulated experiments where students can practice techniques, analyze data, and develop scientific knowledge and skills.

- **MERLOT Virtual Labs:** MERLOT (Multimedia Educational Resource for Learning and Online Teaching) is a platform that hosts a collection of virtual labs across different disciplines. These labs cover various topics, including physics, chemistry, engineering, and environmental science.

- **Journal of Virtual Experiments (JOVE):** JOVE is a journal that publishes peer-reviewed virtual experiments in various fields. It offers detailed video demonstrations of experiments, allowing students to observe and analyze scientific procedures.

Conclusion

Virtual laboratories enhance the learning experience by providing students with opportunities to engage in hands-on scientific exploration, experimentation, and analysis. They offer unique advantages in terms of accessibility, flexibility, safety, and cost-effectiveness. While virtual laboratories cannot replace physical laboratories entirely, they serve as valuable complements to traditional laboratory experiences. By incorporating virtual laboratories into educational settings, teachers can create a more engaging and inclusive learning environment, enabling students to develop a deeper understanding of scientific concepts.

Simulations and Games

Simulations and games have become increasingly popular in education as they offer unique opportunities for engagement, hands-on learning, and skill development. This section will explore the various uses of simulations and games in the classroom, their benefits, as well as some important considerations for implementation.

Understanding Simulations

Simulations are computer-based tools that replicate real-life scenarios or systems and allow students to interact with them in a controlled environment. These interactive simulations provide a safe space for students to experiment, make decisions, and observe the consequences of their actions.

Simulations can be used in various subjects, such as science, mathematics, social studies, and even language arts. They enable students to explore complex concepts, engage in problem-solving, and develop critical thinking skills.

Benefits of Simulations

The use of simulations in education offers several benefits to students:

- **Active Learning:** Simulations encourage active participation, as students take an active role in the learning process by making choices and seeing the outcomes in real-time.

- **Authentic Experience:** Simulations provide students with authentic and relevant experiences that mimic real-world situations, allowing them to apply their knowledge and skills in a practical context.

- **Hands-on Exploration:** Simulations allow for hands-on exploration without the limitations of time, resources, or safety concerns. Students can conduct virtual experiments and manipulate variables to observe the impact on the outcomes.

- **Immediate Feedback:** Simulations provide instant feedback to students, allowing them to assess their understanding, reflect on their choices, and make improvements in real-time.

- **Collaborative Learning:** Simulations can facilitate collaboration and teamwork, as students can work together to solve problems, discuss strategies, and make joint decisions.

- **Motivation and Engagement:** The interactive nature of simulations, along with the gamified elements, can enhance student motivation and engagement, making learning more enjoyable and immersive.

Examples of Simulations

Let's explore a few examples of how simulations can be used in different subjects:

- In **Science**, students can use virtual lab simulations to conduct experiments and explore phenomena that may be difficult or expensive to replicate in a physical lab.

- In **Mathematics**, simulations can help students visualize and understand complex mathematical concepts by providing interactive models and virtual manipulatives.

- In **Social Studies**, historical simulations can immerse students in historical events, allowing them to make decisions and experience the consequences of those decisions.

- In **Language Arts**, simulations can be used to create interactive storytelling experiences, where students can explore different story paths and outcomes based on their choices.

Implementing Simulations

Here are some considerations when implementing simulations in the classroom:

- **Alignment with Learning Objectives:** Ensure that the chosen simulation aligns with the learning objectives and curriculum goals.

- **Clear Instructions and Guidance:** Provide clear instructions and guidance to students on how to navigate and interact with the simulation.

- **Integration with Instruction:** Integrate simulations into lesson plans and use them as a supportive tool to enhance instruction and reinforce concepts.

- **Opportunities for Reflection:** Incorporate reflection activities to help students analyze their experiences, evaluate their decisions, and apply their learning to real-life contexts.

- **Assessment of Learning:** Create appropriate assessment strategies to evaluate student understanding and skill development through the use of simulations.

Considerations and Challenges

While simulations offer many benefits, educators should also be mindful of a few considerations and challenges:

- **Accessibility and Equity:** Ensure that the simulations are accessible to all students, taking into account factors such as varied learning styles, physical disabilities, and limited access to technology.

- **Cost and Resources:** Some simulations may require specific software, hardware, or licenses, which may come at a cost. Consider the availability of resources and the sustainability of incorporating simulations in the long run.

- **Training and Support:** Educators may require training and support to effectively use simulations in the classroom. Professional development opportunities and access to technical support can help address any challenges.

- **Balancing Time:** Simulations can be time-consuming. It is important to strike a balance between hands-on exploration through simulations and other instructional activities.

Conclusion

Simulations offer a powerful tool for engaging and immersive learning experiences. By incorporating simulations into the classroom, educators can create an environment that promotes active learning, critical thinking, and problem-solving skills. With careful consideration of implementation strategies and addressing potential challenges, simulations can positively impact student learning outcomes.

Additional Resources

For further exploration of simulations and games in education, consider these resources:

- Sheppard Software - `https://www.sheppardsoftware.com/`
- PhET Interactive Simulations - `https://phet.colorado.edu/`
- Teach with Portals - `https://teachwithportals.com/`
- Minecraft: Education Edition - `https://education.minecraft.net/`

Collaborative Online Platforms

Collaborative online platforms play an essential role in modern education, facilitating communication, interaction, and collaboration among students and teachers. These platforms provide a digital space where learners can work together, share resources, and engage in meaningful discussions. In this section, we will explore the benefits of collaborative online platforms, discuss various types of platforms, and examine how they can enhance the learning experience.

Benefits of Collaborative Online Platforms

Collaborative online platforms offer several advantages that contribute to a more engaging and effective learning environment. These benefits include:

- **Enhanced collaboration**: Collaborative online platforms empower students to work together on projects and assignments, regardless of their physical location. They facilitate group work, enabling students to collaborate and communicate in real-time, fostering teamwork and shared learning experiences.

- **Improved communication**: Effective communication is crucial for successful collaboration. These platforms provide various communication tools, such as discussion boards, chat rooms, and video conferencing, enabling seamless interaction between learners and instructors. They allow for immediate feedback and clarification, promoting effective communication among participants.

- **Increased access to resources**: Collaborative online platforms enable learners to access a wide range of resources, including documents, videos, and presentations. Students can easily share and exchange materials, enhancing the learning experience and exposing individuals to diverse perspectives.

- **Flexibility in scheduling**: Online platforms eliminate the constraints of physical proximity and time zones. Learners can connect and collaborate at their convenience, making education more accessible and flexible.

- **Promotion of digital literacy**: Engaging with collaborative online platforms enhances students' digital literacy skills. They learn how to navigate the digital space, use different communication tools effectively, and engage in online discussions professionally.

Types of Collaborative Online Platforms

There are various types of collaborative online platforms available, each with its own unique features and advantages. Let's explore some of the commonly used platforms in education:

1. **Learning Management Systems (LMS)**: LMS platforms provide a centralized hub for online learning. They offer features such as discussion forums, assignment submission, grade tracking, and content sharing. Popular LMS platforms include Moodle, Canvas, and Blackboard.

2. **Collaborative Document Editing Platforms**: These platforms allow multiple users to collaborate on the same document simultaneously. Google Docs, Microsoft Office Online, and Zoho Docs are examples of such platforms. Collaborative editing eliminates the need for sending files back and forth and enables real-time collaboration.

3. **Social Learning Networks**: Social learning networks combine social media elements with educational functionality. They foster social interaction and

TECHNOLOGY AND INQUIRY-BASED LEARNING

collaboration among learners by providing features such as communities, groups, and discussion boards. Edmodo, Schoology, and Ning are popular social learning network platforms.

4. **Video Conferencing Platforms:** Video conferencing platforms facilitate real-time communication and collaboration using audio and video. These platforms are particularly useful for synchronous online discussions, virtual classrooms, and guest lectures. Zoom, Skype, and Google Meet are widely used video conferencing platforms.

5. **Project Management Platforms:** Project management platforms enable students to plan, organize, and collaborate on projects effectively. They offer features such as task assignment, progress tracking, and document sharing. Trello, Asana, and Basecamp are popular project management platforms.

Examples and Applications

Collaborative online platforms can be applied across various educational contexts and disciplines:

- In language learning, students can use collaborative document editing platforms to co-create documents, provide feedback on each other's work, and practice writing skills.

- In science and engineering courses, virtual laboratories integrated into online platforms allow students to conduct experiments and simulations collaboratively, regardless of their physical location.

- In literature or history classes, social learning networks provide a space for students to engage in discussions, share interpretations, and collaborate on research projects.

- Video conferencing platforms enable guest speakers from around the world to engage with students, providing them with diverse perspectives and unique insights.

- Project management platforms help students work collaboratively on group projects, dividing tasks, setting deadlines, and tracking progress efficiently.

Challenges and Considerations

While collaborative online platforms offer numerous benefits, there are also challenges and considerations to keep in mind:

- **Digital divide:** Not all students may have access to reliable internet connections or appropriate devices, leading to disparities in participation and engagement. It is important to address these inequities to ensure inclusive learning opportunities for all learners.

- **Technical difficulties:** Collaborative online platforms rely on technology, and technical issues can arise. Students and teachers should be prepared to troubleshoot and have alternative communication channels in case of technical difficulties.

- **Privacy and security:** Online platforms involve the sharing and storage of personal information and student data. It is essential to choose platforms that prioritize data privacy and follow industry best practices for security.

- **Digital etiquette:** In online environments, it is important to establish clear guidelines for communication and collaboration. Educators should promote and model digital etiquette to ensure respectful and productive interactions among participants.

Conclusion

Collaborative online platforms offer a wealth of opportunities for enhancing learning experiences and promoting collaboration. These platforms enable students to transcend physical boundaries and engage in meaningful interactions with peers and instructors. By leveraging the benefits of collaborative online platforms and addressing the associated challenges, educators can create dynamic and inclusive virtual learning environments that foster collaboration and engagement.

Data Analysis Tools

In the digital age, data has become an invaluable resource in various domains, including education. With the advent of technology, educators have access to vast amounts of data that can be used to inform and improve teaching practices. Data analysis tools provide educators with the means to analyze and interpret this data, allowing them to make data-driven decisions to enhance student learning outcomes. In this section, we will explore the different types of data analysis tools available to educators and their applications in the classroom.

Types of Data Analysis Tools

Data analysis tools encompass a wide range of software and platforms designed to collect, store, process, and visualize data. Let's explore some of the commonly used data analysis tools in education:

1. **Spreadsheet Software:** Spreadsheet software, such as Microsoft Excel or Google Sheets, is a versatile tool for data analysis. Educators can use spreadsheets to organize and manipulate data, perform calculations, and generate charts and graphs to visualize trends and patterns.

2. **Statistical Software:** Statistical software packages like SPSS, R, or Python with data analysis libraries provide advanced statistical analysis capabilities. These tools allow educators to conduct complex analyses, such as regression analysis, hypothesis testing, and data modeling.

3. **Learning Analytics Platforms:** Learning analytics platforms are specifically designed for educational data analysis. These platforms collect and analyze data from various sources, such as learning management systems, online assessments, and student information systems. They provide detailed insights into student performance, engagement, and behavior, helping educators identify areas for improvement and personalize instruction.

4. **Data Visualization Tools:** Data visualization tools, such as Tableau or Power BI, enable educators to present data in visually compelling ways. By creating interactive charts, graphs, and dashboards, educators can communicate complex data effectively and facilitate data-driven discussions.

5. **Text Mining Tools:** Text mining tools use natural language processing techniques to analyze and extract information from text-based data. Educators can use these tools to analyze student responses, essays, or feedback, uncovering patterns or sentiment analysis to gain deeper insights into student understanding and engagement.

Applications in Education

Now that we have explored the types of data analysis tools available, let's delve into their applications in education:

1. **Assessment Analysis:** Data analysis tools can help educators analyze assessment data to evaluate student performance and identify areas of strength and weakness. By examining item-level analysis, educators can uncover patterns of student misconceptions and adjust instructional approaches accordingly.

2. **Personalized Learning:** Data analysis tools play a crucial role in implementing personalized learning approaches. Educators can utilize these tools to track individual student progress, identify learning gaps, and provide targeted interventions to meet students' specific needs.

3. **Predictive Analytics:** By analyzing historical data and student performance trends, data analysis tools can provide insights into student outcomes. Educators can use predictive analytics to identify students at risk of falling behind or dropping out, allowing for early intervention and support.

4. **Curriculum Evaluation:** Data analysis tools enable educators to assess the effectiveness of existing curricula and instructional materials. By analyzing student performance and engagement data, educators can make data-driven decisions to improve curriculum alignment and pedagogical approaches.

5. **Educational Research:** Data analysis tools are invaluable in educational research. Researchers can use these tools to analyze large datasets, uncover correlations, and conduct sophisticated statistical analyses to investigate the impact of educational interventions and programs.

Considerations and Challenges

While data analysis tools offer significant benefits, educators need to consider certain factors and address potential challenges:

1. **Data Privacy and Security:** When using data analysis tools, educators must prioritize student data privacy and comply with relevant data protection regulations. It is crucial to ensure that data is stored securely and accessed only by authorized individuals.

2. **Data Quality and Reliability:** Data analysis is only as valuable as the data it relies on. Educators must ensure the accuracy, completeness, and reliability of data sources to obtain trustworthy insights. Proper data collection and cleaning procedures are essential.

3. **Professional Development:** Educators need training and professional development to effectively leverage data analysis tools. They must develop data

literacy skills, including understanding statistical concepts and interpreting data visualizations, to make informed decisions based on the analyzed data.

4. **Ethical Use of Data:** When analyzing data, educators should consider ethical implications, such as ensuring data anonymity and avoiding biases in data interpretation. Ethical considerations include using data to support students' well-being and avoiding the misuse of data for discriminatory purposes.

Example: Using Learning Analytics for Intervention

Let's consider an example of how learning analytics can be used to support intervention strategies. Imagine a high school teacher using a learning management system (LMS) that provides data on student engagement and performance. Through data analysis tools within the LMS, the teacher can identify students who are consistently struggling with a particular topic or falling behind their peers.

By analyzing these students' engagement patterns, completion rates, and assessment scores, the teacher can gain insights into potential reasons for their struggles. The teacher can then create personalized interventions, such as additional resources, small group instruction, or one-on-one mentoring, to support these students and address their specific needs.

Throughout the intervention, the teacher continues to use data analysis tools to monitor the effectiveness of the interventions. By analyzing student progress over time, the teacher can determine if the interventions are helping the targeted students improve their understanding and performance.

By leveraging learning analytics and data analysis tools, educators can make data-informed decisions, personalize instruction, and facilitate targeted interventions to support student success.

Conclusion

Data analysis tools are powerful resources for educators, enabling them to leverage data for informed decision-making and improving student outcomes. By utilizing spreadsheet software, statistical tools, learning analytics platforms, and data visualization tools, educators can gain valuable insights into student performance, engagement, and behavior. However, it is important to consider data privacy, quality, professional development, and ethical use while utilizing these tools. With a well-rounded understanding of data analysis tools, educators can unlock the potential of data to transform teaching and learning.

Artificial intelligence in Inquiry-Based Learning

Artificial intelligence (AI) has been making waves in various industries, and education is no exception. In the context of inquiry-based learning, AI can play a significant role in enhancing the learning experience for students. By harnessing AI technologies, educators can provide personalized guidance, facilitate data-driven decision making, and create engaging learning environments.

Understanding Artificial Intelligence

Artificial intelligence refers to the development of computer systems that can perform tasks that would typically require human intelligence. In the context of education, AI encompasses various technologies such as machine learning, natural language processing, and computer vision. These technologies enable machines to analyze data, recognize patterns, understand and process language, and make predictions or recommendations.

Benefits of AI in Inquiry-Based Learning

AI can offer several benefits in the context of inquiry-based learning:

1. **Personalized Learning:** AI algorithms can analyze students' performance data and provide personalized recommendations for their learning path. By adapting the content and pace to individual needs, AI enhances the effectiveness of inquiry-based learning.

2. **Support for Teachers:** AI can assist teachers in managing and assessing inquiry-based learning. It can provide real-time feedback on student progress, suggest suitable resources, and help in identifying knowledge gaps or misconceptions.

3. **Enhanced Collaboration:** AI-powered platforms can facilitate collaborative inquiry by connecting students with similar interests or skill sets. Virtual collaborative spaces can enable students to work together on projects, share ideas, and provide feedback to each other.

4. **Data Analysis:** AI can analyze large amounts of data generated during inquiry-based learning activities. By identifying patterns and trends, AI can offer insights to educators, enabling them to improve instructional strategies and tailor interventions to student needs.

Examples of AI Applications in Inquiry-Based Learning

1. **Natural Language Processing (NLP) for Inquiry Design:** AI-powered NLP algorithms can assist students in formulating effective research questions by analyzing existing resources, identifying relevant keywords, and suggesting modifications to enhance their inquiry process.

2. **Intelligent Tutoring Systems (ITS):** ITS uses AI algorithms to provide personalized support to students. These systems can identify areas where students are struggling and offer immediate feedback, resources, and guidance tailored to their needs.

3. **Virtual Learning Assistants:** AI-powered virtual assistants can answer students' questions, offer explanations, and provide additional resources. These assistants simulate human interaction, offering a conversational and interactive learning experience.

4. **Automated Assessment Systems:** AI can automate the assessment process in inquiry-based learning. By analyzing student responses and comparing them to predefined criteria, AI algorithms can provide instant feedback and generate detailed assessment reports for both students and teachers.

Challenges and Ethical Considerations

While AI holds great promise in inquiry-based learning, there are challenges and ethical considerations that need careful consideration:

1. **Data Privacy and Security:** AI systems collect and analyze large amounts of student data. It is crucial to ensure that data is securely stored, protected, and used ethically. Institutions must establish clear guidelines and policies regarding data privacy.

2. **Algorithm Bias:** AI algorithms can be influenced by biased data, leading to biased recommendations or assessments. It is essential to regularly monitor and address any biases in AI systems to ensure fair and equitable learning experiences for all students.

3. **Loss of Human Interaction:** AI integration should not replace human interaction in inquiry-based learning. Students still benefit from collaborative discussions, peer feedback, and teacher guidance. AI should augment human teaching rather than replace it.

The Future of AI in Inquiry-Based Learning

As AI technology advances, it will continue to shape the future of inquiry-based learning. Here are some trends and directions to watch for:

1. **Adaptive Learning Environments:** AI will enable the creation of adaptive learning environments that dynamically adjust content, pacing, and instructional strategies to meet the individual needs of each student.
2. **Intelligent Learning Analytics:** AI-powered analytics will provide deeper insights into student learning, enabling educators to make data-informed decisions to improve inquiry-based learning experiences.
3. **Natural Language Conversational Interfaces:** AI-driven conversational interfaces will become more sophisticated, allowing students to interact with educational technologies using natural language, further enhancing engagement and personalized learning.
4. **Ethical AI Use in Education:** The ethical use of AI in education will become a prominent concern. Institutions and educators must keep a close eye on emerging policies and guidelines to ensure responsible implementation.

Conclusion

Artificial intelligence has the potential to revolutionize inquiry-based learning by providing personalized support, enhancing collaboration, and leveraging data analytics. However, careful consideration of ethical considerations and monitoring of algorithm bias is essential. As AI technology continues to develop, it is crucial to use it responsibly to create inclusive and effective educational experiences.

Chapter 3: Integrating Technology in the Classroom

Benefits and Challenges of Technology Integration

Enhancing Student Engagement

Enhancing student engagement is a crucial aspect of integrating technology in the classroom. When students are engaged in the learning process, they are more likely to be motivated, focused, and active participants in their own education. This section will explore various strategies and techniques that teachers can employ to enhance student engagement using technology.

Gamification

One effective way to enhance student engagement is through the use of gamification. Gamification refers to the application of game design elements and principles in non-game contexts, such as education. By introducing elements like points, levels, badges, and leaderboards, teachers can make learning more interactive and enjoyable for students.

For example, a language learning app may award points to students for completing exercises, and allow them to level up as they progress. This creates a sense of achievement and encourages students to continue practicing. Additionally, a leaderboard can be displayed to foster healthy competition among students.

Gamification promotes engagement by tapping into students' natural desire for competition, rewards, and a sense of accomplishment. It can also provide instant feedback, which is crucial for motivation and learning.

Interactive Multimedia

The use of interactive multimedia is another powerful tool for enhancing student engagement. Multimedia can include videos, animations, simulations, and interactive quizzes. These resources can be accessed through online platforms or integrated into the classroom through projectors or interactive whiteboards.

For example, a history lesson on World War II can be supplemented with a video documentary that brings the events to life. Students can actively engage with the content by answering questions, participating in virtual discussions, or even creating their own multimedia projects.

Interactive multimedia captures students' attention, provides visual and auditory stimulation, and caters to different learning styles. It also allows for self-paced learning, enabling students to explore topics at their own speed.

Collaborative Online Platforms

Collaboration is an essential skill in the 21st century, and technology provides various opportunities to foster collaborative learning. Collaborative online platforms, such as Google Docs, Padlet, or Moodle, allow students to work together on projects, assignments, and presentations.

For instance, a science teacher can create a collaborative platform where students can collaborate on a virtual lab experiment. Each student can contribute their observations and analysis, while also engaging in real-time discussions with their peers.

Collaborative online platforms promote active participation, as students are actively involved in the learning process and accountable to their peers. They also encourage communication and teamwork, as students work together to achieve a common goal.

Real-World Connections

Technology offers numerous opportunities to connect classroom learning to the real world, which enhances student engagement. Teachers can facilitate real-world connections through virtual field trips, video conferences with experts, or online research on current events.

For example, a geography lesson on ecosystems can be enriched by connecting with a scientist who conducts field research in a particular ecosystem. Students can engage in a live conversation, asking questions and exploring the practical applications of their knowledge.

Real-world connections help students see the relevance of what they are learning, making it more meaningful and engaging. It also broadens their perspective and allows them to develop a deeper understanding of the subject matter.

Problem-Based Learning

Problem-based learning is an instructional approach that presents students with real-world problems to solve. By engaging students in authentic and complex problems, technology can significantly enhance their engagement.

For instance, in a math lesson, students can use online tools to simulate scenarios where they need to apply their mathematical skills to solve problems. This hands-on approach encourages students to actively think, analyze, and strategize.

Problem-based learning promotes engagement by giving students ownership over their learning. It fosters critical thinking skills, collaboration, and creativity, as students tackle open-ended problems that can have multiple solutions.

In conclusion, enhancing student engagement is vital for effective teaching and learning. Technology can play a significant role in achieving this goal by incorporating gamification, interactive multimedia, collaborative online platforms, real-world connections, and problem-based learning. By utilizing these strategies, teachers can create a more stimulating and interactive learning environment that fosters student engagement and ultimately improves learning outcomes.

Facilitating Differentiated Instruction

In order to meet the diverse needs of students in the classroom, teachers need to employ differentiated instruction techniques. Differentiated instruction is an approach that recognizes and responds to the individual strengths, interests, and learning styles of each student. By providing a variety of instructional strategies, materials, and assessments, teachers can ensure that all students are challenged and engaged in their learning.

Understanding Differentiated Instruction

Differentiated instruction is based on the understanding that learners have unique needs and preferences. It involves tailoring the content, process, and product of instruction to meet these needs. The goal is to create a learning environment that supports individual growth and maximizes student achievement.

To effectively implement differentiated instruction, teachers need to gather information about their students' strengths, interests, and learning profiles. This can be done through formal assessments, informal observations, and conversations with students. By understanding their students' needs, teachers can develop appropriate strategies and activities to support their learning.

Strategies for Differentiated Instruction

There are several strategies that teachers can use to facilitate differentiated instruction:

1. **Flexible Grouping**: Teachers can form groups based on student readiness, interests, or learning styles. This allows for targeted instruction and collaboration among students with similar needs or interests.

2. **Tiered Assignments**: Teachers can provide different levels of complexity or depth in assignments to accommodate varying levels of student readiness. This allows students to work on tasks that are appropriate for their skill level.

3. **Learning Stations**: Teachers can set up different learning stations around the classroom, each focusing on a different topic or skill. Students can rotate through the stations, choosing activities that match their interests or needs.

4. **Choice Boards**: Teachers can provide students with a menu of options for completing assignments or projects. This allows students to choose activities that align with their interests or learning preferences.

5. **Flexible Assessments**: Teachers can offer a variety of assessment options to allow students to demonstrate their knowledge and skills in different ways. This can include written assignments, presentations, projects, or performances.

Benefits of Differentiated Instruction

By implementing differentiated instruction, teachers can create a positive and inclusive learning environment that benefits all students. Some of the key benefits include:

- **Increased Student Engagement**: When instruction is tailored to students' needs and interests, they are more likely to be engaged and motivated to learn.

- **Higher Academic Achievement**: By addressing students' individual strengths and weaknesses, differentiated instruction can lead to improved academic performance.

- **Enhanced Self-Esteem:** When students experience success and feel valued in the classroom, their self-esteem and confidence in their abilities can improve.

- **Development of 21st Century Skills:** Differentiated instruction promotes the development of critical thinking, problem-solving, and collaboration skills, which are essential for success in the modern world.

- **Inclusive Learning Environment:** Differentiated instruction recognizes and values the diversity of learners, creating a classroom where all students feel included and supported.

Challenges of Differentiated Instruction

While differentiated instruction offers many benefits, it also presents some challenges for teachers. These challenges include:

- **Time Constraints:** Planning and implementing differentiated instruction can be time-consuming, as it requires creating multiple materials and activities to meet the needs of diverse learners.

- **Classroom Management:** Managing different groups or stations in the classroom can be challenging, as teachers need to ensure that students stay on task and make effective use of their learning time.

- **Assessment and Grading:** Assessing and grading students' work in a differentiated classroom can be complex, as teachers need to evaluate students' progress based on their individual goals and needs.

- **Professional Development:** Teachers may require additional training and support to effectively implement differentiated instruction strategies in their classrooms.

Strategies for Overcoming Challenges

To overcome the challenges associated with differentiated instruction, teachers can employ the following strategies:

- **Collaboration and Co-teaching:** Collaborating with other teachers or specialists can provide additional support and resources for differentiated instruction.

- **Effective Planning and Organization:** Careful planning and organization can help maximize instructional time and ensure smooth transitions between activities or groups.

- **Professional Development and Training:** Engaging in professional development opportunities can help teachers enhance their understanding and implementation of differentiated instruction.

- **Reflection and Feedback:** Regular reflection and feedback from students, colleagues, and administrators can help teachers refine their differentiated instruction practices.

Conclusion

Differentiated instruction is a powerful approach that allows teachers to meet the diverse needs of students in the classroom. By tailoring instruction to address individual strengths, interests, and learning styles, teachers can create a supportive and inclusive learning environment where all students can thrive. While it presents challenges, with the right strategies and support, differentiated instruction can lead to improved student engagement, academic achievement, and overall success.

Promoting Collaboration and Communication

Promoting collaboration and communication in the classroom is essential for creating an engaging and interactive learning environment. These skills are not only crucial for academic success but also for preparing students for the real-world challenges they will face. In this section, we will explore various strategies, tools, and techniques that can be used to foster collaboration and communication among students.

Importance of Collaboration and Communication

Collaboration and communication are key 21st-century skills that students must develop to thrive in a rapidly changing world. These skills enable students to work effectively in teams, solve complex problems, and express their ideas confidently.

Collaboration promotes active learning and helps students develop important social skills such as teamwork, negotiation, and compromise. It allows students to learn from each other by sharing ideas, perspectives, and resources. Furthermore, collaboration encourages critical thinking and creativity as students engage in meaningful discussions and explore different solutions.

Communication, on the other hand, is the foundation of successful collaboration. Effective communication skills enable students to express their thoughts clearly, listen actively, and provide constructive feedback. It improves their ability to understand and empathize with others, enhancing their interpersonal relationships.

Strategies for Promoting Collaboration

There are several strategies educators can employ to promote collaboration in the classroom. Here are a few effective approaches:

- **Group Work:** Assigning group projects or activities where students work together towards a common goal encourages collaboration. It allows students to learn from each other, leverage their individual strengths, and develop teamwork skills.

- **Peer Teaching:** Encourage students to teach or explain concepts to their peers. This not only promotes collaboration but also reinforces understanding of the material. Peer teaching empowers students and builds their confidence in sharing their knowledge.

- **Cooperative Learning:** Structured activities that require students to work in small groups on specific tasks promote collaboration and peer interaction. Cooperative learning fosters a sense of shared responsibility and encourages students to actively participate and contribute.

- **Problem-Solving Activities:** Engage students in problem-solving activities that require them to brainstorm ideas, evaluate alternatives, and work collaboratively to find solutions. This enhances teamwork, critical thinking, and communication skills.

- **Discussion-Based Learning:** Incorporate class discussions into lessons to encourage students to share their thoughts, debate ideas, and actively listen to their peers. Effective facilitation of these discussions can create a cooperative and inclusive learning environment.

Tools and Technologies for Collaboration

Advancements in technology have provided educators with a wide range of tools and technologies to facilitate collaboration in the classroom. Here are a few examples:

- **Online Collaboration Platforms:** Platforms such as Google Classroom, Microsoft Teams, or Slack provide virtual spaces for students to collaborate, share documents, and communicate in real-time. These platforms allow for easy file sharing, group discussions, and collaborative editing.

- **Video Conferencing:** Tools like Zoom or Microsoft Teams enable synchronous communication and collaboration in real-time, regardless of geographical locations. These video conferencing platforms can be used for virtual group discussions, project presentations, or guest speaker sessions.

- **Collaborative Document Editing:** Tools like Google Docs, Microsoft Office 365, or Etherpad enable students to collaborate on the same document simultaneously. This allows for real-time feedback, editing, and revision of documents, fostering collaboration in the writing process.

- **Virtual Whiteboards:** Applications like Miro or Jamboard provide virtual whiteboards that allow students to collaborate and brainstorm ideas visually. These platforms enable real-time collaboration, annotation, and sharing of ideas, promoting creativity and teamwork.

- **Project Management Tools:** Tools like Trello or Asana can be used to assign tasks, track progress, and facilitate collaboration among students. These platforms help students organize their work, set deadlines, and collaborate effectively on group projects.

Challenges and Considerations

While collaboration and communication are incredibly valuable, there are some challenges and considerations educators must address:

- **Group Dynamics:** Collaborative activities may face challenges related to conflict resolution, unequal contribution, or domination by certain group members. Educators should provide guidance and support to ensure equitable participation and effective collaboration.

- **Technology Barriers:** Not all students may have access to the necessary technology or reliable internet connection for online collaboration. It is important to consider alternative strategies or provide resources to overcome these barriers.

- **Assessment of Individual Contributions:** Assessing individual contributions in group projects can be challenging. Clear criteria and guidelines for assessing collaboration should be established to ensure fairness and accountability.

- **Digital Citizenship:** Promoting responsible and ethical behavior in online collaboration is crucial. Educators should address topics such as digital etiquette, privacy, and online safety to ensure students develop appropriate online communication skills.

Real-World Example

To illustrate the importance of collaboration and communication, let's consider the field of architecture. In architectural design projects, collaboration among architects, engineers, and clients is crucial for successful outcomes. Architects need to communicate their ideas effectively, collaborate with team members, and align their vision with the client's requirements. Through effective collaboration and communication, architects can create innovative and sustainable designs that meet the needs of the community.

Exercises

1. Divide the class into small groups and assign each group a topic. Ask them to collaboratively create a presentation on the topic using a collaborative document editing tool like Google Docs. Each group member should contribute equally to the presentation.

2. Organize a class debate on a controversial topic. Divide the class into two teams and assign each team a stance. Encourage students to collaborate within their teams to gather evidence, articulate arguments, and present their viewpoints during the debate.

3. Create a virtual gallery of students' artwork or projects using a virtual whiteboard platform. Provide students with an opportunity to collaborate and provide feedback on each other's work. This exercise encourages collaboration and constructive communication.

4. Assign a group research project where students have to collectively gather and analyze data, and present their findings. Teach them how to use online collaboration platforms or project management tools to effectively divide tasks, track progress, and collaborate on the project.

Resources

- **Book:** "Collaborative Learning Techniques: A Handbook for College Faculty" by Elizabeth F. Barkley

- **Website:** Edutopia - Collaboration Resources (https://www.edutopia.org/article/collaboration-resources)

- **Webinar:** "Promoting Student Collaboration and Communication in the Classroom" by ASCD

Developing Critical Thinking Skills

Critical thinking is an essential skill for students to develop as it enables them to analyze, evaluate, and synthesize information effectively. This skill is crucial in today's information-rich society, where the ability to think critically allows individuals to make informed decisions, solve complex problems, and navigate various academic and professional challenges. In this section, we will explore the importance of critical thinking skills, strategies for developing these skills, and the role of technology in enhancing critical thinking.

The Importance of Critical Thinking Skills

Critical thinking skills are fundamental to academic success and lifelong learning. These skills go beyond memorization and rote learning, enabling students to engage with content more deeply and critically evaluate information. Here are some key reasons why developing critical thinking skills is crucial:

- **Problem-Solving:** Critical thinking skills empower students to identify, analyze, and solve problems effectively. They learn to question assumptions, gather evidence, evaluate alternatives, and make informed decisions.

- **Decision Making:** By honing their critical thinking skills, students become better decision-makers. They are able to weigh the pros and cons, recognize biases, consider multiple perspectives, and make reasoned judgments.

- **Effective Communication:** Critical thinking skills enhance students' ability to articulate their thoughts and ideas clearly and persuasively. They learn to present logical arguments, support claims with evidence, and engage in constructive discussions.

- **Analytical Thinking:** Developing critical thinking skills enables students to analyze complex information, identify patterns and relationships, draw logical conclusions, and evaluate the credibility of sources.

- **Creativity and Innovation:** Critical thinking nurtures creativity and fosters innovative thinking. It encourages students to explore unconventional ideas, think divergently, and develop unique solutions to problems.

In summary, critical thinking skills empower students to become active, independent learners who can navigate a rapidly changing world.

Strategies for Developing Critical Thinking Skills

To facilitate the development of critical thinking skills, educators can employ a variety of strategies and techniques. Here are some effective approaches to help students enhance their critical thinking abilities:

1. **Questioning Techniques:** Encourage students to ask probing questions that stimulate critical thinking. Teach them various types of questions, such as open-ended questions, probing questions, and Socratic questioning, to promote deeper analysis and reflection.

2. **Problem-Based Learning:** Incorporate problem-based learning activities where students are presented with real-world problems or scenarios. This approach challenges students to think critically, apply knowledge, and work collaboratively to find solutions.

3. **Scaffolding:** Provide students with scaffolding support to develop their critical thinking skills gradually. Start with simpler tasks and gradually increase the complexity, allowing students to build their problem-solving and analytical abilities.

4. **Analysis and Evaluation:** Encourage students to analyze and evaluate information from multiple sources. Teach them to assess the credibility and reliability of sources, identify biases, and evaluate the strength of arguments.

5. **Active Learning Strategies:** Incorporate active learning strategies such as discussions, debates, case studies, and group activities to engage students in critical thinking. These strategies facilitate peer-to-peer learning, promote critical analysis, and encourage students to defend their positions.

6. **Metacognition:** Foster metacognitive skills by teaching students to reflect on their thinking processes. Encourage them to monitor their own learning, identify areas of improvement, and adapt their strategies accordingly.

By integrating these strategies into teaching practices, educators can create an environment that nurtures critical thinking skills in students.

Role of Technology in Enhancing Critical Thinking

Technology offers a wide range of tools and resources that can enhance critical thinking skills in students. Here are some ways technology can be integrated to promote critical thinking:

1. **Online Research:** Students can use the internet to access a vast amount of information for analysis and evaluation. However, it is crucial to teach them how to critically evaluate online sources and distinguish reliable information from unreliable sources.

2. **Collaborative Online Platforms:** Technology enables students to collaborate and engage in discussions beyond the boundaries of the classroom. Online platforms facilitate group projects, peer feedback, and global connections, fostering critical thinking through diverse perspectives.

3. **Simulation and Problem-Solving Applications:** Interactive simulations and problem-solving applications allow students to apply critical thinking skills in a virtual environment. These tools provide opportunities for experimentation, exploration, and decision-making, promoting the development of analytical and problem-solving abilities.

4. **Data Analysis Tools:** Technology provides access to a wide range of data analysis tools that can help students interpret and manipulate data for critical analysis. Students can learn to identify trends, patterns, and correlations, enabling them to draw evidence-based conclusions.

5. **Online Discussion Forums:** Virtual discussion forums allow students to engage in thoughtful discussions, present arguments, and provide feedback. These platforms encourage critical thinking by promoting intellectual discourse and challenging students' perspectives.

While technology can enrich the critical thinking process, it is important to ensure its appropriate and responsible use. Educators should guide students in using technology tools effectively, critically evaluating digital resources, and being mindful of online privacy and security.

In conclusion, developing critical thinking skills is essential for students in the modern era. By employing effective strategies and leveraging technology, educators can foster critical thinking abilities that will empower students to excel academically and thrive in their personal and professional lives.

Addressing Technological Barriers

In today's digitally-driven world, integrating technology in the classroom has become essential to provide students with modern learning experiences. However, along with the numerous benefits that technology brings, there are also several barriers that need to be addressed to ensure effective technology integration. This section will explore some common technological barriers and provide strategies to overcome them.

Limited Access to Technology

One of the major barriers to technology integration is the limited access to devices and internet connectivity. Not all students have access to personal computers or mobile devices at home, which can create a digital divide. To address this barrier, schools can implement the following strategies:

- Providing a sufficient number of devices: Schools can invest in a set of devices, such as laptops or tablets, that can be used by students who do not have access to their own devices. These devices can be shared among students during classroom activities.

- Establishing technology lending programs: Schools can set up programs that allow students to borrow devices for a certain period, such as overnight or weekends, to ensure that they have equal access to technology.

- Collaborating with community organizations: Schools can partner with community organizations, such as libraries or local businesses, to provide computer labs or Wi-Fi hotspots for students who do not have internet access at home.

By implementing these strategies, schools can bridge the technological gap and ensure that all students have equal opportunities to benefit from technology in their learning.

Lack of Technical Support

Another challenge in implementing technology integration is the lack of technical support. Teachers and students may encounter technical issues or difficulties in operating devices and software, which can hinder the learning process. To address this barrier, schools can take the following steps:

- Providing training to teachers: Schools can offer professional development sessions to train teachers in using educational technologies effectively. This training can include troubleshooting common technical issues and providing guidance on software and hardware utilization.

- Establishing a technical support team: Schools can have a dedicated team of technical support staff who can assist teachers and students in resolving technical issues quickly. This team can provide on-site or remote support depending on the needs of the school.

- Creating a knowledge base: Schools can develop a centralized repository of troubleshooting guides, FAQs, and best practices that teachers and students can refer to when encountering technical difficulties. This knowledge base can be in the form of a website or an online portal.

By offering adequate training and technical support, schools can empower teachers and students to overcome technical barriers and effectively utilize technology for learning.

Cybersecurity and Privacy Concerns

As technology becomes more prevalent in classrooms, there is a growing need to address cybersecurity and privacy concerns. Protecting students' personal information and ensuring a safe online environment is crucial. Schools can take the following measures to address these concerns:

- Implementing strong security measures: Schools should invest in robust security measures, including firewalls, antivirus software, and regular software updates, to protect students' data from online threats and unauthorized access.

- Teaching digital citizenship and internet safety: Schools should incorporate digital citizenship education into their curriculum to educate students about responsible online behavior, internet safety, and protecting their personal information.

- Familiarizing with privacy regulations: Schools should stay updated with privacy regulations, such as the Family Educational Rights and Privacy Act (FERPA), to ensure compliance and protect students' privacy. Teachers should be trained on handling and storing student data securely.

By prioritizing cybersecurity and privacy, schools can create a safe digital environment that encourages exploration and learning.

Resistance to Change

Resistance to change is a common barrier that hinders the effective integration of technology in education. Teachers, students, and even parents may resist the adoption of new technologies due to various reasons such as fear, lack of awareness, or discomfort with change. To address this barrier, schools can take the following steps:

- Providing comprehensive training and support: Schools should provide ongoing training and support to teachers to build their confidence and competence in using technology. Teachers should be given opportunities to explore and experiment with new tools in a supportive environment.

- Involving stakeholders in decision-making: Schools should involve teachers, students, and parents in the decision-making process when selecting and implementing new technologies. Engaging stakeholders and addressing their concerns can help alleviate resistance to change.

- Sharing success stories: Schools can showcase success stories of technology integration to demonstrate its positive impact on student learning outcomes. Sharing these stories can inspire teachers, students, and parents to embrace technology as a valuable educational tool.

By addressing resistance to change through training, involvement, and communication, schools can create a culture of innovation and ensure the successful integration of technology in the classroom.

Conclusion

To harness the full potential of technology in education, it is crucial to address the technological barriers that hinder effective integration. By providing equal access to technology, offering technical support, prioritizing cybersecurity and privacy, and addressing resistance to change, schools can create an environment where technology enhances teaching and learning experiences. With careful planning and implementation, technology can empower students to become active learners in the digital age.

Ensuring Privacy and Safety in the Digital Age

In today's digital age, where technology is deeply integrated into our daily lives, ensuring privacy and safety is of utmost importance. With the increasing use of educational technology in classrooms, it becomes crucial to protect the privacy of students and educators and promote a safe learning environment. In this section, we will explore the key considerations and strategies for safeguarding privacy and maintaining safety in the digital age.

Understanding Privacy Concerns

Privacy concerns arise due to the collection, storage, and use of personal information in digital systems. In the context of educational technology, it is essential to address the following privacy concerns:

- **Data Security:** Ensuring that student data is securely stored and protected from unauthorized access is crucial. Educational institutions must implement robust security measures to prevent data breaches and protect sensitive information, such as student records, grades, and contact details.

- **Third-Party Services:** Many educational platforms and software tools integrate third-party services, such as cloud storage or learning management systems. It is vital to review the privacy policies and terms of service of these services to ensure they align with privacy regulations and safeguard student data.

- **Data Sharing:** Educational institutions and teachers must be cautious about sharing student data with external entities. Before sharing any student information, obtaining consent from parents or guardians is essential, and data should be anonymized whenever possible to protect student identities.

- **Online Tracking:** Educational websites and applications often incorporate tracking mechanisms that collect data on students' online behavior. It is crucial to inform students and obtain their consent for any data tracking activities, while ensuring compliance with legal requirements, such as the Children's Online Privacy Protection Act (COPPA).

- **Cybersecurity Threats:** The digital realm is fraught with cybersecurity threats, including phishing attacks, malware, ransomware, and hacking attempts. It is important for educational institutions to implement the necessary security measures, such as firewalls, antivirus software, and regular data backups, to protect against these threats.

Strategies for Ensuring Privacy and Safety

To address privacy concerns and promote a safe digital learning environment, educational institutions and educators can adopt the following strategies:

- **Compliance with Privacy Laws:** Stay up to date with privacy laws and regulations, such as the Family Educational Rights and Privacy Act (FERPA) in the United States or the General Data Protection Regulation (GDPR) in the European Union. Ensure that all practices and policies are aligned with these regulations to protect student privacy.

- **Data Minimization:** Collect and store only the necessary data required for educational purposes. Avoid excessive data collection and retain data only for the required duration. Regularly review data storage practices and delete any outdated or unnecessary information.

- **Transparency and Consent:** Clearly communicate data collection and usage practices to students, parents, and educators. Obtain explicit consent before collecting personal information and provide an option to opt-out whenever possible. Be transparent about the third-party services used and their privacy policies.

- **Secure Infrastructure:** Ensure that the digital infrastructure, including networks, systems, and devices, is secure. Implement strong encryption protocols, multi-factor authentication, and regular security updates. Conduct regular security audits and assessments to identify and address potential vulnerabilities.

- **Educating Students:** Teach students about digital literacy, online safety, and data privacy. Empower them to make informed decisions about sharing personal information and educate them about the risks associated with online activities. Encourage responsible digital citizenship and provide resources for reporting any potential safety concerns.

- **Professional Development and Training:** Provide ongoing professional development and training to educators on privacy best practices and emerging threats. Educators should be aware of the latest privacy and security guidelines and ensure they are effectively implementing them in their classrooms.

- **Monitoring and Reporting:** Regularly monitor digital platforms and tools used in the classroom to ensure compliance with privacy policies. Encourage students, parents, and educators to report any privacy or safety concerns promptly. Establish clear procedures for addressing and resolving such concerns.

Case Study: Safeguarding Student Data

To illustrate the importance of privacy and safety in the digital age, let's consider a case study. Imagine a school district that has recently implemented a learning management system (LMS) to enhance digital teaching and learning. To ensure the privacy and safety of student data, the district takes the following measures:

- The district carefully reviews the privacy policies and terms of service of the LMS provider to ensure compliance with privacy regulations. They choose a provider that has robust security measures in place and guarantees the protection of student data.

- Before implementing the LMS, the district conducts thorough training sessions for educators to educate them about data privacy, security protocols, and responsible data handling practices. Teachers are made aware of their responsibilities in ensuring the privacy and safety of student data.

- The district implements strict access control measures for the LMS, ensuring that only authorized users can access student information. Strong passwords and multi-factor authentication are enforced to prevent unauthorized access.

- Students and their parents are provided with clear information about the data collected, how it will be used, and the security measures in place to safeguard their data. Consent is obtained from parents or guardians before student data is collected or shared with third-party services.

- The district monitors the LMS regularly for any potential security vulnerabilities or privacy breaches. They conduct periodic audits to ensure continued compliance with privacy regulations and best practices.

By implementing these strategies, the school district can ensure the privacy and safety of student data, creating a secure digital learning environment for all stakeholders involved.

Additional Resources

To further explore the topic of privacy and safety in the digital age, you may find the following resources helpful:

- The U.S. Department of Education's Privacy Technical Assistance Center (PTAC) provides guidance, best practices, and resources on student data privacy: https://studentprivacy.ed.gov/

- Common Sense Education offers a variety of resources, including lesson plans, videos, and articles, on teaching digital citizenship and online safety: https://www.commonsense.org/education/digital-citizenship

- The International Society for Technology in Education (ISTE) provides a range of resources on privacy, including webinars, guides, and professional development opportunities: https://www.iste.org/topics/privacy

---

In conclusion, ensuring privacy and safety in the digital age is a critical aspect of educational technology integration. By understanding privacy concerns, implementing appropriate strategies, and staying informed about the latest best practices, educational institutions and educators can create a secure learning environment that respects student privacy and fosters responsible digital citizenship.

Blended Learning and Flipped Classroom Models

Optimizing Face-to-Face Instruction

In the context of integrating technology in the classroom, optimizing face-to-face instruction plays a vital role in enhancing the effectiveness of teaching and learning. While technology offers various opportunities for interactive and engaging learning experiences, the presence of a skilled and knowledgeable teacher remains crucial in guiding students and nurturing their understanding. This section explores strategies and best practices for optimizing face-to-face instruction within the framework of technology integration.

Understanding the Role of the Teacher

In an era where information is readily available through technology, the role of the teacher has evolved to become more facilitative and instructional rather than solely delivering content. The teacher serves as a guide, mentor, and facilitator of learning experiences, ensuring students' active engagement and comprehension of the subject matter. By leveraging their expertise and experience, teachers can optimize face-to-face instruction by employing effective instructional strategies alongside technology integration.

Creating a Supportive Learning Environment

To optimize face-to-face instruction, it is essential to create a supportive learning environment that promotes active student participation and collaboration. The physical arrangement of the classroom can be designed to foster interaction and teamwork, such as by arranging desks in clusters or circles that facilitate group discussions. Teachers can also use classroom management techniques, such as establishing clear expectations and routines, to create a positive and conducive learning atmosphere.

Using Differentiated Instruction

Differentiated instruction is a teaching approach that recognizes and accommodates the diverse learning needs and preferences of students. By tailoring instruction to address individual strengths, weaknesses, interests, and readiness levels, teachers can optimize face-to-face instruction and promote deeper understanding. This approach ensures that every student receives personalized attention and support, resulting in improved learning outcomes.

For example, in a mathematics class, a teacher can use differentiated instruction by providing multiple pathways for students to understand a concept. Some students might benefit from hands-on activities, while others might prefer visual representations or collaborative problem-solving. By catering to these diverse learning styles and preferences, the teacher can optimize their face-to-face instruction and ensure all students have an opportunity to engage with the content.

Engaging Students in Authentic Learning Experiences

To optimize face-to-face instruction, it is important to engage students in authentic learning experiences that connect classroom learning to the real world. By incorporating practical applications and real-life examples, teachers can make the content more meaningful and relevant for students. This can be achieved through the use of case studies, simulations, role-playing activities, or field trips.

For instance, in a history class, instead of merely lecturing about World War II, the teacher can organize a mock debate where students assume the roles of historical figures and present their perspectives on the causes and consequences of the war. This hands-on and interactive approach not only enhances students' understanding but also fosters critical thinking, communication, and collaboration skills.

Assessing Student Learning

To ensure effective face-to-face instruction, it is essential to regularly assess student learning. Assessments provide valuable feedback to both teachers and students, enabling them to monitor progress and make necessary adjustments. By using a variety of assessment methods, such as quizzes, projects, presentations, and class discussions, teachers can gather comprehensive evidence of student understanding and identify areas that require further reinforcement or clarification.

It is important to leverage technology tools to streamline the assessment process and provide timely feedback. Learning management systems, online quizzes or surveys, and digital portfolios are examples of tools that can enhance the efficiency and effectiveness of assessing student learning. By using these tools, teachers can provide immediate feedback, track individual progress, and identify areas for improvement.

Building Relationships and Communication

Building strong relationships with students plays a crucial role in optimizing face-to-face instruction. When students feel supported, valued, and respected, they are more likely to actively engage in the learning process. Teachers can foster positive relationships by showing genuine interest in students' lives, providing a safe and inclusive classroom environment, and integrating social-emotional learning activities into the curriculum.

Effective communication with students and parents is also instrumental in optimizing face-to-face instruction. Teachers should regularly communicate with students to provide feedback on their progress, answer questions, and address concerns. Additionally, maintaining open lines of communication with parents or guardians through newsletters, parent-teacher conferences, or digital platforms ensures a collaborative approach to student success.

Professional Development for Teachers

To optimize face-to-face instruction, ongoing professional development is crucial for teachers. By staying updated with the latest educational research, instructional strategies, and technological advancements, teachers can continually enhance their teaching practice. Professional development can take various forms, such as workshops, conferences, webinars, online courses, or collaborative learning communities.

Schools should prioritize providing opportunities for teachers to expand their knowledge and skills in technology integration and effective pedagogical practices. By investing in professional development, schools empower teachers to optimize face-to-face instruction and create impactful learning experiences for their students.

Summary

Optimizing face-to-face instruction within the framework of technology integration is vital for effective teaching and learning. By understanding the evolving role of the teacher, creating a supportive learning environment, using differentiated instruction, engaging students in authentic learning experiences, assessing student learning, building relationships and communication, and investing in professional development, teachers can maximize the benefits of face-to-face interaction and leverage technology to enhance student learning outcomes. Through this holistic approach, students receive the necessary guidance and support while benefiting from the advantages offered by technology in the classroom.

Using Learning Management Systems

In the modern era of education, technology plays a crucial role in enhancing teaching and learning experiences. One of the key tools that has revolutionized the way educators manage their courses and interact with students is a Learning Management System (LMS). A Learning Management System is a software application that provides a platform for delivering online courses, managing learning materials, tracking student progress, and facilitating communication between instructors and learners.

Benefits of Learning Management Systems

Learning Management Systems offer numerous benefits to both educators and students. Let's explore some of the key advantages of using an LMS in the classroom:

1. **Centralized Course Management:** An LMS allows instructors to organize and manage course materials in one centralized location. This simplifies the process of uploading, organizing, and distributing course content such as lecture notes, assignments, and readings. Students can easily access these materials anytime, anywhere, fostering a more flexible and convenient learning experience.

2. **Efficient Communication:** LMS platforms provide various communication tools, such as discussion forums, messaging systems, and email integration. These features enable instructors to efficiently communicate with students and facilitate class discussions beyond traditional classroom settings. Students can ask questions, participate in discussions, and seek clarification on course content, leading to more active engagement and collaborative learning.

3. **Flexible Assessment and Feedback:** With an LMS, instructors can create and deliver assessments, such as quizzes and exams, electronically. This streamlines the grading process and provides instant feedback to students, allowing them to monitor their progress and areas for improvement. The LMS can also generate detailed analytics and reports, aiding instructors in tracking student performance and identifying areas of concern.

4. **Personalized Learning:** Learning Management Systems offer features for customization and personalization. Instructors can tailor course materials and learning activities based on individual student needs, accommodating diverse learning styles and preferences. This personalized approach enhances student engagement and fosters a more inclusive learning environment.

5. **Collaborative Learning:** LMS platforms promote collaboration among students by facilitating group work and project-based learning. Students can collaborate on assignments, share resources, and engage in online discussions, thereby developing essential teamwork and communication skills. The LMS offers tools for peer assessment, allowing students to provide feedback and evaluate their classmates' work.

6. **Data-driven Decision Making:** Learning Management Systems generate a wealth of data on student engagement, progress, and performance. Instructors can utilize this data to make informed decisions, such as identifying areas for instructional improvement and implementing targeted interventions. The LMS analytics also help administrators and policymakers to assess the effectiveness of educational programs and initiatives.

Implementing Learning Management Systems

To effectively use a Learning Management System, educators should consider the following steps:

1. **LMS Selection:** Choose an LMS that aligns with your instructional needs and preferences. Consider factors such as ease of use, compatibility with existing technology infrastructure, available features, and scalability for future growth.

2. **Course Setup:** Set up your course in the LMS by organizing modules, uploading course materials, and creating assignments or assessments. Ensure that the course structure is intuitive and aligns with the learning objectives.

3. **Orientation and Training:** Provide students with an orientation to the LMS interface and functionalities. Offer training sessions or tutorials to familiarize students with the platform, ensuring they can navigate and utilize LMS features effectively.

4. **Communication Strategies:** Establish clear communication channels within the LMS, such as discussion forums, announcement boards, or dedicated messaging systems. Inform students about the etiquette and expectations for online communication.

5. **Assessment Design:** Design assessments that align with the course objectives and take advantage of the interactive features offered by the LMS. Consider incorporating a variety of assessment types, such as quizzes, discussions, and multimedia projects.

6. **Monitoring Student Progress:** Regularly monitor students' progress using the analytics and reporting features of the LMS. Identify at-risk students and intervene as necessary to ensure they receive the support they need.

7. **Continuous Improvement**: Gather feedback from students and reflect on your own experiences using the LMS. Continuously refine and improve your course materials, instructional strategies, and assessment design based on this feedback and data analytics.

Considerations and Best Practices

While Learning Management Systems offer immense benefits, it is essential to consider some common challenges and best practices for successful implementation:

- **User Support**: Provide ongoing technical support and resources to help students and instructors navigate the LMS effectively. Offer training sessions, tutorials, and a help desk for troubleshooting common issues.

- **Accessibility and Inclusion**: Ensure that the LMS and course materials are accessible to all students, including those with disabilities. Follow universal design principles and provide alternative formats and accommodations as needed.

- **Usability and Interface Design**: Choose an LMS with a user-friendly interface and intuitive navigation. Optimize the layout and organization of course materials to enhance usability and ease of access for students.

- **Data Privacy and Security**: Protect student data and privacy by following best practices in data security. Familiarize yourself with relevant privacy regulations, such as the Family Educational Rights and Privacy Act (FERPA), and ensure that the LMS complies with these regulations.

- **Pedagogical Alignment**: Align the use of the LMS with pedagogical principles and instructional strategies. Integrate the LMS as a tool to enhance learning outcomes rather than relying solely on technology-driven approaches.

Conclusion

Learning Management Systems have transformed the way educational content is delivered, assessed, and managed. By leveraging the benefits of LMS platforms, educators can create engaging and personalized learning experiences for students. Effective implementation of an LMS requires careful planning, training, and continuous improvement to fully leverage its potential in supporting student success. As technology continues to evolve, Learning Management Systems will remain a vital tool for educators in the digital age of education.

Implementing Multimedia in Teaching

In today's digital age, teachers have an array of tools at their disposal to enhance the learning experience for their students. One such tool is multimedia, which refers to the combined use of various forms of media, such as text, images, videos, and audio, to convey information and engage learners. Implementing multimedia in teaching can have numerous benefits, including increased student engagement, improved retention of information, and enhanced critical thinking skills. In this section, we will explore the principles and strategies for effectively integrating multimedia into the classroom.

Principles of Multimedia Integration

When incorporating multimedia into teaching, it is important to consider some fundamental principles:

1. **Alignment with learning objectives:** Multimedia should be aligned with the intended learning outcomes. It should reinforce key concepts and provide relevant examples to enhance understanding.

2. **Engagement and interactivity:** Multimedia should be designed to captivate students' attention and promote active participation. Interactive elements, such as quizzes or simulations, can aid in the exploration and application of knowledge.

3. **Accessibility and inclusivity:** It is essential to ensure that multimedia resources are accessible to all students, including those with disabilities. Captions, transcripts, and alternative formats should be provided when necessary.

4. **Integration with existing pedagogy:** Multimedia should be seamlessly integrated into instructional practices, complementing rather than replacing traditional teaching methods. It should be used as a tool to enhance teaching and learning processes.

5. **Consistency and organization:** Multimedia materials should be well-structured and consistently formatted. Clear navigation options and logical sequencing will help students navigate and make sense of the content.

6. **Appropriate use of media:** The choice of media should align with the content and learning objectives. Different media formats can be employed to cater to different learning styles and preferences.

Strategies for Implementing Multimedia

To effectively implement multimedia in teaching, educators can employ various strategies:

1. **Selecting and Creating Multimedia Materials:** Teachers can choose from a wide range of multimedia resources available online or create their own. It is essential to evaluate the quality, accuracy, and relevance of the materials before using them in the classroom. When creating multimedia content, teachers should consider the principles of design, including visual appeal, clarity of information, and appropriate use of colors and fonts.

2. **Integrating multimedia in presentations:** Multimedia elements can be incorporated into presentations to make them more engaging and interactive. Teachers can enhance traditional PowerPoint slides by adding images, videos, and audio clips. They can use animations and transitions to emphasize key points and guide students' attention.

3. **Flipped classroom approach:** In a flipped classroom model, students learn new content outside of class through multimedia resources, such as videos or online modules. In-class time is then devoted to discussions, collaborative activities, and problem-solving. This approach allows for more personalized and interactive learning experiences.

4. **Multimedia projects and assignments:** Assignments that involve creating multimedia projects can encourage students to actively explore and apply knowledge. For example, students can create videos, podcasts, or interactive presentations to demonstrate their understanding of a particular topic. This not only reinforces their learning but also develops their creativity and digital literacy skills.

5. **Virtual simulations and games:** Virtual simulations and educational games can provide immersive learning experiences by allowing students to apply concepts in a realistic and engaging environment. For example, a virtual chemistry lab can allow students to conduct experiments without the need for physical equipment. These tools can enhance problem-solving skills while making learning enjoyable.

6. **Online discussion platforms and collaboration tools:** Utilizing online discussion platforms and collaboration tools can foster communication and collaboration among students. Multimedia elements, such as videos or images, can be shared and discussed, allowing for a deeper understanding of the topics. These platforms also provide opportunities for students to provide feedback and support their peers.

Example: Multimedia Integration in a History Lesson

Let's consider an example of how multimedia can be effectively integrated into a history lesson on World War II. The learning objective is for students to understand the causes and consequences of the war. Here are some strategies for implementing multimedia:

- **Selecting multimedia resources:** The teacher can curate a collection of videos, images, and audio recordings that provide different perspectives on the war. These resources can include documentaries, interviews with veterans, historic photographs, and speeches.

- **Interactive presentation:** The teacher can create an engaging PowerPoint presentation that incorporates multimedia elements. For instance, they can include maps with animated arrows to show the progression of the war, audio clips of significant speeches, and photographs of key events.

- **Virtual tour:** To deepen students' understanding, the teacher can utilize virtual reality technology to take students on a virtual tour of important historical sites. This immersive experience can help students visualize the locations and gain a greater appreciation for the events that occurred.

- **Role-playing game:** Students can participate in a role-playing game where they assume the roles of political leaders or soldiers during the war. This game can be facilitated through an online platform that incorporates multimedia elements, such as video clips or audio recordings of simulated conversations.

- **Collaborative multimedia project:** As a culminating activity, students can work in groups to create multimedia presentations about specific aspects of the war, such as the Holocaust or major battles. They can combine images, videos, and audio recordings to convey their research findings and present their projects to the class.

By implementing these strategies, the history lesson becomes a multimodal learning experience that caters to different learning styles and encourages active engagement. The use of multimedia elements not only enhances students' understanding of the subject matter but also promotes critical thinking, creativity, and collaboration skills.

Conclusion

Multimedia integration in teaching offers exciting possibilities to create dynamic and engaging learning experiences. By aligning multimedia with learning objectives, employing interactive strategies, and utilizing appropriate technologies, educators can optimize student engagement and foster deeper understanding. However, it is important to ensure that multimedia resources are accessible, well-organized, and integrated thoughtfully into existing pedagogical practices. By leveraging the power of multimedia, educators can empower their students with a rich and immersive learning environment.

Engaging Students in Online Discussions

Engaging students in online discussions is a crucial aspect of technology integration in the classroom. Online discussions provide a platform for students to collaborate, exchange ideas, and deepen their understanding of the subject matter. In this section, we will explore various strategies and considerations for effectively engaging students in online discussions.

Benefits of Online Discussions

Online discussions offer several advantages over traditional face-to-face discussions. First and foremost, they provide a space for all students to participate and contribute actively. In a physical classroom setting, some students may feel hesitant to speak up or may be overshadowed by their more vocal peers. Online discussions give every student an equal opportunity to express their thoughts and insights.

Additionally, online discussions encourage critical thinking and increase student engagement. By discussing topics asynchronously, students have more time to reflect on their ideas and compose well-thought-out responses. This leads to deeper learning and more meaningful discussions.

Furthermore, online discussions promote collaboration and peer learning. Students can provide feedback, ask questions, and learn from their classmates' perspectives. This collaborative approach fosters a sense of community and encourages students to build on each other's ideas.

Strategies for Effective Online Discussions

To promote effective online discussions, teachers can implement the following strategies:

Establish clear expectations and guidelines: Before beginning online discussions, it is essential to establish clear expectations and guidelines for participation. This includes guidelines for respectful communication, required frequency of contributions, and expectations regarding the quality of responses. Clear guidelines ensure that students understand their responsibilities and contribute meaningfully to the discussions.

Pose open-ended questions: To spark thoughtful discussion, teachers should pose open-ended questions that encourage critical thinking and multiple perspectives. Open-ended questions invite students to analyze, evaluate, and apply their knowledge, fostering deeper engagement and stimulating meaningful conversations among students.

Encourage active participation: Teachers can encourage active participation by ensuring that every student has an opportunity to contribute. This can be achieved by using the "think-pair-share" technique, where students first think about and prepare their responses individually, then discuss their ideas in pairs or small groups before sharing with the larger online discussion forum. This approach increases student confidence and promotes active engagement.

Promote peer interaction: Teachers should actively facilitate peer interaction by encouraging students to respond to each other's posts. This can be done through structured prompts or explicitly assigning students the task of providing feedback to their peers. Peer interaction enhances collaboration, encourages diverse perspectives, and builds a sense of community within the online discussion forum.

Provide timely feedback: Teachers should provide timely and constructive feedback on students' contributions to the online discussions. Timely feedback acknowledges students' involvement, reinforces desired behavior, and corrects misconceptions. Feedback should be specific, encouraging, and focused on the quality of thinking and communication.

Overcoming Challenges

While online discussions offer numerous benefits, they can also present challenges. Here are some common challenges and strategies for overcoming them:

Lack of participation: Some students may be reluctant to participate in online discussions or may struggle to articulate their thoughts in writing. To encourage participation, teachers can provide scaffolding activities, such as brainstorming or concept mapping, to help students organize their ideas before contributing. Additionally, teachers can create a supportive and inclusive online environment where students feel comfortable expressing their opinions.

Superficial responses: In some cases, students may provide brief or superficial responses to online discussion prompts. Teachers can address this issue by modeling high-quality responses and providing rubrics that outline expectations for depth and thoughtfulness. Encouraging students to ask probing questions and challenging them to support their arguments with evidence can also promote deeper engagement and analysis.

Time management: Teachers need to manage the time students spend on online discussions effectively. Setting clear deadlines and guidelines for participation can help ensure that all students have an opportunity to contribute. Additionally, teachers can provide time-management strategies and resources to help students allocate their time effectively between online discussions and other assignments.

Example Activity: Debating Ethical Dilemmas

To illustrate the engaging potential of online discussions, let's consider an example activity on debating ethical dilemmas.
  1. The teacher introduces a current ethical dilemma relevant to the subject (e.g., genetic engineering). 2. Students are divided into groups and assigned different perspectives on the issue (e.g., pro-genetic engineering, anti-genetic engineering). 3. Each group conducts research to gather evidence supporting their assigned perspective. 4. Students share their findings and arguments in an online discussion forum. 5. Students engage in respectful debate, responding to each other's arguments and providing counterarguments supported by evidence. 6. The teacher moderates the discussion, highlighting strong arguments and facilitating constructive dialogue. 7. After the debate, students reflect on their learning, identifying new insights gained and considering alternative perspectives.

This activity promotes critical thinking, research skills, and respectful communication while also leveraging the benefits of online discussions.

Additional Resources

For further exploration of engaging students in online discussions, the following resources are recommended:

- *Enhancing Online Discussions: A Pedagogical Handbook* by Jennifer C. Richardson
- *Online Teaching at Its Best: A Merger of Instructional Design with Teaching and Learning Research* by Linda B. Nilson and Ludwika A. Goodson
- *Discussion-Based Online Teaching to Enhance Student Learning: Theory, Practice, and Assessment* edited by Tisha Bender
- *Facilitating Online Learning: Effective Strategies for Moderators* by George Collison, Bonnie Elbaum, Sarah Haavind, and Robert Tinker

These resources provide comprehensive guides and practical tips for engaging students in online discussions.

In conclusion, engaging students in online discussions is an effective way to promote collaboration, critical thinking, and active learning. By implementing strategies like establishing clear expectations, posing open-ended questions, encouraging peer interaction, and providing timely feedback, teachers can create meaningful and vibrant online learning communities. Through well-designed activities and thoughtful facilitation, online discussions can significantly enhance the educational experience and deepen students' understanding of the subject matter.

Assessing Student Learning in Blended Learning Environments

Assessing student learning is a crucial aspect of education, as it allows teachers to gauge the effectiveness of their instruction and helps students understand their progress and areas for improvement. In blended learning environments, where both online and face-to-face instruction are combined, assessment strategies need to be tailored to accommodate the unique characteristics of this approach. This section explores various methods and considerations for assessing student learning in blended learning environments.

Importance of Assessment in Blended Learning

In a blended learning environment, students engage with content and interact with their peers and teachers in both online and face-to-face settings. With this blended approach, traditional assessment methods may not be sufficient to capture the full range of learning experiences and outcomes. Therefore, it is essential to employ a variety of strategies that align with the blended learning model to assess student learning effectively.

Assessment in blended learning serves several purposes:

- **Monitoring student progress:** Regular assessment allows teachers to monitor individual student progress and identify areas where additional support or intervention may be needed.

- **Providing feedback:** Timely and constructive feedback is crucial for student growth and improvement. Assessments provide an opportunity for teachers to offer feedback on students' strengths and areas for development.

- **Demonstrating mastery of content:** Assessments in blended learning help students demonstrate their understanding and mastery of course content and competencies.

- **Informing instruction:** Assessment data can inform instructional decisions, such as adjusting the pace, content, or delivery methods, to better meet students' needs.

Given the diverse nature of blended learning environments, assessment strategies should reflect the integration of online and offline learning activities, as well as the use of technology tools and resources.

Multiple Assessment Methods

To ensure a comprehensive understanding of student learning in blended environments, a combination of assessment methods should be utilized. Here are some effective assessment methods for blended learning:

1. **Online quizzes and tests:** Online quizzes and tests can be used to assess students' understanding of content covered in online modules. These assessments can provide immediate feedback to students and track their progress over time.

2. **Projects and presentations:** Assigning project-based tasks or presentations that require students to apply knowledge gained from both online and face-to-face components can assess their ability to synthesize information and effectively communicate their findings.

3. **Discussion forums and online participation:** Monitoring students' participation in online discussion forums and their contributions to collaborative activities can provide insights into their engagement and understanding of the material.

4. **Peer assessment and self-reflection:** Encouraging students to assess and provide feedback to their peers' work can promote self-reflection and improve critical thinking skills. This can be done through online platforms or in face-to-face discussions.

5. **Traditional assessments:** While blended learning emphasizes the use of technology, traditional assessments like in-class exams and quizzes should not be overlooked. These assessments can help gauge students' understanding and retention of face-to-face instruction and provide a balanced evaluation.

By incorporating a variety of assessment methods, teachers can obtain a holistic view of students' learning in blended learning environments.

Challenges and Solutions

Assessing student learning in blended learning environments comes with its own set of challenges. Here are some common challenges and practical solutions:

1. **Ensuring integrity in online assessments:** Online assessments may raise concerns about academic integrity, as students can access external resources. To address this, teachers can design assessments that require critical thinking and problem-solving skills rather than simple recall of information. Additionally, tools like online proctoring and plagiarism checkers can help maintain academic integrity.

2. **Balancing assessment load:** Blended learning often involves a combination of online and face-to-face activities, which may result in an increased assessment load. Teachers should carefully plan and distribute assessments to avoid overwhelming students with a heavy workload. They can also

utilize technology tools for auto-grading and providing immediate feedback to save time.

3. **Adapting assessments for diverse learners:** Blended learning caters to diverse learners with varying needs and preferences. Assessments should be designed to accommodate different learning styles, multiple intelligences, and accessibility requirements. Providing options for assessment formats and allowing students to demonstrate their understanding through various means can promote inclusivity.

4. **Collecting and analyzing data:** Blended learning generates a vast amount of data, which can be overwhelming for teachers to analyze and utilize effectively. Teachers can leverage learning management systems and data analytics tools to streamline data collection and gain valuable insights into student learning. Professional development opportunities and collaboration with data specialists can also enhance teachers' data literacy skills.

Case Study: Assessing Problem-Solving Skills in Blended Learning

To illustrate the assessment process in a blended learning environment, let's consider a case study focused on assessing problem-solving skills in a mathematics course.

In this scenario, the online component of the course includes video lessons, interactive problem-solving simulations, and online exercises for students to practice mathematical concepts. The face-to-face component involves group discussions and problem-solving tasks that promote collaboration and real-world application of mathematical skills.

To assess students' problem-solving skills, a multi-faceted approach can be implemented:

1. **Online quizzes:** Regular online quizzes can assess students' understanding of mathematical concepts and problem-solving techniques covered in online modules. The immediate feedback provided by the quizzes can guide students' learning and help them identify areas for improvement.

2. **Group problem-solving tasks:** In the face-to-face sessions, students can work collaboratively on open-ended problem-solving tasks. This assesses their ability to apply mathematical knowledge and communicate their problem-solving strategies effectively. Teachers can observe and provide feedback during these sessions.

3. **Portfolio assessment:** Students can maintain a digital portfolio that showcases their problem-solving skills. They can document their approaches to solving complex problems and reflect on the strategies used. This provides students with an opportunity for self-assessment and helps teachers evaluate their metacognitive skills.

By utilizing a blend of online quizzes, group problem-solving tasks, and portfolio assessment, teachers can gain insights into students' problem-solving abilities from different angles.

Conclusion

Assessing student learning in blended learning environments requires a thoughtful and diversified approach that aligns with the unique characteristics of this instructional model. By combining multiple assessment methods, addressing inherent challenges, and leveraging technology tools, teachers can effectively evaluate student progress and inform instructional decisions. Blended learning provides an opportunity to assess students' learning in a holistic manner, taking into account both online and face-to-face experiences. Embracing these assessment strategies will help foster a more engaging and inclusive learning environment.

Professional Development for Technology Integration

In order to successfully integrate technology into the classroom, teachers must undergo professional development to enhance their skills and knowledge. Professional development plays a crucial role in preparing educators for the effective use of technology in instruction and creating a technology-rich learning environment. This section will explore the importance of professional development for technology integration, strategies for implementation, and the evaluation of its impact.

Importance of Professional Development for Technology Integration

Technology is constantly evolving, and educators must keep up with the latest tools and strategies to effectively incorporate them into their teaching practices. Professional development provides teachers with the necessary skills and knowledge to integrate technology in meaningful and innovative ways. It helps them stay current with emerging technologies, improves their digital literacy skills, and boosts their confidence in using technology in the classroom.

Additionally, professional development for technology integration helps teachers develop pedagogical skills that align with the use of technology. It guides educators in understanding how to leverage technology to enhance student engagement, differentiate instruction, promote collaboration and communication, and develop critical thinking skills. By providing teachers with the necessary training and support, professional development empowers them to become effective facilitators of technology-enhanced learning experiences.

Strategies for Professional Development

Effective professional development for technology integration should be ongoing, collaborative, and tailored to the specific needs of educators. Here are some strategies for implementing professional development in this area:

1. **Needs Assessment:** Conduct a needs assessment to identify the technology skills and knowledge gaps of educators. This can be done through surveys, interviews, or observations. The results of the needs assessment will help guide the development of targeted professional development activities.

2. **Individualized Learning Plans:** Create individualized learning plans for teachers based on their needs and goals. Consider their current skill level, comfort with technology, and the specific needs of their students. These plans can include a combination of self-paced online courses, workshops, conferences, and coaching.

3. **Collaborative Learning Communities:** Establish collaborative learning communities where educators can share ideas, resources, and experiences related to technology integration. This can be done through professional learning networks, online forums, or regular team meetings. Encourage teachers to collaborate with their peers and learn from each other's successes and challenges.

4. **Hands-on Workshops:** Provide hands-on workshops that allow teachers to explore new technologies and instructional strategies. These workshops should be interactive and provide opportunities for educators to experiment with technology tools, practice integrating them into their lessons, and receive feedback from their peers.

5. **Coaching and Mentoring:** Offer one-on-one coaching or mentoring for teachers who need additional support in implementing technology in their classrooms. Trained coaches or mentors can provide personalized guidance, model effective technology integration strategies, and help teachers troubleshoot challenges.

6. **Just-in-Time Support:** Provide just-in-time support and resources to teachers as they integrate technology into their instruction. This can include quick

reference guides, online tutorials, video demonstrations, and access to an online community where teachers can ask questions and seek advice.

7. **Peer Observations:** Encourage teachers to conduct peer observations focused on technology integration. This allows educators to learn from each other by observing how technology is used in different classrooms and sharing feedback and reflections.

8. **Partnerships with External Experts:** Collaborate with external experts, such as technology specialists or educational consultants, to provide specialized training or workshops on specific technologies or instructional strategies.

Evaluation of Professional Development

To ensure the effectiveness of professional development for technology integration, it is important to evaluate its impact on educators and students. Here are some evaluation strategies to consider:

1. **Surveys and Interviews:** Gather feedback from teachers who have participated in professional development activities. Use surveys and interviews to assess their perceived skill growth, confidence in using technology, and the impact on their instructional practices.

2. **Classroom Observations:** Conduct classroom observations to observe how teachers are integrating technology into their lessons. Look for evidence of effective technology integration, student engagement, and the use of technology to enhance learning outcomes.

3. **Student Feedback:** Seek feedback from students to understand their experiences with technology integration in the classroom. Use surveys or focus groups to gather their perspectives on how technology has impacted their learning, engagement, and motivation.

4. **Student Performance Data:** Analyze student performance data to assess whether technology integration has had a positive impact on student achievement. Compare performance data before and after the implementation of technology-rich instructional practices.

5. **Teacher Reflections and Portfolios:** Encourage teachers to reflect on their experiences with technology integration and document their growth through portfolios or reflective journals. This provides valuable insights into their professional development journey and can inform future initiatives.

6. **Long-term Evaluation:** Evaluate the long-term impact of professional development for technology integration by tracking the career trajectories of participating teachers. Determine whether they continue to effectively integrate

technology, lead technology initiatives, or serve as technology mentors to their colleagues.

Addressing Challenges and Ethical Considerations

While professional development is essential for technology integration, there are challenges and ethical considerations to be mindful of. Some challenges include lack of funding, limited access to technology resources, time constraints, and resistance to change. It is important to address these challenges through thoughtful planning, resource allocation, and support from administration.

Ethical considerations include ensuring equity of access to technology resources, promoting digital citizenship and responsible use of technology, and maintaining student privacy and data security. Professional development should address these ethical considerations by providing teachers with guidance, strategies, and resources to navigate these issues in their classrooms.

Conclusion

Professional development plays a critical role in preparing educators for effective technology integration. By providing teachers with ongoing support, guidance, and training, professional development empowers them to incorporate technology in ways that enhance student engagement, promote collaboration and critical thinking, and prepare students for the digital age. Through a combination of targeted strategies, thoughtful evaluation, and addressing challenges and ethical considerations, professional development can create a culture of technology integration and ensure positive outcomes for both educators and students.

Evaluating the Impact of Technology Integration

One of the key aspects of integrating technology in the classroom is evaluating its impact on teaching and learning. This process involves assessing the effectiveness of technology tools and strategies in achieving learning objectives, improving student outcomes, and enhancing the overall educational experience. In this section, we will explore various approaches and methods for evaluating the impact of technology integration in the classroom.

Importance of Evaluation

Evaluation plays a crucial role in determining whether technology integration initiatives are successful and if they are aligned with the intended goals. By evaluating the impact of technology, educators can make informed decisions regarding the adoption, implementation, and improvement of technology integration strategies. Additionally, evaluation provides valuable insights into the strengths and weaknesses of different technologies and their suitability for specific learning contexts.

Key Considerations

When evaluating the impact of technology integration, certain factors should be taken into account to ensure a comprehensive and meaningful assessment. These considerations include:

1. **Alignment with Learning Objectives:** Evaluate how well the technology aligns with the learning goals and objectives of the curriculum. Assess whether it enhances the desired outcomes and supports the development of key competencies.

2. **Engagement and Participation:** Measure the level of student engagement and active participation facilitated by the technology. Evaluate whether it promotes collaboration, critical thinking, problem-solving, and creativity among students.

3. **Effectiveness of Instructional Design:** Assess the effectiveness of the instructional design in utilizing technology tools and resources. Evaluate whether the technology enhances instruction, differentiates learning, and provides opportunities for personalized learning experiences.

4. **Student Learning Outcomes:** Evaluate the impact of technology integration on student learning outcomes. Measure improvements in knowledge and skills acquisition, information retention, and the ability to transfer learning to real-world contexts.

5. **Assessment and Feedback:** Assess how technology supports and enhances the assessment and feedback processes. Evaluate whether it enables ongoing formative assessment, timely feedback, and opportunities for self-assessment and reflection.

6. **Teacher and Student Perspectives:** Gather feedback from teachers and students regarding their experiences with technology integration. Consider their perceptions, attitudes, and opinions on the effectiveness, usability, and relevance of the technology.

Methods of Evaluation

To evaluate the impact of technology integration, a variety of methods and tools can be employed. Here are some commonly used evaluation methods:

1. **Surveys and Questionnaires:** Administer surveys and questionnaires to collect quantitative and qualitative data on students' and teachers' experiences with technology integration. This can provide valuable insights into attitudes, perceptions, and satisfaction levels.

2. **Observations and Interviews:** Conduct classroom observations and interviews with teachers and students to gather firsthand information on the impact of technology integration. This qualitative data can provide deeper insights into the dynamics of teaching and learning with technology.

3. **Data Analysis:** Analyze student performance data, such as test scores, assignments, and projects, to assess the impact of technology integration on learning outcomes. Compare performance data before and after technology implementation to identify trends and improvements.

4. **Case Studies:** Conduct in-depth case studies to examine the impact of technology integration in specific educational settings or subject areas. Case studies provide a holistic view of the benefits and challenges associated with technology integration.

5. **Focus Groups:** Organize focus group discussions with teachers, students, and other stakeholders to gather multiple perspectives on the impact of technology integration. This interactive method allows for rich discussions and a deeper understanding of the experiences and outcomes.

6. **Action Research:** Implement action research projects where teachers systematically investigate the impact of technology integration in their own classrooms. This collaborative and iterative approach allows for continuous reflection and improvement.

Challenges and Strategies

Evaluating the impact of technology integration can present several challenges. These challenges include the complex nature of educational environments, the lack of standardized evaluation frameworks, and the dynamic and ever-evolving nature of technology itself. To address these challenges, educators can employ various strategies:

1. **Establish Clear Evaluation Goals:** Clearly define the evaluation goals and objectives to ensure a focused and purposeful evaluation process. This will guide the selection of evaluation methods and the collection of relevant data.

2. **Use Multiple Measures:** Employ a combination of quantitative and qualitative measures to gather a comprehensive understanding of the impact of technology integration. This multi-dimensional approach provides a more nuanced view of the outcomes.

3. **Adopt Longitudinal Approaches:** Consider conducting evaluations over an extended period to capture the long-term impact of technology integration. This allows for the identification of sustained effects and the exploration of evolving trends.

4. **Engage Stakeholders:** Involve teachers, students, parents, administrators, and other stakeholders in the evaluation process. Their input and perspectives can provide valuable insights and ensure the evaluation captures a diverse range of experiences.

5. **Continuously Improve:** Emphasize a culture of continuous improvement by using evaluation findings to inform decision-making and enhance technology integration strategies. Regularly review and update evaluation plans based on emerging needs and priorities.

Real-World Example

To illustrate the evaluation of technology integration, let's consider a real-world example. Imagine a high school implementing a flipped classroom model with the use of online instructional videos and collaborative digital tools. The school administration wants to evaluate the impact of this technology integration initiative on student engagement and academic achievement.

To assess engagement, the school conducts surveys among students to gather their perceptions of the flipped classroom experience, their level of active participation, and the impact on their motivation to learn. The data collected from the surveys provides insights into the effectiveness of the technology in promoting engagement and collaboration.

To measure academic achievement, the school compares student performance data, such as test scores and homework completion rates, before and after implementing the flipped classroom model. The analysis reveals any improvements in academic outcomes and knowledge retention attributed to technology integration.

Additionally, the school organizes focus group discussions with teachers and students to gather qualitative feedback on the strengths and weaknesses of the flipped classroom model. This information helps identify areas for improvement and informs future decision-making regarding technology integration.

By utilizing a combination of surveys, data analysis, and focus groups, the school can comprehensively evaluate the impact of technology integration and make informed decisions regarding the continuation and improvement of the flipped classroom model.

Conclusion

Evaluating the impact of technology integration in the classroom is essential for ensuring its effectiveness and identifying areas that require improvement. By aligning technology with learning objectives, assessing engagement and participation, measuring student learning outcomes, and gathering feedback from teachers and students, educators can gain valuable insights into the impact of technology on teaching and learning. By employing various evaluation methods, addressing challenges, and continuously improving technology integration strategies, educators can maximize the benefits of technology in the classroom and create a more engaging and effective learning environment.

Ethical Considerations in Technology Integration

As technology becomes more prevalent in educational settings, it is crucial to consider the ethical implications of its integration. While technology offers numerous benefits in enhancing teaching and learning experiences, it also raises ethical concerns that need to be addressed to ensure its responsible use. In this section, we will explore some of the key ethical considerations in technology integration and discuss strategies for mitigating potential risks.

Student Data Privacy and Security

One of the primary ethical concerns in technology integration is the protection of student data privacy and security. With the increasing use of digital tools and online platforms, student information is often collected, stored, and shared electronically. It is essential to safeguard this data to prevent unauthorized access and misuse.

To address this concern, educators and school administrators must establish clear policies and procedures for data collection, storage, and sharing. They should ensure that student data is only used for educational purposes and that it is collected with parental consent. Additionally, schools should employ robust security measures to protect the data from cyber threats and regularly update their systems to address any vulnerabilities.

Furthermore, educators should educate students about the importance of data privacy and digital citizenship. Teaching students about responsible online behavior and the potential risks associated with sharing personal information can empower them to make informed decisions and protect their privacy.

Equitable Access to Technology

Integrating technology in the classroom raises ethical concerns regarding equitable access for all students. Not all students may have the same access to technology resources outside of school, which can create a digital divide and impact their learning opportunities.

To address this concern, educators can implement strategies to ensure equitable access to technology. This may include providing devices and internet access to students who do not have them at home or leveraging school resources to ensure equal opportunities for all. Additionally, educators should design activities that allow for both digital and non-digital participation to accommodate students with limited access to technology.

Moreover, it is crucial to consider the potential bias in relying heavily on technology for instruction. Educators must be mindful of not assuming that all students have the same level of technological proficiency or access, and they should provide support and resources to bridge any gaps.

Digital Citizenship and Responsible Technology Use

Technology integration in education necessitates the development of digital citizenship skills in students. Digital citizenship refers to the responsible and ethical use of technology, including appropriate online behavior, digital literacy, and the ability to evaluate information critically.

Educators should incorporate digital citizenship education into their curriculum and teach students about the rights and responsibilities of using technology. This includes topics such as online etiquette, responsible use of social media, digital footprints, and understanding the consequences of cyberbullying and online harassment.

Furthermore, educators should model responsible technology use and provide guidance on navigating the digital world. They can create opportunities for discussions about ethical dilemmas related to technology and guide students in making ethical decisions in different scenarios.

Intellectual Property and Copyright Issues

Technology integration often involves using digital resources, such as educational software, multimedia content, and online materials. Ethical considerations arise regarding the fair use of these resources and respecting intellectual property rights.

Educators should ensure that they are using digital resources in compliance with copyright laws and licensing agreements. They should guide students on the importance of giving credit to the original creators of the content and teach them how to cite and reference sources appropriately.

To address these concerns, educators can also provide lessons on digital literacy and critical evaluation of online sources. Teaching students how to identify credible sources, avoid plagiarism, and respect intellectual property rights is essential in promoting ethical behavior in technology use.

Technology Addiction and Mental Health

Technology integration should also take into account the potential risks of technology addiction and its impact on students' mental health. Excessive use of technology can lead to issues such as decreased attention spans, sleep disturbances, and social isolation.

Educators should promote a healthy balance between technology use and other activities. They can incorporate digital wellness practices into their curriculum, such as regular breaks from screens, mindfulness exercises, and fostering face-to-face interactions.

Moreover, educators should be vigilant in identifying signs of technology addiction or mental health issues related to technology use. They should collaborate with school counselors and support services to provide guidance and intervention when needed.

Professional Ethics and Boundaries

Lastly, ethical considerations in technology integration extend to the professional conduct of educators. Maintaining professional ethics and appropriate boundaries when using technology in educational settings is essential.

Educators should adhere to professional codes of conduct and follow school policies regarding technology use. They should avoid engaging in inappropriate or unprofessional online interactions with students and maintain a respectful and safe online environment.

Furthermore, educators should strive for continuous professional development and stay informed about emerging technologies and their ethical implications. This will enable them to make informed decisions and implement responsible and ethical technology integration practices.

In conclusion, the integration of technology in education brings numerous benefits but also raises ethical concerns. By addressing and mitigating these concerns, educators can ensure the responsible and ethical use of technology in promoting student learning and well-being. Through clear policies, education on digital citizenship, equitable access, and professional ethics, technology integration can be harnessed to its full potential while ensuring the protection, privacy, and well-being of students.

Building Digital Citizenship Skills

In the digital age, the ability to navigate and utilize technology responsibly has become increasingly important. This section focuses on building digital citizenship skills, which refer to the appropriate and responsible use of technology. Digital citizenship encompasses various elements, including online etiquette, digital rights and responsibilities, cyberbullying prevention, and digital literacy.

Understanding Digital Citizenship

Digital citizenship involves the responsible and ethical use of technology, ensuring that individuals are active participants in the digital world while understanding its potential risks and challenges. It is essential for students to develop these skills to protect themselves and others and to make informed decisions in the online environment.

Digital Rights and Responsibilities

Digital citizenship includes understanding one's digital rights and responsibilities. This includes the right to privacy, freedom of speech, and the responsibility to respect copyright laws. Students should be aware of their digital footprints, the information they share online, and the potential consequences of their actions.

Online Etiquette

Online etiquette, also known as netiquette, refers to the proper behavior and manners when engaging with others online. It encompasses aspects such as being respectful, using appropriate language and tone, and understanding cultural differences in online interactions. Teaching students about online etiquette fosters positive and respectful online communication.

Cyberbullying Prevention

Cyberbullying is a significant issue in the digital age. Building digital citizenship skills involves teaching students how to prevent and respond to cyberbullying incidents. This includes educating them about the impact of cyberbullying on individuals and communities, promoting empathy and kindness online, and teaching strategies for safe reporting and intervention.

Digital Literacy

Developing digital citizenship skills also involves promoting digital literacy. Digital literacy encompasses the ability to find, evaluate, and utilize information online effectively. Students should be taught critical thinking skills to assess the credibility of online sources, distinguish between reliable and unreliable information, and understand the ethical use of digital content.

Resources and Strategies

Building digital citizenship skills requires a comprehensive approach that integrates various resources and strategies. Here are a few examples:

- **Digital Citizenship Curriculum:** Implement a structured curriculum that covers the different aspects of digital citizenship, providing students with a foundation of knowledge and skills.

- **Open Discussions:** Engage students in open discussions about digital citizenship, allowing them to express their opinions, share their experiences, and learn from one another.

- **Real-World Examples:** Use real-world examples of digital citizenship issues, such as online privacy breaches or cyberbullying cases, to illustrate the importance of responsible digital behavior.

- **Role-Playing Activities:** Organize role-playing activities where students can practice responding to challenging online situations, such as a friend asking for personal information or witnessing cyberbullying.

- **Collaborative Projects:** Encourage collaborative projects that require students to work together online, promoting teamwork, communication, and respectful online behavior.

- **Guest Speakers:** Invite guest speakers, such as cybersecurity experts, educators, or individuals who have experienced cyberbullying, to share their expertise and personal stories with students.

- **Digital Citizenship Pledge:** Have students create a digital citizenship pledge, outlining their commitment to responsible and ethical online behavior. Display the pledges in the classroom as a reminder of the importance of digital citizenship.

Challenges and Solutions

Building digital citizenship skills can present challenges, but there are strategies to address them:

Limited Resources: Some schools may have limited resources to dedicate to digital citizenship education. In such cases, leveraging free online resources, collaborating with community organizations, or integrating digital citizenship topics into existing subjects can help overcome these limitations.

Keeping Up with Technology: Technology evolves rapidly, and it can be challenging for educators to keep up. Engaging in professional development opportunities, joining online communities, and staying updated on the latest trends and tools can help educators stay ahead and provide relevant information to students.

Parental Involvement: Educating parents about digital citizenship and involving them in the process is crucial. Holding workshops, providing resources for parents, and encouraging open communication can foster a collaborative approach to digital citizenship education.

Exercises

1. Research and prepare a short presentation on a real-world case of cyberbullying. Discuss the impact of cyberbullying on the victim, the community, and the potential legal consequences for the perpetrator.

2. Conduct a group activity where students evaluate the credibility of online sources. Provide them with various websites and articles and ask them to identify the reliable sources based on specific criteria.

3. Organize a debate on the topic of freedom of speech online. Divide the class into two groups, one supporting unrestricted freedom of speech and the other advocating for limitations in certain situations. Encourage students to present their arguments based on real-life examples and ethical considerations.

4. Create an infographic or poster highlighting the key principles of digital citizenship. Include information about rights and responsibilities, online etiquette, and strategies for addressing cyberbullying. Display the final products in the classroom or school to raise awareness among students and staff.

Conclusion

Building digital citizenship skills is essential in today's technology-driven world. By focusing on digital rights and responsibilities, online etiquette, cyberbullying prevention, and digital literacy, educators can empower students to become responsible digital citizens. Through targeted resources, open discussions, and practical activities, students can develop the necessary skills to navigate the digital landscape safely and ethically.

Creating Technology-Rich Learning Environments

In today's digital age, integrating technology in the classroom has become increasingly important to enhance student engagement, promote collaboration, and develop critical thinking skills. A technology-rich learning environment provides students with opportunities to explore, create, and connect with the world beyond the classroom walls. In this section, we will discuss various strategies and considerations for creating such an environment.

The Role of Technology in Education

Before diving into the specifics of creating technology-rich learning environments, let's first understand the role of technology in education. Technology can serve as a powerful tool to support teaching and learning in several ways:

1. Enhancing Student Engagement: Technology offers interactive and multimedia resources that can grab students' attention and make learning more enjoyable. For example, educational apps, online quizzes, and gamified learning platforms can motivate students to actively participate in their own learning process.

2. Facilitating Differentiated Instruction: Technology provides opportunities for personalized learning experiences. With the help of adaptive learning software and online platforms, educators can tailor instruction based on individual students' needs, interests, and learning styles.

3. Promoting Collaboration and Communication: Technology enables students to collaborate with peers, both locally and globally. Virtual classrooms,

BLENDED LEARNING AND FLIPPED CLASSROOM MODELS

video conferencing tools, and online discussion platforms foster communication and collaboration among students, breaking down geographical barriers.

4. Developing Critical Thinking Skills: Technology-rich environments encourage students to analyze, synthesize, and evaluate information. With access to online research tools, students can engage in higher-level thinking tasks, such as analyzing data, solving complex problems, and evaluating the reliability of sources.

Now, let's explore some strategies for creating technology-rich learning environments.

Strategies for Creating Technology-Rich Learning Environments

1. Providing Access to Technology: To create a technology-rich learning environment, it is essential to ensure that every student has access to the necessary devices and connectivity. This may involve securing funding for devices like laptops or tablets, establishing a reliable internet connection in the classroom, or implementing a bring-your-own-device (BYOD) policy.

2. Integrating Technology Across the Curriculum: Technology should not be viewed as a separate subject but rather an integral part of the curriculum. Educators should identify opportunities to infuse technology in different disciplines and subject areas. For example, science students can use virtual laboratories to conduct experiments, while language arts students can participate in online collaborative writing projects.

3. Providing Professional Development: Educators must be equipped with the necessary skills and knowledge to use technology effectively in the classroom. Professional development programs should be offered to teachers to enhance their digital literacy and introduce them to new tools and resources. These programs can be delivered through workshops, online courses, or mentoring.

4. Creating Flexible Learning Spaces: Technology-rich learning environments should include flexible spaces that accommodate different types of activities. Design classrooms that facilitate collaboration, provide areas for small group work, and offer comfortable seating arrangements. This flexibility allows students to work in various settings, both individually and collaboratively.

5. Ensuring Digital Citizenship: As students navigate the digital world, it is crucial to teach them about responsible and ethical technology use. Incorporate discussions about digital citizenship, online safety, and information literacy into the curriculum. Students should understand their rights, responsibilities, and the potential consequences of their online actions.

6. Encouraging Exploration and Experimentation: Technology-rich environments should foster a culture of exploration and experimentation.

Encourage students to explore new tools, experiment with different digital resources, and create their own content. This freedom to explore enhances creativity, problem-solving skills, and digital literacy.

Considerations and Challenges

While creating technology-rich learning environments offers numerous benefits, educators need to be mindful of potential challenges and considerations. Here are a few to keep in mind:

1. Access and Equity: Ensuring equal access to technology can be a challenge, especially in schools with limited resources or in rural areas with inadequate internet connectivity. Efforts must be made to bridge the digital divide and provide equitable learning opportunities for all students.

2. Technological Support: Technology can sometimes be unreliable or introduce unexpected technical issues. Schools should have a robust technical support system in place to address any technical glitches promptly. Regular maintenance, software updates, and adequate device management are crucial for a smooth learning experience.

3. Privacy and Security: With the integration of technology comes the need for data privacy and security. Schools must have policies and procedures in place to protect students' personal information and ensure safe online environments. Educators should teach students about cybersecurity and responsible online behavior.

4. Distractions and Digital Overload: While technology enhances learning, it can also be a source of distraction. Students may be tempted to engage in non-educational activities or multitask during class time. Educators should establish clear expectations and guidelines for technology use and monitor students' engagement.

Real-World Example

Let's consider a real-world example of creating a technology-rich learning environment in a social studies classroom. The teacher wants to integrate technology to enhance students' understanding of historical events and promote critical thinking. Here's how they do it:

1. Access to Technology: The school secures a set of laptops for the classroom, ensuring that every student has access to a device. The classroom is also equipped with a projector and a smart board, enabling the teacher to display multimedia resources.

2. Integrating Technology: The teacher incorporates online research tools, interactive timelines, and digital maps to supplement traditional textbooks. Students use laptops to conduct research, analyze primary sources, and create multimedia presentations. They also participate in online discussions to engage with their peers and discuss historical events.

3. Professional Development: The school provides professional development workshops for teachers to enhance their knowledge of technology integration in social studies. The teacher learns about new resources, strategies, and assessment tools that can be used to create a technology-rich learning environment.

4. Digital Citizenship: The teacher incorporates lessons on digital citizenship and the responsible use of online resources. Students learn about evaluating the reliability of online sources, respecting copyright, and protecting their personal information online.

5. Collaboration and Communication: The teacher promotes collaboration among students by assigning group projects that require online research and multimedia presentations. Students use collaborative online platforms to work together, share resources, and provide feedback to their peers.

By integrating technology in this way, the social studies classroom becomes a technology-rich learning environment that promotes active engagement, critical thinking, and collaboration among students.

Conclusion

Creating technology-rich learning environments is crucial in preparing students for the digital world and equipping them with the necessary skills for the 21st century. By providing access to technology, integrating it across the curriculum, offering professional development to teachers, and addressing concerns of access, equity, privacy, and digital citizenship, educators can create vibrant, engaging, and effective learning environments. Remember, the goal is not just to use technology for the sake of it, but to leverage its power to transform and enhance teaching and learning.

Emerging Technologies in Education

Virtual Reality and Augmented Reality

Virtual Reality (VR) and Augmented Reality (AR) are two groundbreaking technologies that have the power to reshape the way we learn, teach, and experience the world. These immersive technologies offer unique opportunities for education by creating simulated environments and enhancing real-world experiences with digital overlays. In this section, we will explore the principles, applications, and challenges of VR and AR in education.

Principles of Virtual Reality and Augmented Reality

Virtual Reality (VR) immerses users in a completely computer-generated environment, whereas Augmented Reality (AR) overlays digital content onto the real world. Both technologies rely on a combination of hardware devices and sophisticated software algorithms to create compelling experiences.

In VR, users typically wear a head-mounted display (HMD) that tracks their head movements, allowing them to explore and interact with the virtual environment in a realistic way. VR systems often include handheld controllers or other input devices that enable users to manipulate objects or navigate within the virtual space.

AR, on the other hand, is usually experienced through a smartphone or tablet, which acts as a window to the real world. By using the device's camera and sensors, AR apps can detect and analyze the user's surroundings. The digital content is then superimposed onto the live video feed, making it appear as if the virtual objects are part of the physical environment.

The key principle behind both VR and AR is immersion. By placing users in an interactive and lifelike environment, these technologies have the potential to enhance learning experiences, engage students, and promote active participation.

Applications of Virtual Reality and Augmented Reality in Education

Virtual Reality and Augmented Reality offer a wide range of applications in education. These technologies can be used across various disciplines and grade levels to bring abstract concepts to life, provide hands-on experiences, and foster deeper understanding.

In science education, VR can simulate complex experiments or phenomena that are difficult or dangerous to replicate in a traditional lab setting. Students can explore the human body in 3D, conduct virtual dissections, or even observe microscopic organisms in their natural habitat. AR, on the other hand, can overlay additional information or labels onto real-world objects, helping students visualize and understand complex structures or processes.

In history and social studies, VR can transport students to different time periods and locations, allowing them to experience historical events firsthand. They can virtually visit ancient civilizations, walk through famous landmarks, or interact with historical figures. AR can enhance field trips by providing additional contextual information or by overlaying virtual artifacts onto real-world exhibits.

In language learning, VR and AR can create immersive environments where students can practice their language skills. They can engage in virtual conversations with native speakers, explore culturally diverse settings, or even role-play in realistic scenarios.

Mathematics and geometry can also benefit from VR and AR. These technologies can help students visualize abstract concepts by providing interactive 3D models or by allowing them to manipulate geometric shapes in a virtual space. AR can overlay virtual measurements or annotations onto real objects, facilitating problem-solving and spatial reasoning skills.

Challenges and Considerations

Although Virtual Reality and Augmented Reality have great potential in education, there are several challenges and considerations that need to be addressed.

First, the cost of VR and AR hardware can be prohibitive for some educational institutions. HMDs, sensors, and other necessary equipment can be expensive, making it difficult for schools with limited budgets to adopt these technologies.

Second, there is a lack of standardized content and applications specifically designed for educational purposes. While there are some VR and AR educational resources available, the market is still in its early stages, and more development and refinement are needed.

Another challenge is the integration of VR and AR into existing curriculum and teaching practices. Teachers need support and training to effectively incorporate these technologies into their instruction. They also need to consider the potential distractions or discomfort that may arise from prolonged use of VR.

Privacy and safety concerns are also important considerations. VR and AR applications often require access to personal data or sensor information, and it is crucial to ensure the protection and ethical use of this data, especially when working with minors.

Lastly, it is important to recognize that VR and AR should not replace real-world experiences or human interactions. They should be used as tools to enhance learning, supplement traditional teaching methods, and provide opportunities for exploration and discovery.

Resources and Tools

Fortunately, there are already a variety of resources and tools available to support the integration of VR and AR in education.

Educational VR platforms, such as Google Expeditions or Nearpod VR, offer pre-made virtual field trips and lessons that cover a wide range of topics. These platforms provide teachers with ready-to-use content and allow students to explore and learn in an immersive virtual environment.

There are also tools and software development kits (SDKs) that allow teachers and students to create their own VR or AR experiences. Unity and Unreal Engine are popular game development engines that support VR and AR, providing a user-friendly interface to create interactive content.

For AR, apps like HP Reveal or Metaverse enable users to create their own augmented reality experiences. These apps allow students to design and integrate digital content into their physical surroundings, encouraging creativity and active participation.

Furthermore, universities and educational institutions are increasingly offering courses and workshops on VR and AR development, providing educators with the necessary skills and knowledge to effectively use these technologies in the classroom.

Conclusion

Virtual Reality and Augmented Reality have the potential to revolutionize education by creating immersive and interactive learning experiences. These technologies can transport students to different places and times, visualize abstract concepts, and provide hands-on experiences that were previously inaccessible.

However, it is important to approach the integration of VR and AR in education thoughtfully and with careful consideration. The cost, availability of content, teacher training, and ethical considerations should all be taken into account when implementing these technologies.

As the field of VR and AR continues to advance, it is crucial for educators to stay updated on the latest developments and best practices. By leveraging these innovative technologies, we can create engaging and meaningful learning experiences that prepare students to thrive in the digital age.

Artificial Intelligence and Machine Learning

Artificial Intelligence (AI) and its subfield, Machine Learning (ML), have become increasingly popular in various industries, including education. AI refers to the development of computer systems that can perform tasks that typically require human intelligence, such as understanding natural language, recognizing patterns, and making decisions. ML, on the other hand, is a subset of AI that focuses on designing algorithms that allow computers to learn and make predictions or decisions without explicit programming.

In the context of education, AI and ML offer great potential for enhancing teaching and learning experiences. They can assist educators in personalizing instruction, automating administrative tasks, and providing adaptive feedback to students. Let's explore the applications and benefits of AI and ML in education.

Automated Grading and Feedback

One of the time-consuming tasks for educators is grading assignments and providing feedback to students. AI and ML can help automate this process, enabling teachers to focus more on instructional planning and individualized support. Natural Language Processing (NLP) algorithms can analyze students' written responses, essays, or even code, and provide instant feedback based on predefined criteria or models trained on existing data. This not only saves time but also provides students with timely feedback, allowing them to improve their work more effectively.

Adaptive Learning Systems

AI and ML can power adaptive learning systems, which adjust instruction and content based on individual students' needs and progress. These systems can analyze data from student interactions, such as quiz responses, learning activities, and performance on assignments, to create personalized learning paths. By identifying students' strengths and weaknesses, adaptive learning systems can recommend appropriate learning materials, provide additional practice or remediation, and scaffold content to suit individual learning styles. This tailored approach promotes more efficient and effective learning outcomes for students.

Intelligent Tutoring Systems

Intelligent Tutoring Systems (ITS) leverage AI and ML to provide personalized guidance and support to students in a variety of subjects and domains. These systems use student data and learning models to create adaptive instruction, simulate human tutoring interactions, and provide real-time feedback and explanations. ITS can adapt to individual learning styles, provide targeted practice, and identify and address misconceptions. By personalizing the learning experience, students receive tailored instruction that meets their specific needs and promotes deeper understanding and mastery of the material.

Predictive Analytics

Predictive analytics is another application of AI and ML in education. By analyzing vast amounts of data, such as student demographics, attendance records, grades, and behavioral patterns, predictive models can forecast student outcomes and identify students who may need additional support. For example, ML algorithms can predict the likelihood of students dropping out or falling behind academically based on historical data. This early identification allows educators to intervene and provide targeted interventions to prevent negative outcomes and promote student success.

Ethical Considerations

While the integration of AI and ML in education brings many benefits, it also raises ethical considerations. It is crucial to ensure that student data privacy and security are protected. Educational institutions need to establish clear policies and guidelines for the collection, storage, and use of student data to prevent misuse or unauthorized access. Additionally, there should be transparency in how AI and ML algorithms reach their decisions to avoid algorithmic bias and to give educators and students the ability to understand and question the results.

Real-World Example

To illustrate the potential of AI and ML in education, consider the use of AI-powered chatbots in online teaching platforms. These chatbots can provide instant support to students by answering frequently asked questions, guiding them through course materials, and suggesting additional resources. The chatbots can analyze students' queries using natural language processing and provide accurate and timely responses. This not only enhances students' learning experiences but also allows educators to focus on higher-level interactions and individualized instruction.

Conclusion

The integration of AI and ML in education has the potential to revolutionize teaching and learning experiences. Automated grading and feedback, adaptive learning systems, intelligent tutoring systems, predictive analytics, and many other applications can enhance personalized instruction, improve learning outcomes, and allow educators to focus on individualized support. However, it is essential to address ethical considerations to ensure student data privacy and minimize algorithmic bias. By harnessing the power of AI and ML, we can create more engaging and effective educational experiences for students.

Mobile Learning Applications

Mobile learning, also known as m-learning, refers to the use of mobile devices such as smartphones and tablets for educational purposes. With the widespread availability of mobile devices and the advancement of technology, mobile learning has become an integral part of modern education. This section explores the various applications of mobile learning and how it can enhance the learning experience.

1. **Anywhere, Anytime Access:** One of the key advantages of mobile learning is its ability to provide learners with access to educational resources anytime and anywhere. With mobile learning applications, students can access course materials, lectures, and interactive content on their mobile devices, allowing them to continue their learning outside the traditional classroom setting. This flexibility in learning ensures that students can engage in learning activities at their convenience, maximizing their learning potential.

2. **Interactive Learning:** Mobile learning applications offer various interactive features that promote active learning. These features include multimedia elements such as images, videos, and audio, as well as interactive quizzes and games. These interactive elements not only make the learning experience more engaging, but also help to reinforce and assess students' understanding of the material.

3. **Collaborative Learning:** Mobile learning applications also facilitate collaborative learning by allowing students to connect and collaborate with their peers. Through features such as discussion boards, group projects, and real-time messaging, students can exchange ideas, collaborate on assignments, and provide feedback to one another. This collaborative aspect of mobile learning promotes social interaction and enhances the learning experience by fostering a sense of community among learners.

4. **Personalized Learning:** Mobile learning applications can be personalized to cater to individual learning needs and preferences. These applications can track students' progress, provide personalized recommendations based on their performance, and offer adaptive learning paths. By tailoring the learning experience to the needs and interests of each student, mobile learning applications enable personalized and customized learning, enhancing overall learning outcomes.

5. **Augmented Reality and Virtual Reality:** Mobile learning applications can leverage augmented reality (AR) and virtual reality (VR) technologies to create immersive learning experiences. AR overlays digital content onto the real world, while VR creates a simulated environment. These technologies allow students to

visualize complex concepts, explore virtual environments, and engage in interactive simulations. By using AR and VR, mobile learning applications provide highly interactive and engaging learning experiences that enhance understanding and retention.

6. **Offline Learning**: Another advantage of mobile learning applications is the ability to access content offline. This is particularly beneficial in areas with limited or no internet connectivity. Students can download course materials, lectures, and interactive content onto their mobile devices, enabling them to continue learning even when they are not connected to the internet. This offline access ensures that learning is not disrupted due to internet connectivity issues.

7. **Real-World Applications**: Mobile learning applications can bridge the gap between theoretical knowledge and real-world applications. These applications can provide real-time data, case studies, and examples from various fields, enabling students to apply their knowledge to real-world scenarios. By incorporating real-world applications into the learning process, mobile learning applications make learning more practical and relevant.

Despite the numerous benefits, there are a few challenges associated with mobile learning applications. These challenges include:

1. **Device Compatibility**: Mobile learning applications need to be compatible with a wide range of devices and operating systems to ensure accessibility for all students. Developers must consider different screen sizes, operating system versions, and device capabilities when designing and optimizing mobile learning applications.

2. **Digital Divide**: The digital divide refers to the gap between those who have access to technology and those who do not. Ensuring equal access to mobile devices and internet connectivity can be a challenge, especially in underserved or economically disadvantaged areas. Efforts must be made to bridge the digital divide and provide equal learning opportunities for all students.

3. **Data Security and Privacy**: When using mobile learning applications, student data may be collected and stored. It is crucial to ensure that strict data security measures are in place to protect sensitive student information. Additionally, privacy concerns regarding the collection and use of student data should be addressed, ensuring compliance with relevant laws and regulations.

In conclusion, mobile learning applications offer a wide range of benefits in education. They provide students with flexibility in accessing educational resources, promote interactive and collaborative learning, enable personalized learning experiences, leverage AR and VR technologies for immersive learning, allow offline access to content, and foster the application of knowledge to real-world scenarios. While challenges such as device compatibility, the digital divide, and data security exist, efforts can be made to overcome these challenges and harness the full potential of mobile learning applications in education.

Resources:

- Mobile Learning Handbook: Provides a comprehensive guide to designing and implementing mobile learning initiatives in educational settings. - Mobile Learning in the Classroom: Offers practical strategies and case studies on integrating mobile learning applications in the K-12 classroom. - Mobile Learning: Transforming Education, Engaging Students, and Improving Outcomes: Explores the impact of mobile learning on student engagement and learning outcomes. - Mobile Learning and Mathematics: Presents research on the use of mobile learning applications to enhance mathematics education. - Mobile Learning Apps for Language Learning: Provides a curated list of mobile learning applications specifically designed for language learning.

Tricks and Caveats:

- Ensure that mobile learning applications are compatible with a range of devices and operating systems to maximize accessibility. - Regularly update and optimize mobile learning applications to incorporate new features and address any compatibility issues. - Establish clear guidelines and protocols regarding data security and privacy to protect student information.

Exercise:

Think of a subject or topic that could benefit from mobile learning applications. Based on your chosen subject or topic, brainstorm different ways in which a mobile learning application can enhance the learning experience. Consider the interactive features, collaborative opportunities, and potential real-world applications that the mobile learning application could provide.

Robotics in Education

Robotics has emerged as a powerful tool in education, providing students with hands-on learning experiences and promoting critical thinking, problem-solving, and creativity. The integration of robotics into the classroom enables students to explore complex concepts in a tangible and engaging way. In this section, we will discuss the principles, benefits, challenges, and applications of robotics in education.

Principles of Robotics in Education

The use of robotics in education is anchored in several principles that guide its implementation and effectiveness.

1. **Experiential Learning:** Robotics provides students with the opportunity to learn through direct experience and hands-on experimentation. By building, programming, and controlling robots, students actively engage with the material and apply their knowledge in real-world scenarios. This promotes a deeper understanding of concepts and enhances their problem-solving skills.

2. **Interdisciplinary Learning:** Robotics integrates various disciplines such as science, technology, engineering, mathematics (STEM), and even art and design. Students learn to work collaboratively, combining their knowledge from different subject areas to design and build functional robots. This interdisciplinary approach fosters a holistic understanding of the underlying principles and encourages creativity.

3. **Critical Thinking and Problem-Solving:** Robotics challenges students to think critically, analyze problems, and develop innovative solutions. They learn to break down complex challenges into smaller, manageable tasks and use logical reasoning to overcome obstacles. This process enhances their problem-solving skills and prepares them for real-world challenges.

4. **Creativity and Innovation:** Robotics encourages students to think outside the box and explore innovative ideas. They have the freedom to design and build their robots, experimenting with different materials, mechanisms, and programming codes. This fosters creativity, imagination, and the ability to innovate, which are essential skills in the evolving landscape of the 21st century.

Benefits of Robotics in Education

Integrating robotics into education offers numerous benefits for students, teachers, and the learning environment as a whole.

1. **Engagement and Motivation:** Robotics sparks students' interest and curiosity, creating an engaging and fun learning environment. The hands-on nature of robotics captivates students, keeping them motivated and eager to explore new concepts and challenges. This high level of engagement leads to deeper learning and improved retention of knowledge.

2. **Collaboration and Communication:** Robotics projects often require collaborative work, allowing students to develop essential teamwork and communication skills. They learn to effectively communicate their ideas, share responsibilities, and work together towards a common goal. This collaboration mirrors real-world scenarios, promoting social skills and preparing students for future careers.

3. **Practical Application of Concepts:** Robotics bridges the gap between theoretical knowledge and practical application. By building and programming

robots, students witness firsthand how concepts learned in textbooks can be applied in real-world situations. This connection enhances their understanding, making learning more meaningful and relevant.

4. **Critical Thinking and Problem-Solving:** Robotics challenges students to think critically and solve problems by using logic, analysis, and creativity. They are encouraged to explore different solutions, make informed decisions, and iterate upon their designs. These experiences hone their problem-solving skills, cultivating a mindset of resilience and adaptability.

5. **Career Readiness:** Robotics education prepares students for the demands of the 21st-century job market. It equips them with technical skills, such as programming and engineering, as well as essential interpersonal skills, such as teamwork, communication, and adaptability. These skills are highly valued in today's technology-driven society.

Challenges and Solutions

While the integration of robotics in education presents numerous benefits, several challenges need to be addressed to maximize its impact.

1. **Limited Resources:** Robotics equipment and materials can be expensive, making it challenging for schools to provide access to all students. To overcome this challenge, schools can seek partnerships with local industries, universities, or organizations to secure funding or sponsorships. Additionally, students can be encouraged to work in teams and share resources, maximizing the utilization of available materials.

2. **Teacher Training:** Integrating robotics into the curriculum requires teachers to acquire the necessary skills and knowledge. Professional development programs, workshops, and online resources can help teachers build their expertise in robotics education. Collaboration among teachers and the sharing of best practices can also contribute to effective implementation.

3. **Curriculum Integration:** Integrating robotics into the existing curriculum can be challenging due to time constraints and predetermined learning objectives. Collaborative planning among teachers from different subjects can help identify areas where robotics can be integrated seamlessly. Robotics projects should align with curriculum standards and learning outcomes, ensuring their relevance and value within the educational framework.

4. **Gender Gap in Robotics:** There is a gender disparity in the field of robotics, with fewer female students showing interest or pursuing careers in robotics. To address this, it is crucial to create an inclusive and supportive environment that encourages all students to participate. Providing female role models, mentorship

programs, and showcasing diverse representations in robotics can help bridge the gender gap.

Applications of Robotics in Education

Robotics has a wide range of applications in various educational settings. Here are some examples:

1. **STEM Education:** Robotics is often used to enhance STEM education by integrating hands-on learning experiences. Students can explore concepts in science, technology, engineering, and mathematics through building and programming robots.

2. **Computer Science Education:** Robotics provides an ideal platform for teaching computer science concepts such as coding, algorithms, and computational thinking. Students can write programs to control their robots and develop their coding skills.

3. **Special Education:** Robotics can be used as a valuable tool to support students with special needs. Robots can act as social companions, assistive devices, or therapy tools, promoting social interactions, communication, and skill development.

4. **Robotics Competitions:** Participating in robotics competitions, such as FIRST Robotics Competition or VEX Robotics, offers students a chance to apply their skills in a competitive setting. These competitions foster teamwork, problem-solving, and creativity while exposing students to real-world challenges.

5. **Creative Arts:** Robotics can be integrated into art and design classes, allowing students to incorporate robotic elements into their artworks. This interdisciplinary approach promotes creativity and innovation, blurring the boundaries between art and technology.

Resources and Tools

To help educators and students explore robotics in education, the following resources and tools are available:

1. **Robot Kits:** Various educational robot kits, such as LEGO Mindstorms and Arduino-based kits, provide an accessible and user-friendly platform for beginners. These kits come with building components and programming interfaces, allowing students to design and control their robots.

2. **Programming Languages:** Scratch, Python, and Arduino are popular programming languages used in robotics education. Scratch offers a visual

programming environment suitable for beginners, while Python and Arduino provide more advanced capabilities for control and experimentation.

3. **Online Platforms:** Online platforms like Robot Virtual Worlds and Tinkercad Circuits offer virtual robotics simulations, allowing students to experiment and program robots without the need for physical hardware. These platforms provide a cost-effective solution for schools with limited resources.

4. **Open-Source Communities:** Open-source communities, such as ROS (Robot Operating System), provide access to a wealth of robotic resources, tutorials, and code libraries. Students and educators can collaborate, learn, and contribute to the open-source community.

5. **Robotics Competitions:** Participating in robotics competitions provides students with opportunities to apply their skills, collaborate with peers, and showcase their achievements. These competitions often have online communities, resources, and mentorship programs to support participants.

Ethical Considerations

As with any technology, the integration of robotics in education raises ethical considerations that should be addressed:

1. **Privacy and Data Security:** Robotics may involve the collection and storage of sensitive data. Educators must ensure robust privacy policies and implement appropriate data security measures to protect student information.

2. **Robot-Human Interaction:** The design and implementation of robots should prioritize the well-being and safety of students. Ethical considerations should include clear guidelines for robot behavior, ensuring that robots do not compromise students' physical or emotional well-being.

3. **Equitable Access:** Efforts should be made to ensure equitable access to robotics education for all students, regardless of their socio-economic background, gender, or disabilities. This promotes inclusivity and prevents further disparities in education.

Conclusion

Integrating robotics in education opens up new avenues for engaging, experiential learning. By promoting critical thinking, problem-solving, and creativity, robotics prepares students for the challenges of the 21st century. While challenges exist, addressing them through proper training, collaboration, and resource management can unlock the full potential of robotics in education. With diverse applications across STEM, computer science, special education, and the arts, robotics offers a dynamic and interdisciplinary approach to learning. Embracing robotics in education equips students with essential skills and prepares them for a future where robotics and automation play an increasingly significant role.

Internet of Things in Education

The Internet of Things (IoT) refers to the network of interconnected devices that communicate and exchange data through the internet. In education, IoT has the potential to revolutionize the learning experience by creating a more connected and personalized environment for students and teachers. This section will explore the applications of IoT in education, the benefits it offers, as well as the challenges and considerations associated with its implementation.

Understanding Internet of Things (IoT)

IoT involves the integration of everyday objects, such as sensors, actuators, and other smart devices, with the internet. These devices can collect and transmit data, enabling them to interact with their environment and other connected devices. In the context of education, IoT can include various technologies, such as smart classrooms, wearable devices, and educational robots, among others.

Applications of IoT in Education

1. Smart Classrooms: IoT can transform traditional classrooms into smart learning environments. For example, smart boards equipped with sensors can capture students' interactions and provide real-time feedback. Smart lighting systems can adjust illumination based on natural light and student preferences, creating an optimal learning environment. Furthermore, IoT can enable automatic attendance systems, personalized learning pathways, and remote access to educational resources.

2. Wearable Devices: IoT-enabled wearable devices, such as smartwatches or fitness trackers, can enhance learning experiences. For instance, they can track students' physical activity levels during physical education classes or monitor their sleep patterns, helping educators make informed decisions regarding health and well-being. These devices can also promote engagement by incorporating gamified elements into educational activities.

3. Educational Robots: IoT can facilitate the integration of robots for educational purposes. Robots equipped with sensors and AI capabilities can support students' learning in various subjects, such as programming, mathematics,

and science. They can provide real-time feedback, guide students through problem-solving tasks, and foster collaboration among peers.

4. Smart Campus Management: IoT can streamline various administrative tasks on educational campuses. For instance, connected devices can monitor energy usage, optimize heating and cooling systems, and manage maintenance schedules. IoT can also enhance campus security through intelligent surveillance systems, access control, and emergency response mechanisms.

Benefits of IoT in Education

1. Personalized Learning: IoT enables the collection of vast amounts of data regarding students' learning habits, preferences, and progress. This data can be used to personalize learning experiences, providing tailored content, adaptive assessments, and individualized support. Through IoT, educators can monitor students' performance in real-time and intervene when necessary.

2. Engaging and Interactive Learning: IoT devices can offer interactive and immersive experiences that promote engagement and active learning. For instance, virtual reality (VR) and augmented reality (AR) technologies can create realistic simulations, allowing students to explore complex concepts and scenarios. IoT-enabled gamification elements can also make learning more enjoyable and motivating.

3. Data-Driven Decision-Making: IoT generates vast amounts of data, which can be analyzed to gain insights into student learning patterns, instructional effectiveness, and resource allocation. Educators can use this data to make informed decisions about curriculum design, teaching methodologies, and educational interventions. Furthermore, data-driven decision-making can lead to continuous improvement and innovation in education.

4. Enhancing Collaboration and Communication: IoT devices enable seamless communication and collaboration among students, teachers, and parents. Online platforms and tools facilitate remote learning, virtual classrooms, and collaborative projects. IoT can also foster partnerships between schools and the community, as information sharing becomes more efficient and accessible.

Challenges and Considerations

1. Privacy and Security: As IoT involves the collection and transmission of personal data, ensuring privacy and security is paramount. Educational institutions must implement robust data protection measures, such as encryption

and authentication protocols, to safeguard sensitive information. Clear policies and guidelines should be established to address data privacy concerns.

2. Infrastructure and Connectivity: IoT implementation requires a reliable infrastructure and robust connectivity. Educational institutions need to invest in appropriate network infrastructure, such as Wi-Fi networks, to support the seamless integration of IoT devices. Adequate bandwidth and scalability are essential to handle the increasing volume of data generated by IoT devices.

3. Cost and Sustainability: Deploying IoT devices and maintaining the necessary infrastructure can be costly. Educational institutions must consider the financial implications of IoT implementation and ensure long-term sustainability. Collaboration with stakeholders, such as government bodies and industry partners, can help mitigate costs and explore funding opportunities.

4. Ethical Use of Data: IoT generates a vast amount of data about students, raising ethical concerns. Schools must adhere to ethical guidelines and policies regarding data usage, storage, and sharing. Transparency and informed consent should be ensured when collecting and processing student data, and data should be used solely for educational purposes.

Resources and Tools

1. Arduino: Arduino is an open-source platform that allows users to build IoT devices and interactive projects. It provides a range of hardware and software tools, making it accessible for educators and students to explore IoT concepts.

2. Raspberry Pi: Raspberry Pi is a credit card-sized computer that can be used for IoT projects. It enables users to connect sensors, actuators, and other components, making it a versatile platform for educational IoT applications.

3. ThingSpeak: ThingSpeak is an IoT analytics platform that allows users to collect, analyze, and visualize data from IoT devices. Educators can use this platform to integrate data-driven projects into the curriculum and facilitate student learning.

4. OpenSensors: OpenSensors is a cloud-based platform that enables the integration of IoT devices for data collection and analysis. It provides real-time insights and visualization, making it useful for educational IoT projects that require data monitoring and analysis.

Conclusion

The integration of IoT in education offers immense potential to transform the learning experience. By leveraging IoT devices and technologies, educators can create personalized and engaging learning environments, while students can benefit from adaptive and immersive learning experiences. However, careful consideration must be given to the challenges associated with privacy, security, infrastructure, and ethical use of data. By addressing these challenges and leveraging the right tools and resources, educational institutions can harness the power of IoT to enhance teaching and learning in the digital age.

Wearable Technology in Education

Wearable technology has become increasingly prevalent in various aspects of our lives, and its integration into education has the potential to revolutionize teaching and learning. Wearable devices, such as smartwatches, fitness trackers, and augmented reality glasses, offer unique opportunities for enhancing educational experiences and improving student outcomes. In this section, we will explore the principles, benefits, challenges, and applications of wearable technology in education.

Principles of Wearable Technology

Wearable technology in education is based on the principles of enhancing engagement, promoting active learning, and providing personalized experiences. These devices enable students to interact with digital content in real-time, allowing for immediate feedback and deeper understanding. Additionally, wearable technology encourages collaboration and communication, as students can easily share and discuss their findings and ideas with peers and teachers.

Benefits of Wearable Technology in Education

The integration of wearable technology in education offers several benefits for both students and educators. Some of these benefits include:

- Enhanced Learning Experiences: Wearable devices provide students with immersive and interactive learning experiences. For example, augmented reality glasses can overlay digital information onto the physical world, allowing students to explore concepts in a more engaging and memorable way.
- Personalized Learning: Wearable technology enables personalized learning experiences by adapting content and pacing to individual student needs. For instance, fitness trackers can collect data on students' physical activity levels and provide personalized recommendations for maintaining a healthy lifestyle.

- Real-Time Feedback: Wearable devices can provide immediate feedback to students, allowing them to monitor their progress and make necessary adjustments. This real-time feedback promotes metacognitive skills and empowers students to take ownership of their learning.

- Collaboration and Communication: Wearable technology facilitates collaboration and communication among students and teachers. For instance, smartwatches can be used for group discussions and notifications, enabling seamless communication and fostering a collaborative learning environment.

- Access to Information: With wearable devices, students have easy access to a vast array of information. This accessibility increases students' ability to explore and research topics of interest, enhancing their critical thinking and problem-solving skills.

Challenges of Wearable Technology in Education

While wearable technology offers numerous benefits, its integration into education also presents some challenges. These challenges include:

- Cost: The cost of wearable devices can be a significant barrier to implementation, especially for schools with limited budgets. However, as technology advances and becomes more accessible, the cost is gradually decreasing.

- Privacy and Security: Wearable devices collect and store personal data, raising concerns about privacy and security. Schools must ensure that appropriate measures are in place to protect student information and comply with relevant data protection regulations.

- Training and Support: Educators may require training and ongoing support to effectively integrate wearable technology into their teaching practices. Professional development programs and resources should be provided to help educators navigate the implementation process.

- Integration with Curriculum: Integrating wearable technology into the curriculum can be challenging, as it requires aligning technology use with learning objectives and pedagogical approaches. Teachers need to carefully plan and design lessons that maximize the benefits of wearable technology.

Applications of Wearable Technology in Education

Wearable technology can be applied in various educational contexts to enhance learning experiences. Here are some examples of how wearable devices can be utilized:

- Language Learning: Wearable devices equipped with translation software can assist students in practicing and improving their language skills. For example, language learners can use augmented reality glasses to receive real-time translations of text or spoken language.

- Science Experiments: Wearable devices can be employed in science experiments to collect and analyze data. For instance, fitness trackers can measure heart rate and physical activity during physical education classes, allowing students to investigate the relationship between exercise and human physiology.

- Virtual Field Trips: Augmented reality glasses or virtual reality headsets can transport students to virtual environments, providing immersive and realistic field trip experiences. Students can explore historical landmarks, natural habitats, or even outer space without leaving the classroom.

- Accessibility and Inclusion: Wearable technology can promote accessibility and inclusion in the classroom. For students with disabilities, wearable devices can provide real-time captioning or sign language interpretation, ensuring equal access to educational content.

Ethical Considerations of Wearable Technology in Education

The integration of wearable technology in education raises ethical considerations that must be addressed to ensure responsible and ethical use. Some key ethical considerations include:

- Data Privacy: Schools must obtain appropriate consent and adhere to data protection regulations when collecting and storing student data through wearable devices. Data should be securely managed and used only for educational purposes.

- Equity and Access: Schools must ensure that all students have equal access to wearable technology to prevent further exacerbation of existing educational inequalities. Efforts should be made to provide devices for students who cannot afford them.

- Digital Well-being: Educators should promote healthy technology use and help students develop a balanced approach to technology. This includes setting boundaries, encouraging breaks from wearable devices, and fostering face-to-face interactions.

Conclusion

Wearable technology has the potential to transform education by providing immersive, personalized, and collaborative learning experiences. While challenges exist, the benefits of wearable technology outweigh the drawbacks. By carefully integrating wearable devices into educational practices and addressing ethical considerations, educators can harness the power of this technology to enhance student engagement, promote active learning, and prepare students for the digital age. So, let's embrace wearable technology and embark on an exciting educational journey!

Index

-effectiveness, 170

ability, 3, 50, 55, 56, 91, 95, 105, 115, 189, 192, 227, 229, 230, 240
academic, 30, 43, 46, 49, 52, 55, 56, 58, 61, 65, 111, 140–143, 160, 162, 164, 166, 188, 192, 225
access, 10, 78, 79, 84, 96, 97, 160–163, 177, 195, 197, 222, 226, 227, 229, 233–235, 237, 240, 242, 248, 249
accessibility, 87, 97, 101, 170, 243
accomplishment, 142, 183
account, 72, 86, 161, 219, 223, 228, 238
accountability, 15
accuracy, 210
achievement, 16, 20, 68, 69, 153, 183, 185, 188, 225
acquisition, 96
act, 103, 132, 147
activity, 12, 13, 41, 47, 121, 214, 215, 231, 248
Adam Grant, 58
adaptability, 55

adaptation, 49
addiction, 228
addition, 49, 116, 152
address, 10, 15, 17, 23, 32, 43, 49, 52, 53, 59, 63, 75, 77–79, 88, 140, 142, 143, 160, 178, 179, 188, 190, 195–199, 202, 203, 214, 222, 224, 226–228, 231, 234, 240, 243, 250
adjustment, 46
administration, 222, 225
adoption, 197, 223
advance, 89, 238
advancement, 241
advent, 177
age, 85, 162, 177, 198, 201, 208, 209, 222, 229, 230, 232, 238, 251, 254
agency, 47
aid, 156
algorithm, 182
allocation, 222, 249
allow, 51, 115, 116, 162, 170, 183, 184, 210, 227, 238, 240, 242
alternative, 117, 161, 214
amount, 162, 250

analysis, 50, 70, 89, 116, 135, 156, 170, 177–179, 184, 214, 225, 226, 250
anatomy, 94, 95
answer, 71, 203
antibiotic, 138
app, 183
appeal, 210
application, 80, 81, 127, 135, 138, 183, 218, 240, 242, 243
approach, 3, 4, 6, 8, 12, 14, 17, 20, 26, 30, 35, 41, 46, 48, 51–54, 67, 74, 77–81, 89, 94, 101, 103, 111, 118, 129, 134, 135, 139, 140, 143, 144, 147, 149, 150, 152, 153, 155, 157, 185, 188, 202–204, 210, 212, 213, 215, 216, 218, 219, 230, 238, 239, 248
architect, 16
architecture, 96, 191
area, 152, 220
arrangement, 202
array, 209
art, 96
asking, 13, 50, 79, 103, 105, 106, 116, 121, 184
aspect, 10, 49, 55, 67, 103, 111, 183, 201, 212, 215
assessment, 6, 8, 17–20, 26, 30, 47, 51, 53, 59, 61, 67–70, 77, 120, 129, 141, 143, 150–152, 154, 156, 161, 179, 203, 215–219, 223, 235
assigning, 47, 77, 213, 235
assistance, 79
atmosphere, 202

attendance, 240, 248
attention, 49, 79, 84, 95, 184, 202, 210, 228, 232
audio, 209, 210
auditory, 91, 184
authentication, 250
automation, 248
autonomy, 3–6, 47, 49, 67, 68, 70, 78, 81
availability, 238, 241
awareness, 128, 142, 197, 232

background, 160
balance, 80, 89, 228
bandwidth, 250
barrier, 195–197
base, 64
beating, 94
beginning, 20, 59, 117, 213
behavior, 61, 179, 213, 227–229, 234
being, 64, 111, 144, 195, 229, 248
belief, 3, 6, 10, 14, 41
belonging, 55, 61
benefit, 14, 41, 58, 195, 202, 237, 243, 250
bias, 89, 182, 227, 240, 241
bibliography, 164
Bing, 162
biology, 12, 39, 94, 95, 127, 128, 138
blend, 219
board, 234
body, 94, 236
box, 55
brain, 91
brainstorm, 52, 243
brainstorming, 214
budget, 48
building, 64, 96, 115, 117, 204, 229

business, 117

camera, 236
campus, 249
Camtasia, 80
capacity, 157
card, 250
career, 49, 63
case, 5, 6, 52, 77, 94, 118, 135, 137–139, 203, 218, 231, 243
cater, 27, 43, 49
Caveats, 243
center, 26, 103
century, 14, 46, 55, 122, 184, 188, 235, 247
challenge, 58, 59, 79, 96, 196, 234, 237
change, 55, 134, 141, 143, 197, 222
channel, 63
chapter, 17
charge, 3
chat, 116
checklist, 156
chemical, 96
chemistry, 96, 155, 156, 210
child, 61–63
choice, 6, 43, 47, 49
citizenship, 141, 201, 222, 227, 229–233, 235
city, 16, 52
clarification, 80, 203
clarity, 210
class, 12, 13, 17, 20, 39, 48, 52, 77–79, 81, 94, 105, 113, 116, 121, 127, 138, 142, 155, 202, 203, 210, 231, 234

classroom, 5, 6, 10, 11, 13–17, 21, 23, 25, 27, 29, 35, 40, 41, 44–47, 49, 50, 54, 55, 57–60, 62–65, 74, 77–81, 115, 116, 118, 119, 121, 132, 140, 145, 146, 150, 156, 160, 161, 170, 171, 173, 177, 183–185, 188, 189, 195, 197, 201–205, 209, 210, 212, 219, 222, 225–227, 232–235, 238, 243
client, 191
cloud, 250
cognition, 95
collaboration, 6, 10, 12–14, 16, 17, 35, 41, 44–46, 52, 58, 59, 64, 66–68, 70, 80, 87, 89, 101, 106, 115–118, 121, 122, 126, 128, 129, 145, 147, 150, 156, 159–161, 173, 176, 182, 185, 188–191, 202, 203, 211–213, 215, 218, 220, 222, 225, 232, 233, 235, 247, 249, 251
collect, 13, 121, 142, 177, 248, 250
collection, 89, 105, 153, 155, 156, 163, 198, 226, 240, 249, 250
college, 143
combination, 16, 20, 70, 91, 104, 118, 141, 157, 216, 222, 226
commitment, 30, 143
communication, 14, 15, 35, 45, 62, 63, 111, 115–118, 121, 122, 140, 162, 173, 184, 188–191, 197, 203, 204,

211, 213, 215, 220, 229, 233, 249, 251
community, 14, 52, 61–64, 67, 115, 117, 128, 140–143, 161, 191, 212, 213, 231, 249
compatibility, 242, 243
competence, 63, 140, 143
competition, 84, 183
completion, 15, 179, 225
complexity, 80, 103
compliance, 228
component, 17, 78, 81, 107, 140, 218
comprehension, 202
compromise, 188
computer, 91, 166, 170, 180, 247, 250
concept, 12, 13, 16, 33, 113, 202, 214
concern, 138, 226, 227
conclusion, 6, 26, 70, 87, 95, 111, 143, 147, 185, 195, 201, 215, 229, 242
conduct, 16, 51, 62, 63, 96, 142, 143, 166, 210, 228, 233, 235, 236
conference, 162
conferencing, 116, 233
confidence, 58, 65, 67, 140, 213, 219
confidentiality, 143
conflict, 14, 15
congestion, 52
connection, 49, 61
connectivity, 195, 234, 250
consensus, 16
consent, 89, 143, 226, 250
conservation, 140
consideration, 89, 95, 133, 137, 173, 181, 182, 238, 251

constructivism, 95
content, 48, 53, 59, 78–81, 88, 96, 97, 118, 125, 140–143, 155, 184, 185, 192, 202, 203, 207, 210, 216, 228, 230, 234, 236–239, 242, 249, 251
context, 15, 86, 95, 180, 198, 201, 239, 248
continuation, 226
control, 47, 78, 249
convenience, 97
conversation, 184
cooperation, 14
copyright, 228, 229, 235
core, 74, 115, 130
cost, 48, 170, 237, 238
course, 68, 218, 240
coverage, 59
creation, 74, 80, 97, 117
creativity, 35, 51, 52, 55–58, 101, 145, 150, 185, 188, 210, 212, 234, 238, 243, 247
credibility, 230, 231
credit, 228, 250
culture, 20, 41, 44–46, 59, 61, 66, 116, 145, 150, 157–160, 197, 222, 233
curiosity, 47, 51, 94, 103, 105, 106, 144, 145, 150, 157
curriculum, 15, 48, 59, 61, 62, 97, 143, 156, 158, 160, 203, 227, 228, 233, 235, 237, 249, 250
cyberbullying, 227, 229–232
cybersecurity, 196, 197, 234

data, 13, 16, 70, 77, 84, 88, 89, 97, 105, 117, 121, 142, 147,

Index

150, 153–157, 177–180, 182, 201, 222, 225–227, 233, 234, 237, 239, 240, 243, 248–251
debate, 50, 203, 214, 231
decision, 3, 16, 50, 51, 62, 64, 117, 135, 139, 161, 179, 226, 249
depth, 214
design, 13, 15, 16, 27, 29, 33, 47, 51, 52, 74, 80, 87, 96, 97, 121, 147, 161, 183, 191, 210, 227, 238, 249
designing, 16, 53, 105, 150, 243
desire, 47, 103, 183
detail, 111
development, 16, 17, 26, 41, 44, 46, 51, 52, 54, 56, 58, 59, 61, 62, 64–67, 84, 88, 96, 97, 103, 104, 106, 124, 142, 143, 151, 161, 167, 170, 179, 180, 193, 204, 219–222, 227, 228, 233, 235, 237, 238
device, 234, 236, 242
dialogue, 214
difference, 140
direction, 80
discipline, 147
discomfort, 197, 237
discovery, 167, 237
discussion, 13, 116, 121, 211, 213, 214, 233
display, 91, 234
disposal, 209
disseminator, 125
distraction, 234
distribution, 15
district, 201

diversity, 161
divide, 195, 227, 234, 243
document, 16
documentary, 184
drive, 73
dynamic, 10, 13, 17, 43, 46, 70, 81, 122, 176, 212, 224, 248

ease, 94
ecosystem, 121, 184
education, 6, 10, 12, 17, 20, 26, 49, 52, 55, 56, 58, 60–64, 74, 84–89, 91–97, 101, 113, 129, 134, 144, 157, 161, 166, 170, 173, 174, 177, 178, 180, 183, 197, 208, 215, 227, 229, 232, 236–254
effect, 108
effectiveness, 49, 66, 67, 69–71, 74, 97, 107, 118, 141, 150, 152, 153, 155, 157, 170, 179, 201, 203, 215, 221, 222, 225, 226, 243, 249
efficiency, 69, 203
effort, 54, 59, 160, 164
emergency, 249
empathy, 52, 115, 140, 143, 230
emphasis, 47
empowerment, 55
encourage, 13, 15, 48, 50, 51, 58, 106, 115, 116, 144, 145, 161, 184, 210, 212–214, 233
encouragement, 145
encryption, 249
end, 20, 68, 77, 117, 151
energy, 16, 249

engagement, 9–14, 16, 17, 20, 30,
    40, 42, 45, 47–49, 53, 59,
    61, 63–65, 67, 78, 79, 81,
    84, 87, 89, 95, 97, 106,
    128, 142, 143, 146, 147,
    153–157, 160, 170, 176,
    179, 183–185, 188, 202,
    209, 212–214, 220, 222,
    225, 226, 232, 234, 235,
    243, 248, 251, 254
engaging, 12, 14, 15, 20, 26, 43,
    47–51, 61, 67, 77–79, 84,
    90, 95, 101, 106, 111, 115,
    116, 118, 129, 134, 139,
    140, 144, 149, 150, 157,
    165, 166, 170, 173, 184,
    185, 188, 201, 204, 207,
    210, 212, 214, 215, 219,
    226, 228, 229, 235, 238,
    241, 243, 247, 250
engineer, 16
enjoyment, 47
entrepreneurship, 55
environment, 4, 6, 10, 12, 13, 15, 20,
    41, 43, 45, 46, 49, 53–55,
    59, 61, 62, 64, 65, 79, 81,
    85, 91, 94, 95, 106, 115,
    121, 144–147, 152, 157,
    160–162, 166, 170, 173,
    185, 186, 188, 194,
    196–199, 201–204, 210,
    212, 214, 216, 218, 219,
    226, 228, 229, 232,
    234–236, 238, 244, 248
equipment, 210, 237
equity, 55, 87, 160, 161, 222, 235
era, 195, 202
etiquette, 227, 229, 232
evaluation, 9, 50, 69–71, 74, 140,
    141, 143, 152–154, 156,
    157, 219, 221–226, 228
evidence, 17, 50, 52, 71, 73, 89, 142,
    153, 203, 214
example, 12, 16, 33, 39, 40, 47, 48,
    52, 95, 96, 108, 113, 117,
    121, 138, 155, 183, 184,
    202, 210, 211, 214, 225,
    232–234, 240, 248
excellence, 160
exchange, 14, 165, 166, 212
exhibit, 61, 142
exit, 116
experience, 6, 16, 49, 74, 77, 78, 81,
    84, 87, 88, 94, 97, 101,
    128, 134, 140–142, 170,
    173, 202, 209, 212, 215,
    222, 225, 234, 236, 241,
    243, 250
experiment, 13, 51, 105, 170, 184,
    234
experimentation, 170, 233
expertise, 16, 62, 65, 96, 202
exploration, 12, 25, 77, 105, 145,
    150, 160, 170, 173, 197,
    215, 233, 237
explore, 6, 10, 17, 20, 27, 34, 41, 46,
    48, 50, 52, 55, 58, 61, 67,
    74, 77, 80, 81, 94–97, 103,
    107, 111, 114, 115, 117,
    118, 131, 140, 144, 147,
    148, 150, 153, 157, 162,
    166, 170, 171, 173, 174,
    177, 183, 184, 188, 192,
    195, 198, 201, 205, 209,
    210, 212, 219, 222, 226,
    232–234, 236–239, 243,
    246, 250, 251
exposure, 165

Index 261

expression, 115

face, 46, 58, 74, 77, 188, 201–204, 212, 215, 216, 218, 219, 228
facilitation, 215
facilitator, 64, 125, 202
fair, 161, 228
fairness, 15
fear, 197
feed, 236
feedback, 15, 17, 20, 48, 62, 66–70, 81, 88, 91, 115–117, 121, 142, 145, 150, 183, 189, 203, 211–213, 215, 226, 235, 239, 240, 248, 249, 251
field, 49, 94, 184, 191, 203, 236, 238
finding, 162, 166
fishbowl, 116
fitness, 248, 251
flexibility, 78, 84, 97, 170, 233, 242
focus, 17, 51, 62, 79, 155, 161, 226, 240
following, 10, 15, 33, 34, 62, 63, 74, 101, 108, 110, 111, 117, 123, 127, 129, 130, 139, 140, 163, 165, 167, 187, 195–199, 201, 206, 213, 215, 246
form, 97, 116, 127
format, 91, 164
forum, 213, 214
foster, 30, 46, 47, 50, 55, 58, 63, 64, 66, 73, 79, 89, 115, 116, 118, 143, 147, 149, 150, 157, 161, 176, 183, 184, 188, 195, 202, 203, 211, 212, 219, 233, 236, 242, 249
foundation, 50, 189
frame, 103
framework, 16, 70, 111, 116, 202, 204
freedom, 47, 229, 231, 234
frequency, 213
funding, 222, 250
future, 10, 20, 26, 49, 56, 58, 60, 90, 97, 111, 139, 153, 156, 181, 226, 248

game, 84, 87, 183
gamification, 84–87, 183, 185
gap, 195
gender, 160
generation, 160
geography, 184
geometry, 237
George Couros, 57
go, 56, 116, 162, 192
goal, 6, 15, 184, 185, 235
government, 141, 250
grade, 236
grading, 88, 240
group, 13–16, 46, 59, 77, 79, 120, 121, 141, 179, 202, 214, 218, 219, 226, 231, 233, 235
growth, 10, 12, 13, 20, 30, 46, 59, 66, 70, 103, 105, 106, 108, 116, 140–143, 153, 156, 185
guest, 49
guidance, 6, 15, 59, 63, 66, 79, 88, 116, 121, 145, 161, 204, 222, 227, 228

guide, 17, 20, 27, 36, 41, 50, 64, 74, 79, 97, 104, 107, 111, 116, 118, 122, 130, 135, 144, 145, 150, 167, 194, 202, 210, 227, 228, 243, 249
guidebook, 143
guiding, 116, 125, 144, 201, 240

habitat, 236
hand, 47, 189, 236
harassment, 227
hardware, 237, 250
health, 63, 228, 248
healthcare, 94, 117, 138
heart, 94
heating, 249
help, 15, 20, 23, 48, 50, 58, 59, 63, 77, 142, 145, 161, 164, 185, 193, 214, 219, 232, 237, 246, 250
history, 95, 96, 184, 203, 211, 212, 236
home, 61, 62, 79, 195, 227
homework, 78, 225
hub, 35
human, 51, 88, 89, 94, 103, 180, 236, 237

idea, 74, 78
identification, 240
illumination, 248
imagination, 49
immersion, 236
impact, 9, 52, 69–74, 89, 96, 121, 140–142, 152–157, 173, 219, 221–228, 230, 231, 243, 245
implement, 15, 17, 20, 23, 33, 42, 51, 58, 61, 64, 66, 67, 76, 77, 81, 119, 129, 141, 161, 185, 195, 210, 213, 227, 229, 249
implementation, 3, 10, 20, 23, 27, 29, 34, 36, 41, 43, 44, 46, 54, 60, 70, 71, 74, 87, 97, 99, 107, 130, 133–135, 137–140, 150, 170, 173, 198, 207, 219, 223, 243, 250
importance, 12, 64, 95, 105, 111, 115, 191, 192, 198, 219, 227, 228
improve, 92, 141, 157, 177, 179, 240
improvement, 17, 20, 51, 66, 70, 71, 73, 74, 88, 89, 116, 203, 207, 215, 223, 226, 249
in, 3, 5, 6, 8, 10–17, 19–21, 23, 25, 27, 29, 30, 35, 36, 39–41, 43–52, 55–58, 60–65, 67–71, 74, 77–81, 84–89, 91, 92, 94–97, 100, 103, 105, 108, 109, 111–119, 121, 122, 125–130, 132, 134, 135, 138–150, 152, 154–157, 160, 161, 163, 164, 166–168, 170, 171, 173, 174, 176–178, 180, 181, 183–185, 188, 189, 192, 194–198, 201–205, 207–210, 212–220, 222, 225–240, 242, 243, 245–251, 253
inclusivity, 54, 62, 63
increase, 14, 47, 64, 212
individual, 15–17, 20, 49, 52–55, 78, 81, 84, 88, 116, 120, 141, 152, 185, 188, 202, 203, 232, 239

Index

individuality, 6, 10
industry, 63, 250
influence, 49
infographic, 232
information, 3, 49, 50, 53, 67, 78, 95, 104, 107, 141, 155, 157, 162, 166, 185, 192, 196, 198, 202, 209, 210, 226, 227, 229, 230, 232–237, 243, 249, 250
infrastructure, 16, 84, 250, 251
initiative, 225
innovation, 35, 55–58, 197, 249
input, 62, 91
inquiry, 13, 17, 103–108, 111, 113–115, 118–122, 144–161, 167, 180–182
instance, 48, 49, 95, 184, 185, 203, 248, 249
instruction, 6, 8–10, 17, 20, 26–30, 53, 55, 64, 67, 74, 81, 84, 140, 161, 179, 185–188, 201–204, 215, 219, 220, 227, 232, 237, 239, 240
integration, 35, 46, 89, 96, 97, 118, 150, 195–197, 201, 202, 204, 212, 216, 219–229, 234, 235, 237, 238, 240, 243, 245, 247, 248, 250–253
integrity, 117
intelligence, 88, 180, 182
intensity, 13
interaction, 42, 46, 78, 89, 173, 202, 204, 213, 215
interest, 6, 47, 78, 94, 203
internet, 79, 162, 195, 227, 234, 248
intervention, 77, 179, 228, 230
investigation, 108

investment, 47
involvement, 10, 63, 157, 197, 213
isolation, 228
issue, 39, 138, 141, 214, 230
it, 10, 15, 23, 27, 30, 32, 38, 49, 52, 53, 58–60, 64, 65, 71, 75, 78–80, 87–89, 97, 99, 103, 110, 118, 122, 140, 148, 150, 152, 157, 158, 161, 166, 179, 181, 182, 185, 187, 188, 192, 194, 197, 198, 202, 203, 207, 209, 212, 213, 215, 216, 221, 226, 227, 233–238, 240, 241, 250

journaling, 117, 141
journey, 3, 17, 36, 40, 47, 78, 88, 111, 112, 115, 134, 160, 166, 254
Julie Hatcher, 143
justice, 141, 143

Ken Robinson, 57, 58
kindness, 230
knowledge, 10, 15–17, 40, 45, 48, 51, 56, 64, 65, 67, 77–80, 88, 89, 94, 95, 103, 105, 107, 111–115, 140, 141, 143, 147, 152, 155, 157, 161, 162, 165, 166, 184, 204, 210, 213, 219, 225, 233, 235, 238, 242

lab, 184, 210, 236
label, 96
laboratory, 167, 169, 170
lack, 63, 196, 197, 222, 224, 237
landscape, 6, 232

language, 5, 6, 53, 63, 64, 88, 96, 170, 180, 183, 229, 233, 237, 240, 243
layout, 16
leaderboard, 183
leadership, 140
learn, 14, 16, 20, 47, 48, 50, 58, 67, 78, 81, 95, 116, 121, 142, 188, 210, 212, 225, 235, 238
learner, 4–6, 27, 53, 55
learning, 3–6, 8–10, 12–23, 25, 26, 30, 35, 40–50, 52–55, 58–65, 67–85, 87–90, 92, 94–101, 103–108, 111–118, 122, 124, 125, 129, 131, 132, 134–158, 160–162, 167, 170, 173, 176, 177, 179–186, 188, 192, 195–199, 201–204, 207, 209–212, 214–220, 222, 223, 226, 227, 229, 232–244, 247–251, 253, 254
lecture, 12, 78–81
length, 80
lesson, 117, 184, 185, 211, 212
level, 13, 62, 116, 143, 156, 183, 225, 227, 233, 240
leverage, 57, 74, 84, 97, 179, 203, 204, 207, 220, 235, 242
licensing, 228
life, 48–50, 58, 140, 170, 184, 203, 231, 236
light, 13, 105, 106, 248
lighting, 96, 248
likelihood, 240
list, 243
listening, 62, 115, 116

literacy, 62, 63, 210, 219, 227–230, 232–234
literature, 163
love, 30, 35, 49

machine, 88, 180
maintenance, 89, 234, 249
making, 3, 16, 48–51, 62, 64, 74, 87, 95, 96, 117, 135, 139, 140, 161, 166, 179, 185, 210, 226, 227, 236, 237, 249, 250
management, 16, 46, 143, 164–166, 202, 203, 214, 234, 247
managing, 59
manner, 48, 95, 161, 219
mapping, 214
market, 237
mastery, 151
material, 78
math, 20, 117, 185
matter, 14, 17, 48, 81, 94, 96, 134, 135, 140, 185, 202, 212, 215
meaning, 111–115
measure, 71, 142, 143, 156, 161, 225
medicine, 94
meeting, 141
member, 15, 16
memorization, 192
mentor, 145, 202
mentoring, 179, 233
mentorship, 63
metacognition, 116
Metaverse, 238
method, 17, 81
mind, 19, 105, 155, 163, 164, 168, 176, 234
mindedness, 58

Index 265

mindfulness, 228
mindset, 53, 61, 64, 79, 156
misuse, 226, 240
ML, 239, 240
Mobile, 97, 98, 101, 241
mobile, 96, 97, 99–101, 195, 241–243
model, 78, 80, 115, 210, 216, 219, 225–227
modeling, 161, 214
module, 77
monitor, 3, 20, 77, 150, 152, 179, 203, 234, 248, 249
monitoring, 8, 88, 182, 250
motivation, 5, 6, 14, 15, 47–49, 61, 84, 87, 89, 95, 146, 156, 183, 225
multimedia, 184, 185, 209–212, 228, 232, 234, 235
multitude, 101

nature, 216, 224
Nearpod VR, 238
need, 15, 23, 43, 49, 59, 64, 72, 79, 80, 89, 93, 96, 97, 99, 117, 160, 161, 178, 181, 185, 191, 195, 196, 210, 214, 215, 226, 234, 237, 240, 245, 250
negotiation, 188
netiquette, 229
network, 250
networking, 165, 166
note, 152
nurture, 143, 145

objective, 153, 211
offer, 16, 51, 63, 79, 81–84, 163, 165–168, 170, 172, 173, 176, 178, 180, 205, 207, 212, 214, 233, 236, 238, 239, 242, 251
offering, 67, 196, 197, 235, 238
on, 3, 10, 12–17, 20, 21, 35, 36, 41, 46–49, 51, 52, 59, 62, 63, 65, 68, 69, 74, 77–80, 88, 89, 91, 94–97, 103, 105–108, 116–118, 121, 122, 130, 134, 135, 140–142, 145, 152, 154–156, 160–162, 166, 167, 170, 179, 184, 185, 189, 202, 203, 211–214, 218, 221, 222, 225–232, 235, 236, 238–240, 243, 248, 249, 251, 254
one, 6, 47, 53, 62, 80, 82, 104, 179, 229, 231
online, 16, 17, 48, 51, 52, 74, 77, 114, 162–166, 173–176, 184, 185, 195, 196, 203, 204, 210–216, 218, 219, 225–235, 240
operating, 196, 243
opportunity, 20, 48, 78, 81, 94, 122, 142, 202, 212–214, 219
order, 17, 23, 41, 43, 185, 219
organization, 142
organizing, 166
orientation, 141
other, 14, 41, 47, 78, 80, 91, 116, 117, 162, 163, 188, 189, 212–214, 228, 231, 236, 237, 240, 248, 250
outline, 214
outreach, 64
overlay, 95, 236, 237
ownership, 5, 6, 10, 14, 20, 26, 30,

40, 46, 47, 63, 78, 101,
103, 157, 185

pace, 20, 77, 78, 81, 84, 88
pair, 116, 213
parent, 62, 63, 204
part, 117, 233, 236, 241
participate, 14, 15, 20, 48, 51, 61,
62, 78, 115, 167, 212, 214,
232, 233, 235
participation, 10, 13, 15, 16, 41, 44,
62, 64, 95, 122, 184, 202,
213, 214, 225–227, 236,
238
partner, 142
pathway, 10
Patti Clayton, 143
peer, 14, 16, 20, 79, 116, 141, 212,
213, 215
people, 140
perception, 88
performance, 17, 77, 88, 89, 120,
141, 161, 179, 225, 239,
249
perpetrator, 231
perspective, 79, 185, 214
Phil Hansen, 58
phone, 62
photosynthesis, 12, 13, 113
physics, 96
place, 143, 234
plagiarism, 228
plan, 9, 13, 15, 16
planet, 96
planner, 16, 52
planning, 8, 17, 23, 26, 29, 30, 35,
44, 46, 48, 59, 62, 105,
129, 133, 134, 137, 139,
143, 150, 198, 207, 222

plant, 12, 13, 105, 106, 108
platform, 64, 77, 184, 212, 250
play, 6, 45, 115, 132, 144, 145, 173,
185, 237, 248
playing, 49, 80, 203
point, 17, 96
pollution, 39, 121, 142
popularity, 97, 157
portfolio, 117, 219
post, 155, 156
poster, 232
potential, 6, 10, 30, 46, 49, 80, 84,
86, 89, 93–95, 97, 100,
134, 142, 143, 159–161,
173, 178, 179, 182, 197,
207, 214, 226–229, 231,
233, 234, 236–240, 243,
247, 250, 251, 254
power, 49, 74, 84, 89, 96, 106, 160,
212, 235, 239, 241, 251,
254
practice, 46, 67, 117, 135, 139, 204,
218, 237, 239
pre, 78–80, 141, 155, 156, 238
presence, 91, 201
present, 5, 43, 51, 63, 79, 83, 142,
203, 214, 224, 231
presentation, 16, 231
prevention, 142, 229, 232
pride, 142
principle, 78, 91, 236
privacy, 10, 84, 89, 97, 179,
195–199, 201, 222, 226,
227, 229, 234, 235, 240,
243, 249–251
problem, 3, 14, 16, 20, 33, 35, 36,
40, 48–52, 59, 77, 78, 88,
104–106, 111, 115, 117,
118, 121, 122, 125–128,

Index 267

135, 139, 140, 144, 147, 149, 150, 157, 160–162, 170, 173, 185, 202, 210, 218, 219, 234, 237, 243, 247, 249
process, 3, 6, 10, 13, 14, 16, 17, 20, 26, 36, 39, 47–49, 52, 61, 67–69, 71, 79, 84, 88, 92, 98, 103–108, 111–113, 115–118, 121–123, 125, 130, 135, 141, 144, 145, 150, 156, 157, 161, 162, 164, 166, 177, 180, 183–185, 194, 196, 203, 218, 222, 232
processing, 53, 96, 180, 240, 250
product, 185
professional, 14, 17, 26, 44, 51, 52, 58, 59, 61, 64–67, 84, 91, 117, 135, 139, 161, 179, 192, 195, 204, 219–222, 228, 229, 235
proficiency, 5, 6, 53, 227
programming, 248
progress, 3, 8, 20, 62, 67, 69, 77, 81, 84, 88, 116, 117, 150, 152, 179, 183, 203, 215, 219, 239, 249
project, 16, 33, 52, 64, 68, 77, 117, 130–132, 134, 141, 142, 151
projector, 234
promise, 23, 181
prompt, 116
property, 228
protection, 226, 229, 237, 249
prototype, 51
punishment, 47
purpose, 15

quality, 80, 96, 106, 141–143, 179, 210, 213, 214
question, 13, 104, 121, 240
questioning, 50, 52, 106, 160, 161
quiz, 239

race, 160
range, 21, 47, 79, 91, 116, 140, 166, 169, 177, 189, 194, 210, 216, 236, 238, 242, 243, 246, 250
rate, 13
readiness, 53, 202
reality, 48, 97, 238, 251
realm, 6, 52, 84
reasoning, 14, 50, 88, 117, 149, 237
record, 80
reference, 164–166, 228
refinement, 237
reflection, 6, 44, 46, 49, 70, 115–118, 121, 122, 139, 141, 142
regulation, 6
reinforcement, 203
relationship, 89
relevance, 13, 48, 50, 80, 185, 210
reliability, 154, 233, 235
remediation, 239
reporting, 230
research, 16, 47, 51, 64, 70, 117, 118, 121, 140, 142, 150, 161, 162, 164–166, 184, 204, 214, 215, 233, 235, 243
resistance, 138, 197, 222
resolution, 14, 15
resource, 16, 96, 177, 222, 247, 249
respect, 62, 115, 145, 161, 228, 229
response, 127, 249

responsibility, 14–16, 30, 48, 63, 64, 79, 80, 122, 128, 140, 141, 229
result, 5, 15
retention, 94, 209, 225
review, 78
rewind, 78
right, 17, 61, 87, 188, 229, 251
risk, 55, 143, 145
river, 39, 142
roadmap, 54
Robert Bringle, 143
role, 6, 13, 16, 41, 45, 49, 61, 63, 64, 67, 74, 80, 89, 95, 125, 132, 144, 145, 147, 150, 173, 185, 192, 201–204, 219, 222, 232, 237, 248
rotate, 15
routine, 89
rubric, 20

safety, 143, 170, 198, 201, 233, 237
sake, 47, 235
sample, 156
satisfaction, 142
say, 47
scaffold, 239
scaffolding, 161, 214
scalability, 250
scale, 9
scenario, 105, 127, 138, 218
school, 20, 39, 61–64, 66, 77, 94, 105, 113, 127, 142, 155, 201, 225–228, 232, 234, 235
science, 12, 52, 77, 94, 96, 105, 113, 117, 121, 142, 147, 170, 184, 233, 236, 247, 249
scientist, 184

search, 162, 166
seating, 233
section, 10, 20, 27, 41, 47, 49, 52, 55, 58, 60, 61, 64, 67, 74, 81, 97, 107, 111, 115, 118, 140, 144, 147, 150, 153, 157, 162, 166, 170, 173, 177, 183, 188, 192, 195, 198, 201, 209, 212, 215, 219, 222, 226, 229, 232, 241, 243, 251
security, 10, 97, 195, 222, 226, 227, 234, 240, 243, 249, 251
seek, 115
self, 6, 20, 51, 59, 69, 78, 80, 117, 140, 141, 184
sense, 14–16, 47, 48, 55, 61–64, 91, 117, 128, 140–142, 157, 183, 212, 213
sensitivity, 64, 141
sensor, 237
service, 63, 140–143
set, 3, 20, 52, 59, 79, 217, 234
setting, 6, 87, 212, 236
shape, 3, 181
share, 14–16, 66, 79, 80, 89, 116, 121, 161, 165, 173, 213, 214, 229, 235, 251
sharing, 16, 44, 45, 89, 142, 145, 188, 213, 226, 227, 249, 250
shift, 61, 64, 79, 80
size, 6, 53, 80, 82
skill, 16, 104, 115, 170, 184, 192
sky, 96
sleep, 228, 248
smartphone, 236
society, 14, 35, 46, 52, 141, 192

software, 177, 179, 196, 228, 232, 234, 250
solving, 3, 14, 16, 20, 35, 36, 48–52, 59, 78, 80, 88, 105, 106, 111, 115, 117, 118, 121, 122, 125, 126, 129, 130, 135, 139, 140, 144, 147, 149, 150, 157, 161, 162, 170, 173, 202, 210, 218, 219, 233, 234, 237, 243, 247, 249
source, 234, 250
space, 91, 116, 170, 173, 212, 237
specific, 6, 13, 15–17, 20, 43, 46, 47, 53, 54, 79, 88, 89, 147, 150, 152, 179, 213, 220, 223, 231
speech, 229, 231
speed, 184
spreadsheet, 179
staff, 63, 232
start, 62, 79, 105
status, 160
step, 71, 161
stewardship, 142
stimulation, 184
storage, 198, 226, 240, 250
store, 177
storing, 164
storytelling, 49
strategy, 48, 51, 116
strength, 17
struggle, 80, 214
student, 6, 8–10, 13, 17, 20, 21, 30, 46–50, 52, 54, 55, 58–62, 64–74, 77, 78, 81, 89, 95, 97, 118, 129, 135, 141, 144, 147, 150–157, 161, 173, 177, 179, 183–185, 188, 201–204, 207, 209, 212, 213, 215–217, 219, 220, 222, 225, 226, 229, 232, 234, 239, 240, 243, 248–251, 254
study, 5, 6, 77, 94, 150, 155, 218
style, 78, 81
subject, 14, 17, 48, 80, 94, 96, 134, 135, 140, 147, 152, 185, 202, 212, 215, 233, 243
success, 6, 10, 13–15, 20, 26, 46, 49, 50, 53, 55, 58, 61, 64, 65, 74, 91, 111, 118, 122, 179, 188, 192, 204, 208, 240
suitability, 223
summary, 59, 193
support, 9, 10, 15–17, 20, 30, 35, 40, 45, 46, 52, 58, 61, 63, 64, 66, 67, 70, 74, 77–80, 88, 89, 97, 100, 106, 109, 112, 116–118, 129, 138, 142, 145, 150, 159–161, 179, 182, 186, 188, 196, 197, 202, 204, 211, 214, 220, 222, 227, 228, 232, 234, 237, 240, 248–250
surface, 116
surveillance, 249
sustainability, 16, 66, 128, 250
system, 21, 22, 31, 94, 96, 234

tablet, 236
tailor, 6, 232
tailoring, 26, 53, 185, 188, 202
taking, 55, 145, 161, 219
tap, 97
target, 30
task, 213
teach, 12, 227, 228, 233, 234

teacher, 5, 12, 13, 20, 62–64, 77–79, 89, 94, 97, 105, 121, 125, 141, 179, 184, 201–204, 214, 234, 235, 238
teaching, 14, 26, 41, 46, 49, 53, 64–67, 78, 79, 84, 89, 97, 111, 117, 150, 152, 153, 157, 161, 177, 179, 185, 194, 198, 201, 202, 204, 209, 210, 212, 219, 222, 226, 230, 232, 235, 237, 239, 240, 249, 251
team, 191
teamwork, 14, 16, 140, 184, 188, 202
technique, 213
technology, 10, 46, 49, 57, 58, 69, 70, 74, 79, 81, 84, 89, 95–97, 116, 118, 150, 161, 166, 177, 181–185, 189, 192, 194–198, 201–204, 208, 212, 216, 219–229, 232–235, 241, 247, 251–254
term, 66, 250
test, 51, 52, 225
testing, 142
text, 209
think, 14, 49–51, 55, 104, 116, 185, 192, 213
thinking, 3, 12–14, 16, 17, 26, 33, 35, 45, 46, 48–52, 55, 58, 59, 67, 68, 70, 77, 78, 80, 94, 103, 105–107, 111, 115, 116, 118, 121, 122, 126, 128, 129, 135, 139, 140, 142, 144, 145, 147, 150, 153, 156, 157, 160, 162, 170, 173, 185, 188, 192–195, 203, 209, 212, 213, 215, 220, 222, 230, 232–235, 243, 247
thought, 50, 212
thoughtfulness, 214
time, 15–17, 46, 59, 78–81, 88, 96, 117, 141, 143, 164, 179, 184, 210, 212, 214, 222, 234, 236, 248–251
today, 14, 49, 55, 162, 192, 195, 198, 209, 232
tone, 229
tool, 20, 48, 89, 96, 140, 173, 184, 208, 209, 232, 243
topic, 12, 47, 77, 80, 117, 201, 210, 231, 243
track, 81, 88, 91, 117, 203, 248
tracking, 84
traffic, 52
training, 58, 91, 97, 141, 196, 197, 207, 220, 222, 237, 238, 247
transition, 64
translation, 63
transmission, 249
transparency, 240
transportation, 16, 64
triangulation, 154
trust, 145
tutoring, 88, 89, 240

ubiquity, 101
understanding, 12–14, 16, 17, 20, 26, 40, 47, 48, 59, 62, 64, 67, 70, 74, 77–79, 81, 88, 94–97, 104, 106, 107, 110, 114–117, 121, 126, 128, 129, 134, 135, 140, 142, 147, 149–152, 154, 155,

157, 170, 179, 185, 186, 201–204, 210–212, 215, 216, 220, 227, 229, 234, 236, 251
unit, 20, 68, 77, 117, 151
up, 49, 183, 212, 219, 247
update, 161, 227, 243
usage, 249, 250
use, 8, 16, 20, 48, 52, 58, 62, 70, 79, 80, 88, 89, 95–97, 116, 161, 167, 170, 179, 182–186, 194, 198, 202, 203, 206, 209, 210, 212, 216, 219, 220, 222, 225–230, 233–235, 237, 238, 240, 241, 243, 249–251, 253
user, 91, 236

validity, 117, 154
value, 48, 58, 121, 161
variability, 30
variety, 11, 42, 43, 51, 59, 62, 91, 106, 152, 161, 185, 193, 203, 216, 217, 224, 237
victim, 231
video, 80, 116, 184, 218, 233, 236
view, 217
vision, 180, 191
visit, 95, 236
visual, 91, 184, 202, 210
visualization, 95, 97, 179, 250
vocabulary, 96
voice, 47, 63, 161

volume, 250

war, 203, 211
water, 39, 142
way, 47, 48, 52, 53, 65, 78, 96, 97, 122, 149, 166, 183, 207, 215, 235, 243
wealth, 176
web, 162
well, 15, 21, 41, 47, 59, 64, 70, 80, 104–107, 111, 118, 170, 179, 212, 215, 216, 229, 248
wellness, 63, 228
whole, 13, 17, 21, 31, 116, 244
window, 236
work, 14–16, 20, 33, 41, 48, 59, 80, 89, 96, 115, 117, 135, 142, 165, 173, 184, 188, 233, 235
workforce, 14, 56
working, 15, 17, 35, 64, 78, 118, 130, 140, 143, 237
workload, 15
world, 13, 14, 16, 17, 33, 35, 40, 48–51, 55, 57, 63, 77, 80, 91, 95–97, 103, 105, 117, 128–130, 135, 139, 140, 150, 157, 162, 184, 185, 188, 193, 195, 203, 218, 225, 227, 229, 231–237, 242, 243
writing, 116, 140, 214, 233

Milton Keynes UK
Ingram Content Group UK Ltd.
UKHW021428011224
451693UK00012B/1021